THE LEGENDS OF THE SAINTS

THE LEGENDS
OF THE SAINTS

Hippolyte Delehaye

translated by
DONALD ATTWATER

with a memoir of the author by
PAUL PEETERS

and a new introduction by
THOMAS O'LOUGHLIN

FOUR COURTS PRESS

Published by
FOUR COURTS PRESS LTD
Fumbally Lane, Dublin 8, Ireland
E-mail: info@four-courts-press.ie
and in North America
FOUR COURTS PRESS
c/o ISBS, 5804 N.E. Hassalo Street, Portland, OR 97213.

A catalogue record for this title
is available from the British Library.

ISBN 1-85182-370-0

Printed in Ireland
by ColourBooks Ltd, Dublin

INTRODUCTION TO THE 1998 RE-PRINT

Christianity is a religion of historians. Other religious systems have been able to found their beliefs and their rites on a mythology nearly outside human time. For sacred books, the Christians have books of history, and their liturgies commemorate, together with episodes from the terrestrial life of a God, the annals of the Church and the lives of the saints.

Marc Bloch[1]

For nearly a century, to those concerned with medieval history, and especially whose investigations touch on religion, the name of Hippolyte Delehaye and of his most famous book, *The Legends of the Saints*, have been common terms of reference. Delehaye has been seen as the great ground-clearer that set out a methodology that would not only help in establishing the historical basis behind a saint's life (a *vita*), but who, more importantly, showed the value of such works as evidence for the concerns—political, economic, religious—of the time which produced them.[2] So, on the one hand, another reprinting to make this book available again to students of medieval history, literature and ideas calls for no comment. On the other hand, no work which first saw the day in 1905, even if it received some revisions from its author (the third French edition is translated here) up to the late 1920s, can be assumed to speak directly as an introductory textbook today. The assumptions and questions of one age cease for the next. What arises as a problem, or even an intellectual crisis, in one place and period, may seem so much otiose in-fighting, so much argument within the rules of a particular Language Game, to another.

The Legends provides us with some telling examples of these shifts in world-view. It was written with a very wide audience in view,[3] and when it was first translated into English (1907)[4] it appeared in a series not directed at those specialising in medieval studies—probably its main readership today—but at ordinary Catholic priests and seminarians.[5] At the time reading passages from the lives of the saints formed a part of the Liturgy. Each day these occurred in the Second Nocturne of Matins in the breviary, and every priest, and many other religious both men and women, had to read them. Indeed, by Delehaye's time, these readings with their fabulous accounts of miracles and other wonders were a source of uncomfortable giggles: one could not but laugh at their contents, yet could one scoff at the official liturgy? Clerical wits might use the phrase 'to lie like a Second Nocturne,' but what was 'the proper attitude' to take in these situations?[6] It is against the backdrop of this practical interest in hagiography by a large group of people that he wrote this introduction. His aim was to keep it simple: he avoided citing cults that had no mention in the liturgy of that time, he steered clear of languages other than Latin and a little Greek, and he noted interesting points of theology rather than of philology or folklore. Today, this might not appear as a user-friendly strategy, but this shows the changes in readership over ninety years. Likewise, Delehaye devoted much energy to sorting out the confusions in the martyrologies (see memoir). Today, these are the province almost solely of the medievalist, yet at the time the martyrology was read, with contradictions, repetitions, and spuria of every sort, each day in most religious houses.[7] Delehaye assumes this level of familiarity with saints' lives and the problems that accompany them, and presumes that many people feel that getting to the bottom of this question is more than academic.

The fact that it was produced by one of the Bollandists can

create the impression that it was a work that is somehow above the religious controversies of its day, yet nothing could be further from being the case.[8] The church-political situation of the day affected *The Legends* just as much as it affected the composition of many a medieval *vita*. And, as with the *vita*, this political agenda does not appear on the surface, but has to be teased out by criticism. The pontificate of Leo XIII (1878-1903) ushered in a new era in Catholic thinking, and nowhere more than in historical studies. It is as part of this general awakening of historical investigations into the Church's past that we must locate the first decade of Delehaye's work. It was a period of intense research and publishing which laid the basis for many projects that bore fruit only much later. Delehaye's sense of being part of this movement is carefully described in the memoir. But by the time that *The Legends* was actually written there was a new pope, Pius X, and a new more suspicious attitude to critical scholarship. Whether in doctrine, scriptural studies, or investigations of Christian origins there was a fear that 'modern' methods would lead to an unravelling of church teaching. And it is against this attitude of suspicion—what became known as the Vatican's 'campaign against Modernism'—that we read the work. So we see an author who was fully cognisant of the latest scholarship in both the French and German, and within the Catholic and non-Catholic worlds: he used the best critical scholarship available to him, such as Harnack, and his work was in turn appreciated by these same scholars. However, we see him carefully using his footnotes. He acknowledged debts where he had borrowed texts, but less so with ideas, and he avoided endorsements or encomia of their work; all lest he be tarnished by association. Likewise, while he clearly saw the implications of his methods for all historical religious texts he sometimes inserted a word of caution lest he fall under one of the condemnations that were then afflicting scholars. An example of this can be seen when he points to distinction between the criticism which can be directed at the works of hagiographers and that appropriate to the books of the Scriptures.

Then he quietly pointed out to those who thought these were watertight compartments (one of which one must believe in all its parts, the other which is one free to disbelieve) that this was one of those quaint ideas which does not belong to the world of those studying hagiography (i.e. the world of 1900), but to the mindset of the ancient hagiographers they are trying to understand![9] This, in the circumstances, amounts to a most carefully staged assault on the obscurantists who were causing havoc among Catholic academics at the time. But one senses that he did not like even this caution, and repeatedly he announced that if you are not willing to have some lovely stories debunked and suffer the pain of having your eyes opened, then perhaps one should not read the work. He taunts those who saw scientific work of the Bollandists as one more attempt to undermine the tradition by saying that these people have already told him that they will not read his book as they want to continue enjoying the stories, but then he rounds firmly on them by pointing out that the tradition is richer and far more robust than these defenders allow. Delehaye is indeed a model of the critical worker on the tradition: he can attack it rigorously precisely because he believes that it will stand all the stronger for having rubble removed from its base and by showing that it is not afraid of open debate on some of its holiest icons.

But if the 'Modernist threat' forms one part of the work's background, then those who were attacking Catholicism from without form another. The last decades of the nineteenth century saw many attacks on the Church based on showing up historical errors in its accepted books of devotion or by 'exposing' the identity of Christian and non-Christian ancient cults. In both strategies, the battleground tended to be hagiography. In the first strategy the arguments tended to run like this: the Church believes this about St X. But St X did not exist or could not have said/done that. This shows that the Church's teaching is full of holes and lies. The other strategy tended to observe the cult associated with this or that saint, find a similar cult in ancient Egyptian or Greek religion and then conclude that the saint's cult was no more than a mutation of the earlier one. Hence the whole cultic base of Christianity is but a variation on that of the religions it replaced. Against both assaults he mounted a defence. To the first, he pointed out the exact amounts that can be known, acknowledging all the errors and confusions that had entered the hagiographical legacy. Indeed, the scientific method he advocated was designed to remove the very basis of this kind of criticism. Against the other attack he did two things. First, he pointed out just how careful one has to be in seeking to identify a Christian and a non-Christian cult. And second, and more importantly, he delved into the then hardly explored waters of what we would call missiology. Since human beings must use human language to speak of things divine, should we not expect to find the same elements of cult in different religions? Are not these common elements no more than parts of a natural religious language which Christians inter alios must use?[10] In this he was drawing on a way of looking at the relationship between Christian and non-Christian that had been promoted by Clement of Alexandria,[11] Augustine of Hippo,[12] and several medieval hagiographers (e.g. the seventh-century Irish writer Muirchú),[13] but which had been dormant since the sixteenth century. Delehaye was aware of these problems and we can detect an apologetic tone in several places in *The Legends*—notably in those sections that are incorporated into the text from earlier articles.[14] So in *The Legends* we do not simply have a technical handbook for a rarefied field of academic research, but a work that buzzed with the life of its own day, a work that is honest and courageous, and that broke more new ground than most of its first readers realised.

THE GREATNESS OF 'THE LEGENDS'

It is the fate of textbooks, introductions, and manuals that they come to be forgotten. If they do their work well what they announce becomes so much part of 'common knowledge' that it appears no more than 'common sense'. And, we forget that what we take for granted was originally the insight of genius. So it is with this work. When we leave aside such matters as his refinements of historical method and his reflections on the nature of religious language, we might note that there are several notions we take for granted about historical narratives, but were then radically innovative.

I would isolate four points. First, that hagiography constitutes a distinct literary genre with its own rules and dynamics; and that within this category of texts there were specific textual units that repeatedly appear. In short, the *vita* is a narrative game where certain commonplaces are to be expected and which vary only in details between one life and another. Since the rise of Form Criticism is scripture studies students with even a passing acquaintance with theology take these ideas for granted, but we forget that this approach to texts—seemingly obvious when one has read more than one text—is part of the revolution in textual studies that has occurred in this century. Twenty years after Delehaye, the 'father' of Form Criticism, Rudolf Bultmann, could make the very same points, as if these were the newest insights on how to read texts.[15]

A second notion central to *The Legends* is that whatever a *vita* tells us, it tells us more about the time of its composition—its theology, spirituality, politics—than of the time of the saint, and more about the mind of the hagiographer than of the mind of the saint.[16] Again this seems so obvious as to be not worth stating. This insight has inspired almost everything that has been written by medieval historians using *vitae* ever since, but at the time it was a revolutionary idea that took many years to really sink in. For example, it was not until 1962 that anyone in Ireland was prepared to apply this maxim of research to the legends of St Patrick.[17] When it was applied it rendered a century of argument, all trying to link or unlink bits of the legends to the fifth-century Roman bishop, obsolete overnight. While at the time Binchy was seen as either a superman or a demon, in fact he was following closely in the steps of Delehaye 'that prince of hagiographers.'[18] And we might note that in his influential *What is history?* of 1961, E.H. Carr states 'the point of view of a writer is more likely to reflect the period in which he lives than that about which he writes'.[19] This was a point brought home more than half a century earlier to those who learned their craft from this handbook.

A third concept Delehaye repeatedly brought before the student was to ask why and for what reason did the hagiographer take up his pen? This notion of authorial intent is central to the work of the historian working with texts.[20] We understand a text to the extent that we understand the questions it answers and the points it author wants to make. While we make many important distinctions within this concept of criticism, for example diverse notions such as 'the hermeneutic of suspicion' and 'the mind of the author' are both derived from it, we should not forget that this approach is recent and these are questions that troubled few before Delehaye's time. Though we cannot say that he was the first to bring these questions into scholarship, he was one of the pioneer generation of textual historians who made these issues part of the scholar's normal apparatus.

Lastly, Delehaye repeatedly pointed out that the legend develops through the continuity of cultus. It is the repetition of story, the celebration of liturgy, and the pattern around tombs and other shrines that leads to the development of the hagiographical myth. And, this *cultic* recollection is one of the most powerful forces in the development of the religious world that produces *vitae* with all their wonders. Again, this is now a commonplace both within the study of Christianity and of other religions. As a fully worked out idea, this only emerged with the Preface to the third edition,[21] but it was there just beneath the surface of *The Legends* from the beginning. Again, we take it for granted and even the novice can now articulate it with more force. Yet, we should recall that Delehaye wrote before Otto, Bultmann, Eliade, or those others whom we usually credit with bringing this aspect of religious thought to our awareness.

THE CORROSION OF TIME

The limitations of a work of this age as a piece of scholarship are obvious: research does not stand still. New discoveries, new editions, different interpretations all contribute to the corrosion of time. But one or two points should be noted as anchoring it in one intellectual epoch. The most obvious is that the work was conceived in the age of 'historical laws.'[22] This was the notion that within human processes there could be discerned 'laws' which governed change/development in the same way that biologists, sociologists, and linguists discovered repeating patterns in their studies. The notion was widely adopted by intellectual historians as a way of seeing the pattern, unfolding or developing, in what otherwise appeared as chance—but chance in matters of thought, particularly the development of religious thought, seemed an inadequate or inappropriate explanation. So Delehaye unhesitatingly spoke of 'the law' that explains that change, this growth, the adoption of that myth, or this sequence of miracles. The whole process by which the cult of individual saints grow seems amenable to understanding and analysis, indeed prediction, in the way that a natural historian describes the annual migration of a species of birds. Today, we have far less trust that in the humanities we can understand our subjects in this way. We may see patterns, we may see phenomena repeatedly, and experienced observers may be able to guess outcomes, or explain what has happened over time, with a moment's acquaintance: but this is not a deduction from a general law.

Another, somewhat irritating, aspect of the work, but common at the time, is the assumption of a radical divide between the world of the 'scientific' observer and the people observed.[23] Thus we find references to 'the popular imagination', 'the psychology of the crowd', and 'the brain of the multitude'. It is the sense that there is a large number of people somewhere out there who think and behave as an unthinking unitary animal. 'It' is the creator and bearer of superstition, false ideas, and confusions; while the scholars are preserved immune from such things. There are, in some way or other, 'collective psyches' or the advertisers and propagandists would not be as powerful as they are; and, academics are somewhat detached from the flow of uncritical opinion or they would be less feared by those who wish to be intellectually coercive; but the situation is far more complex than Delehaye's working model—and, alas, scholars have far less immunity that he imagined.

In common with so much writing of the time, there is a tone of historical positivism about the work: the facts can be ascertained, the problems solved, the true history written down. Few historians today share that faith, but in Delehaye's defence it might be noted that in textual matters, as opposed to the writing of historical narrative, the notion of an ever increasing mass of evidence does have meaning. The process of untangling strands in vitae, editing, in explaining coincidences in cult, detecting sources and influences is an on-going one; and if Delehaye wished to train new practitioners, then there is still much left to be done.

'LET US NOW PRAISE ...'

Given that this work contains a biographical memoir of Delehaye there is no need to set out the details of his life,[24] but an introduction could not omit some mention of the man whose religious and academic personality shines through it. The most telling aspect of this was his devotion to the belief that the truth is greater than any human artefact—be that an ancient vita or a modern piece of research. Because of this anyone who desires to know with accuracy cannot assume that truth can be easily found in ancient or modern writings: steady research, slow and pains-taking, is what is required. While his output was prodigious, he was not the modern academic churning out books or textbooks on a sequence of production deadlines. Instead, we see someone who did what he could, added notes on this or that detail, pointed out those problems which could not yet be tackled and brought to a solution, collaborated, and worked to produce guides and tools for others. The enterprise of knowing was for him greater than single individuals or moments: each was filling in those parts of a larger picture as best he could. The full picture lay somewhere in the future. This is an attitude to the corporate nature of scholarship that is a challenge in every generation, but which today is in danger of being ignored completely even as an ideal. Delehaye not only belonged to one of the 'great historical enterprises'[25] but was the individual who lead that enterprise, the Bollandists, during one of its most illustrious periods. Delehaye's work reminds us that steady research, problem solving, laying out the materials upon which others can build—this was the aspect of his work that most impressed Marc Bloch—is ultimately more fruitful than meteoric 'solo runs' that flame the imagination until, a moment later, the next author with 'hype' and razzmatazz claims the stage. We applaud trilling re-interpretations and scoff at projects whose term is longer than a few years, applaud originality and decry well-written textbooks; but we must ask ourselves if the materials we deal with as historians are that simple and straight-forward? Is truth that rapidly attainable? If not, we are, in hasty projects and singular displays, merely contributing to the fragmentation of understanding—and to label the resulting jumble 'post-modernity' is simply to delude ourselves with the magical notion that 'if I can name something then I am in control of it.'

Delehaye did not see himself as a popularizer—see the memoir—yet he did see it as part of his task to produce overviews of his subject that were syntheses of what he had learned about studying the documents he worked upon. These not only gave a sense of direction, but formed an entry for others into hagiography by giving them tools which would sharpen their own critical awareness of what they were reading. While *The Legends* is by far the best known, we should remember that it is but the general guide, the portico to his more elaborate introductions: *Les Origines du culte des martyres* (2nd ed., Brussels 1933); *Les Passiones des martyrs et les genres littéraires* (Brussels 1921); *Sanctus: Essai sur le culte des Saints dans l'antiquité* (Brussels 1927) and *Cinq leçons sur la méthode hagiographique* (Brussels 1934).[26] Taken together these works should be viewed as a single complex organon outlining an appropriate critical method for dealing with vitae. Seen in this way we appreciate Delehaye's full greatness as the someone who almost single-handedly opened up a research path into one of the largest, by volume, categories of pre-modern literary documents both Latin and Greek. In his preface to the third French edition (p. xvi) Delehaye said he desired to be remembered as doing for hagiography what Mabillon did for official documents. It was Jean Mabillon (1632-1707) who set out in his *De re diplomatica* the criteria for distinguishing genuine ancient documents from forgeries, and gave subsequent scholars a framework for understanding them. In like fashion Delehaye set out the criteria for analysing hagiographical documents as well as providing a context in which we might understand them. Looking through his bibliography of more than 200 items, but especially these handbooks, we see that 'the Mabillon of hagiography' is the most fitting tribute we can pay to him.

Finally, the enduring value of Delehaye's work surely lies in the fact that he was not only a great student of hagiography as one particular research task, but that he was interested in the reflexive question of the method to be adopted in this. He wanted useful tools for the detective work of the historian, yet was also concerned that the methods used be valid in themselves and applied consistently so that the documents could be questioned with rational control. He kept that most awkward question of the historian always in mind: how can I know what I am going to say?[27] This being the case, the final lines of *The Legends* take on an added significance:

> The saints show forth every virtue in superhuman fash-
> ion ... they make virtue attractive and ever invite
> Christians to seek it. Their life is indeed the concrete
> manifestation of the spirit of the Gospel; and, in that it
> makes this sublime ideal a reality for us, legend, like all
> poetry, can claim a higher degree of truth than history.

Every methodology, each particular approach to questioning reality, each human manifestation of understanding, is limited and co-ordinated to other things. No discipline, be it philology, history or theology, is absolute and final in its possession of truth. Each pursues the truth within its own confines, and achieves it only in so far as it removes ignorance, error and falsehoods from its conclusions. But the fullness of under-standing, like the fullness of reality, is always beyond what any or all of these paths of investigation can reveal: *veritas semper maior.*

Thomas O'Loughlin

Father Delehaye's *Les Légendes hagiographiques* was first published, at Brussels, in 1905 and a second edition in the following year. A third edition, revised by the author, appeared in 1927; this was reprinted in a fourth edition in 1955, with the addition of a memoir and bibliog-raphy of Father Delehaye by Father Paul Peeters. An English transla-tion of the second edition, by Mrs V. M. Crawford, was published in 1907 under the title *The Legends of the Saints: An Introduction to Hagiography*. The present new translation has been made from the 1955 edition.

The numerous footnotes of reference have been collected togeth-er at the end of each chapter. Those notes which add something to the text are distinguished by an asterisk in the textual reference.

NOTES ON INTRODUCTION

[1]*The Historian's Craft* (ET: P. Putnam, Manchester, rept 1992), p. 4; it should be noted that Bloch was indebted to Delehaye's work and admired him as a scholar. Bloch praised the kind of documentary research and the production of guides that Delehaye and his fellow Bollandists were engaged in, indeed he took their industry as a model that others should imitate (op. cit., p. 58). He quoted from *The Legends* (p. 74 below) the example of St Ignatius and St John Colombini to show the danger confusing coincidence with identity (op. cit., pp. 102 and 108). A more curious link is that both men held Daniel Papebroch (1628-1714) as an academic hero: Delehaye took him as his model of dedication to the task of understanding hagiography (see the Memoir); Bloch held him to be one of the originators of critical method (op. cit., pp. 68-9).

[2]Bloch wrote, 'At least three fourths of the lives of the saints of the high Middle Ages can teach us nothing concrete about those pious personages whose careers they pretend to describe. If, on the other hand, we consult them as to the way of life or thought peculiar to the epoch in which they were written (all things which the biographer of the saint had not the least intention of revealing), we shall find them invaluable' (op. cit., pp. 52-3). This could be seen as a synopsis of Delehaye as he was taken up by medieval historians in general, but most especially by 'the Annales school' who revolutionised the study of the Middle Ages in this century.

[3]That it was not primarily aimed at academics can be seen from the fact that it was translated into German and Italian, along with English (see the Memoir, p. 208).

[4]Over the years (I first read *The Legends* in 1979 as an undergraduate studying Early Irish History in University College Dublin) I heard on several occasions that this early translation was technically faulty and, more significantly, that it was expurgated of the full rigour of Delehaye's argument lest it be 'offensive to pious ears.' Hence in preparing this introduction one of my tasks was to compare the texts (original and third editions, the 1907 and 1962 translations) to ascertain how far they diverged. Somewhat to my regret—as speculating about omissions and additions is one of the more savoury pleasures of scholarship—there proved to be almost nothing of note. The French editions hardly vary at all (see Delehaye's own comments in the Preface to the third edition, below), and the English translations hardly vary. V.M. Crawford in 1907 produced an accurate and careful (if somewhat stilted) translation of the whole text—omitting nothing. However, the 1962 translation is reprinted here as first, it represents a later edition as approved by the author; second, based as it is on the fourth French edition (1955) it contains a memoir of Delehaye and a bibliography of his works; and third, while it was influenced by the earlier translation, it is translated with a verve that more closely captures the force of the original. However, lest we fall into the fallacy of 'the more recent, the better,' we should note that in some ways it is less useful than the earlier translation. For one thing in the first translation the notes were proper footnotes and where they added texts or comment one had only to glance downwards, in this translation they are presented as endnotes requiring extra fingers, energy, and patience. More importantly, the 'Index of Saints Mentioned' is SERIOUSLY INCOMPLETE (pp. 247-52) and should not be relied upon as a guide to

what is to be found in the work: e.g. in the 1907 translation there are three references given to the 'Seven Sleepers of Ephesus': pp. 36, 58, and 188; while in this index there is only one: p. 144. *Caveat lector!*

[5]It appeared in 'The Westminster Library: A Series of Manuals for Catholic Priests and Students.'

[6]The problem dragged on until the Second Vatican Council's reform of the liturgy (cf. Vatican II, *Sacrosanctum concilium*, n. 92c) when in the reform of the Liturgy of the Hours it was decreed that any extract from a *vita* read in the Office of Reading was to be carefully checked to see that fabulous elements were expunged and that biographical notices of saints in the Sanctoral Cycle were to be 'strictly historical' by which they meant that anything presented there was to be in accord with what any historian could check (*Instructio generalis liturgiae horarum*, 3, 8 nn. 166-8). It is regrettable that in some of the parts of the new Office composed in vernacular languages this has not been followed: e.g. in the Irish 'national proper' many 'early Irish' saints where we have nothing but the name (*nudum nomen*) are still presented with their legendary dates, foundations, and other 'facts.'

[7]The Second Vatican Council desired a revision of the martyrology (and other documents presuppose this, e.g. the above cited *Instructio*, n. 244), but it has not yet appeared and few younger clergy would have even heard of it.

[8]For the history of the Bollandists. cf. Delehaye's *L'oeuvre des Bollandistes à travers trois siècles 1615-1915* (2nd ed., Brussels 1913) [ET: *The Work of the Bollandists through Three Centuries, 1615-1915* (Princeton 1922)]; other introductions are D. Knowles, *Great Historical Enterprises London*, n.d. = 1963), pp. 3-32, and D. Hay, *Annalists and Historians: Western Historiography from the VIIIth to the XVIII Century* (London, 1977), pp. 159-61; and for a guide to their work, both past and ongoing, visit their website: http://www.kbr.be/~socboll

[9]See the last paragraphs on pp. 54-5.

[10]See ch. 6 *passim*.

[11]Cf. E.F. Osborn, 'Teaching and Writing in the first chapter of the Stromateis of Clement of Alexandria,' *Journal of Theological Studies* 10 n.s. (1959) 335-43.

[12]De doctrina christiana, bk 2, *passim*.

[13]Cf. T. O'Loughlin, 'St Patrick and an Irish Theology,' *Doctrine and Life* 44 (1994) 153-9.

[14]Ch. 6, section III, IV, and V (especially the last two sections).

[15]Bultmann in his piece from 1926: 'The New Approach to the Synoptic Problem.' This is can be found in ET in S.C. Ogden, *Existence and Faith: Shorter Writings of Rudolf Bultmann* (London 1961), pp. 35-57; for his statement on the value of Form Criticism, see p. 38.

[16]See the valuation of the historical value of vitae by Bloch quoted in n. 2, above.

[17]D.A. Binchy, 'Patrick and his Biographers, Ancient and Modern,' *Studia Hibernica* 2 (1962) 7-173.

[18]The phrase is Binchy's, loc. cit., p. 17. In the article he quotes Delehaye on several occasions as enunciating the principles he was using (e.g. on p. 18 and again on p. 19), he refers to him on numerous other occasion, but his intellectual debt to him is still more widespread.

[19]E.H. Carr, *What is history?* (London 1964). p. 111, n. 1.

[20]I am aware that the current fashion among those who describe themselves as 'Post-Modern' is to consider this question meaningless. But I am

merely modern—yet I suspect that when we have moved past the post-modern and are in the post-post-modern (or if you prefer: 'the near future'), one of the interesting questions we might ask is what inspired the Post-modernists to write as they did.

[21]p. xix.

[22]For an insightful comment on this attitude to 'laws,' see the foreword by Bernard Botte to the 1952 French reprint of Anton Baumstark's *Liturgie Comparée* (in the ET by F.L. Cross (*Comparative Liturgy*, London 1957) this can be found on pp. viii-ix). Baumstark in his classic on the methodology for studying the history and development of the liturgy adopted a similar attitude to 'evolutionary laws' as Delehaye. It should be noted that Baumstark was an admirer of Delehaye's work, cf., *Comparative Liturgy*, pp. 175-6.

[23]When Delehaye uses words like 'scientific' they carry with them a notion of perfect observational detachment.

[24]But see also the useful entry 'Delehaye, Hippolyte' by P. Roche in the *New Catholic Encyclopaedia* 4 (NY 1967), p. 731.

[25]This is the phrase used by David Knowles, op. cit., to describe, among others, the work of the Bollandists.

[26]Unfortunately these works have not yet found their English translators.

[27]Bloch, op. cit., p. 59.

CONTENTS

CONTENTS—*contd.*

PREFACE TO THE FIRST EDITION

The recent advances in scientific hagiography have given rise to more than one misunderstanding. The application of historical criticism to the Lives of the saints has achieved results which contain nothing very surprising for anyone used to working on written documents and interpreting other records; but they have not failed to upset the ideas of many other people.

There are religious people who have just the same reverence both for the saints themselves and for everything that has to do with them; and they have shown alarm at certain conclusions which, they think, are inspired by an innovating spirit at work even within the Church, and are highly prejudicial to the good name of the heroes of the faith. This feeling is often expressed in trenchant style.

If you are of the opinion that the biographer of a saint has been unequal to his task, or that he has not attempted to write history, you are accused of attacking the saint himself, because, it seems, he is so powerful that he would never allow himself to be compromised by an inadequate panegyrist.

Or if you express doubt about some marvellous happening, which is well-calculated to enhance the saint's glory but has been reported by the writer on insufficient evidence, you are at once suspected of lack of faith.

You are accused of bringing rationalism into history, as though it were not above all else necessary to weigh the evidence when dealing with questions of fact. How often accusations of destructive criticism, of being iconoclasts, are hurled at men whose sole concern is to find out the true worth of the various records of the cultus of saints, who are never happier than when they are able to say that one of God's friends has found a biographer worthy of him!

It might be supposed that the application of such considerations to the attitude of suspicion that so many good people take up towards historical criticism would be enough to show how unjust their prejudices are. But it is not all that easy to overcome a reaction which they think true piety requires.

The conditions in which many accounts of martyrs and lives of saints were composed are too little known to people in general to allow of a ground of understanding. Many readers are not enough on their guard against the vague notion that hagiographers have a mysterious privilege which exempts them from those mistakes of human frailty to which every other kind of writer is liable.

We therefore believe we shall be doing a useful work by trying to set out, more clearly than usual, the various kinds of writings our pious authors produced, by outlining the origins of their compositions and by showing how far they were from being protected from making errors that exact history is bound to point out.

It will be well to caution the reader once for all against an impression which might be got from a study which is mainly concerned with the weak points of hagiographical writings. To give help in recognizing material that is of poor quality is not to deny what there may be of good; tares are sometimes mingled with the wheat to an alarming extent, and to draw attention to them is to save the crop.

Those simple narratives of the heroic age which one would say were written with a pen dipped in the blood of martyrs, those unaffected stories, fragrant with religion and goodness, in which eyewitnesses relate the heroism of dedicated maidens and ascetics, these call for our unreserved respect and admiration.

But for that very reason they must be most carefully differentiated from a numerous class of laboriously elaborated writings in which the saint's features are clouded in a thick mist of rhetoric, and his voice stifled by the voice of his biographer. The distance between these two classes of writing is infinite. The one is easily recognized and carries its own recommendation; the other is too often overlooked, and does harm to the first.

It will be obvious that there is a big difference between the simple process of sorting-out, the need for which we are trying to demonstrate, and the wholesale work of destruction which we may be suspected of undertaking.

Moreover, if we recommend anyone who feels drawn to hagiographical studies to pursue them in a resolutely critical spirit, we do not advise him to do so blindfold; we should not dream of disguising the fact that to misapply methods of research, however good in themselves, can lead to deplorable results.

This may easily be seen by reading through the chapter in which we examine some questions touching that mythological exegesis which is so much in vogue nowadays. Certain glittering performances in this field have dazzled the eyes of people who are more impressed by novel conclusions than concerned about their trustworthiness. We were bound to ask for them to be checked, and to indicate how it can be done.

It has not been our aim to write a full treatise on hagiography. Many questions that may suggest themselves to the reader have not even been referred to, and we do not profess to have exhausted any of the subjects on which we have touched.

Quotations and examples could have been multiplied indefinitely. It surely was not wrong to resist the temptation to dazzle the reader by a cheap display of learning, and to avoid everything that might complicate the exposition without adding anything necessary to the argument.

The aim of this book is briefly to show the spirit in which hagiographical documents should be read, to sketch the method for discriminating between materials that the historian can use and those that he should leave to poets and artists as their property, and to put readers on their guard against being led away by formulas and preconceived ideas.

So far as possible, controversy—a bad counsellor—has been kept out of the book. At the same time we have here and there had to draw attention to other people's mistakes. Unhappily, faulty methods often take shelter under respected names, and sometimes, when criticizing errors, it looks as if one is attacking persons. It is a proper matter of regret for the critic that in the thick of the fight he sometimes hits those at whom he is not aiming. Please understand, we have not aimed at anybody.

Some chapters of this study first appeared in the *Revue des Questions historiques* for July 1903. They have been touched up and added to in a few places.

Brussels
    13 March 1905

PREFACE TO THE THIRD EDITION

The Legends of the Saints has been out of print for a long time, and we have decided on a new edition because there has been an insistent demand for it. Naturally, the text has had to be re-examined. Scientific hagiography has progressed during the past twenty years, and we cannot ignore this.

On the other hand, the book in general remains just as it was before. To work over it again from top to bottom, to bring in all the developments that might be wished, would have entailed the repetition of what we have had occasion to say in special works, to which we take the liberty of referring the reader.

The bibliography called for some bringing up to date. It would have been easy to lengthen it by adding from sources that can now be found anywhere. We have preferred not to over-burden it.

Several well-wishers have communicated the impression which they have received from reading *The Legends of the Saints* and have suggested various ways of improving certain chapters. I am sincerely grateful for their observations; at the same time they leave me rather puzzled. Some find that the book is not clear enough; others, that it is too clear. It is difficult to please everybody, but I will try to clear up at any rate some misunderstandings.

In the first place, there is no question whatever of the saints being put on trial. They are often mentioned, as Achilles would be in a study of Homer. But Achilles is not Homer; and the shadowy, nameless persons who are the proper object of our researches are not saints. If fault can be found with them, it casts no reflection on the citizens of Heaven.

It is also worth recalling that hagiographical texts are not the only documents we have on the history of saints; they form a separate category, but there are others. The *Bibliotheca hagiographica latina* is a very long list indeed of saints' Passions, Lives, Translations, Miracles, and at its beginning the Bollandists remark: "It is not infrequent for more trustworthy or older evidence to be found in a chronicle, in annals or some similar work, in a poem, an epitaph or an inscription. Thus the history of the emperor St Henry must be sought in Thietmar of Merseburg's Chronicle and the Annals of Hildesheim much more than in his Life; the history of the queen St Clotildis in Gregory of Tours rather than in the Vita Chrotildis". Many more examples could be given.

Some readers complained that our work had a too uniformly destructive tendency; they would like to have seen, by the side of debased hagiography (which they would not dream of defending), more space given to those writings about the saints of which no one questions the value.

We must confess that this opinion surprises us. If there is the least attempt at destruction in these pages, it is wholly directed against the notion—as widespread as it is stubborn—that in these matters there is a close connexion between the subject of a narrative and its value as history. It would be difficult to exaggerate the disintegrating effect of this principle, which is implicitly accepted by very diverse kinds of people, though not openly admitted. In virtue of it, credit is given to too many stories that are incompatible with the seriousness of true religion; in virtue of it, we often hear talk of saints who in fact never existed, of saints who are the successors of the ancient gods, even of saints who are gods in disguise.

Unless I am mistaken, it is eminently constructive to explain how authentic documents may be recognized, to show what signs distinguish them from those that are not authentic. Has Mabillon ever been blamed for having, in his *De re diplomatica*, set out rules which convict very many documents of being forgeries, documents which before his time were commonly confused with authentic state papers? Is it possible to build up an old city without doing a certain amount of demolition?

It is a serious mistake, and a very common one, to think that when a saint's story is declared to be legendary all is lost, that that discovery brings the saint himself into disrepute. Christian saints are not like Turnus or Dido. Saints have a real existence, outside written documents. Their memory is perpetuated and lives on in the very life of the Church, and it is not without reason that the Bollandists so carefully gather up, side by side with the saints' Acts, the facts which establish what is called their posthumous glory.

We have shown what can be learned from these facts by giving a concrete example. The current legend of St Procopius provides no data for a grasp of his individuality. A few lines by Eusebius and the indisputable vestiges of his ancient cultus enable us to place him in the full light of history.

It is perhaps timely to recall another result of this method, possibly a more important one. For reasons that are easily understood, the Life of St Paul of Thebes was received with scepticism by contemporaries; this vexed St Jerome, but he did not trouble to combat the view. The result of this strange silence was to perpetuate down to our own time an opinion which was shared until lately by moderate critics. Since then, evidence independent of the legend, bringing St Antony's contemporary Paul into the light of history, appears to have settled all doubts.

There have been other examples, no less encouraging. If we are asked why we have not given more of them, and whether a special chapter on authentic Acts was not called for, the answer is easy. In our opinion, it was desirable not to burden this book with a mass of details that were superfluous to it and would have upset its arrangement; instead, we did something better: we devoted two whole volumes to these special questions—the subject is as big as all that. In *Les origines du culte des martyrs* (Brussels, 1912) texts are brought together which, better than the legends, prove the antiquity of the cultus of the more famous martyrs and of many others less well known. In *Les Passions des martyrs et les genres*

littéraires (Brussels, 1921) hagiographical documents of every kind
are analysed and valued, historical Acts having the first place. It
would have been impossible to treat all these matters with the
necessary detail in a few pages.

And, having just referred to literary *genres,* it may here be
emphasized that most of the difficulties met in the study of hagiographical texts arise from forgetfulness of an elementary rule : the
rule of not confusing the poet with the historian.

For it is poets that the common run of hagiographers must be
called. We shall be told that this is to do them too much honour.
Does is not profane a noble designation, one that is associated
with some of the greatest works of the human mind, in which the
deepest thoughts are clothed in magnificent images and lovely
sounds? It is true that a few exceptional hagiographers, more
talented than the rest and carried away by the grandeur of their
subject, have, perhaps unconsciously, reached a high level of
poetry, telling sublime stories in the unpolished language of their
age. But it must be acknowledged that most hagiographers were
hardly endowed with the lofty gifts which make a true poet, and if
one decides to put them in such good company it is for want of a
better way of marking the contrast between their work and that of
the historians.

Inspiration apart, hagiographers do just as poets do : they affect
complete independence of, sometimes a lordly contempt for, historical facts; for real persons they substitute strongly-marked types;
they borrow from anywhere in order to give colour to their narratives and to sustain interest; above all, they are ever mindful of the
marvellous, so apt for heightening the effect of an edifying subject.

Or they can be called painters, if you wish, and be accorded the
prerogatives which are granted to artists everywhere :
Pictoribus atque poetis
quidlibet audendi semper fuit aequa potestas.
Here is an old edition of the Aeneid; in accordance with the
custom of his time, the printer has prefaced it with an engraving
representing Virgil. You do not hesitate for a moment, do you, to
to say that it is not a portrait? And nobody will take you to task

for so lightly deciding a question of likeness, which calls for a comparison between the original and the representation. You for your part will not say that the man who wrote Virgil's name under a fanciful picture is a swindler. The artist was following the fashion of his time, which allowed conventional portraits.

Or take Leonardo da Vinci's "Last Supper". Nobody will think of saying that if the apostles returned to earth they would not recognize themselves in the painting, or their divine Master, or the supper-room or the table or anything else in it. We know perfectly well that the idea of an archaeological reconstruction never entered the artist's head. What he aimed at doing was to bring back to mind the poignant feelings of that tragic night when the Saviour said to his disciples, "One of you is to betray me": and how well he succeeded. But where is the exegete who would think of going to the painter for any elucidation whatever of the gospel account?

When we are faced with a written text we are liable to forget what would instinctively suggest itself were it a pictorial representation, and so it often happens that we look in the text for what the writer had no idea of putting there.

May I here recall an already distant memory? One of the first copies of *The Legends of the Saints* had a reception I was far from expecting. The friend who had received the complimentary copy informed me that he would put the book in his library, but that he would never read it. "What do you expect?" he said, "I love the legends of the saints, and I do not want anything to spoil my pleasure in them." That may be the psychology of more than one of my readers. If so, they should read no further. We do not wish to spoil anybody's pleasure.

There is no question whatever of our waging war on legends. It would be a senseless thing to do. All the learned societies can join together and proclaim that St Lawrence could not have been tortured in the way that is said; but till the end of the world the gridiron will be the only recognized emblem of that famous Roman deacon. The work of legend can be numbered amongst the great unconscious natural forces. It is impossible for the people's mind to be strongly impressed by some great event or by some powerful personality without their feelings finding expression in stories in which popular fancy is given full play. To say that legend has flourished luxuriantly in the neighbourhood of shrines is simply to underline the importance of the cultus of saints in the life of peoples. Legend is a homage that the Christian community pays to its patron saints. As such, one cannot ignore it. Only, do not mistake it for history. Zeal for the glory of the saints does not require any such confusion of mind, and it presents serious disadvantages.

Brussels
    13 August 1927

THE LEGENDS OF THE SAINTS

CHAPTER I

GENERAL IDEAS

Hagiographical documents. Imaginative narratives. Literary compositions. The romance. Creations of the people. The myth. The tale. The legend. The hagiographical legend; its two chief factors.

FIRST OF all let us try to get clear what we mean by a *hagiographical document.*

The term should not be applied indiscriminately to any and every writing that bears on the saints. Tacitus's vivid picture of the sufferings of the earliest Roman martyrs is not a hagiographical document, any more than are those pages of Eusebius's *Ecclesiastical History* in which the victims of the great persecutions pass before our eyes in massed ranks. Eusebius wrote a panegyric in four books of the first Christian emperor, who in the Eastern Orthodox Church is given the honours reserved to saints. Yet that Life of Constantine is not a life of a saint; whereas the same writer's *Martyrs of Palestine,* written with the object of edifying the faithful by recounting the sufferings of those martyrs, is a hagiographical document; it is an historical document too, and one of the first order. From the point of view of hagiography, the same must be said of the Acts of St Theodore, though in the form that we have them there is nothing historical about them. The calendars and martyrologies in which the martyrs' anniversary days are recorded must be included in the same classification, but in a special category of it, and with them the formal inscriptions (such as those of Pope Damasus) engraved on their tombs.

So we see that to be strictly hagiographical the document must be of a religious character and aim at edification. The term then must be confined to writings inspired by religious devotion to the saints and intended to increase that devotion.

The important thing to be emphasized at the outset is the

3

distinction between hagiography and history. The work of the hagiographer may be historical, but it is not necessarily so. It may take any literary form suited to honouring the saints, from an official record adapted to the needs of the faithful to a highly exuberant poem that has nothing whatever to do with factual reality.

Obviously no one would dare to maintain that hagiographers always and everywhere observe the strict rules of historical writing. But how are their deviations to be gauged? This is what has to be decided in each particular case. And before going any further in this matter we will try to clarify certain notions that are less commonplace than they seem at first sight.

Narratives that are not factually true are referred to as myths, fables, tales, romances, legends. These terms are taken in a wide sense and often used synonymously. This may lead to all sorts of confusion, which we will try to avoid by means of more careful definitions.[1]

We need say but little about *fable*. In its widest sense the word designates any imaginative story; in a more exact sense it is the equivalent of apologue or allegory, especially when the characters in the story are represented by animals. Not that hagiographers have wholly disdained this imaginative form. The writer of the Life of SS. Barlaam and Joasaph included several apologues in his compilation; these have been the object of particular studies.[2] But they are exceptions, and in general hagiographical criticism does not have to concern itself with imitators of Aesop or La Fontaine.

Myth, tale, legend and romance all belong to the class of imaginative story, but may be divided into two categories: there are those that are the spontaneous impersonal expression of a people's genius or native disposition, and those that are the product of deliberate literary artifice.

In the usual sense of the word, a *romance* belongs to the second category. The author chooses and ponders his subject, and brings his abilities and imagination to bear on the work of art he has conceived. If his theme is the character and doings of an historical

person, or the events of an historical period, the result is an historical romance or novel. If the characters and events in the work are
wholly fictitious, it will be an imaginative romance. If the writer's
aim is to depict the life and spirit of a saint honoured by the
Church by means of a series of happenings that are partly real and
partly imaginary, then the work may be called a hagiographical
romance, though that expression has not passed into common use.

Romances of this last kind are very numerous, and some of
them go back to very early times :[3] for example, the Acts of Paul
and Thecla, and that collection of apocryphal Acts of the Apostles
which had so long and remarkable a vogue. And there are the
Clementine romances (Homilies and Recognitions),[4] of which a
summary for long formed part of the best-known hagiographical
collections.

The tale and the legend cannot strictly speaking be included in
the family of artificial compositions. It is true that short works of
fiction are often called tales, and the writer at his desk sometimes
sets out to produce a story in a form that recalls the legend or tale
properly so called. Such sophisticated imitations have just to be
mentioned here, but there is no need to dwell on them. Our concern is with those works of fiction which are without individual
character, the anonymous product of that abstraction which is
called a people's genius.

And first, the *myth*. This term is often applied to anything
which has no real existence, and the hero who never lived outside
a poet's imagination is called a mythical personage. That is not
the word's proper sense; Joad's confidant, Abner, in *Athalie,* is a
pure invention of Racine, but it is wrong to classify Abner and
similar characters as "mythical beings".

The essence of myth is the personification of a power or of an
abstract idea, or, if it be preferred, a myth is simply the explanation of a natural phenomenon as it presents itself to a people in a
primitive stage of development.[5]* Whether we choose to regard
myths as poetical symbols, or whether, as has been ingeniously
suggested, we look on mythology as the treatise on physics of primitive times, it is certain that natural phenomena are the proper

subject of myth. Sun, moon, stars, lightning, day and night, the changing seasons, all are represented by gods and heroes and the adventures attributed to them. Rosy-fingered Dawn opening the doors of the East, Phaethon driving the chariot of the sun, a dozen other charming fables with which the study of antiquity has made us familiar—these are myths.

I do not want to multiply examples, for before classifying a narrative it is needful to make up one's mind about its real meaning, and were we to follow a certain school there would be very few fictional items that could not be included under the heading of mythology. A cantankerous critic has said that there are people who cannot see a cat and dog fight without beginning to chatter about the conflict between light and darkness. This quip was aimed at extravagances that are only too real, and we shall take care not to use the word myth without a good reason.

Are there such things as hagiographical myths? Have hagiographers at any rate made use of mythical elements? I see no difficulty in admitting it, and I shall show that more than one element belonging to ancient mythology has been carried over to saints.

The *tale,* properly speaking, is an invented story that is not associated with any real person or real place. "Once upon a time there were a king and a queen who had a very beautiful daughter . . ." This classical beginning by the teller[6*] characterizes the kind of story exactly, one in which everything is subordinate to the plot, which is meant solely for the pleasure of the hearer or, in the case of a moral tale, to bring out some practical truth.

It might be supposed that there is an endless variety of popular tales, but this is not so. They can all be brought under one or other of a certain number of types, of which not one seems to belong exclusively to a particular people or even to a race: they are a common heritage of mankind.

A great deal has been written about the origin of these tales.[7] Without going into details of the theories put forward by experts, we may mention two principal ones which have been well received and can be considered extreme solutions. Some scholars explain the repetition of identical themes and the similarity of their forms by the sameness of the human mind. Others prefer a less simple and less metaphysical solution, one which corresponds more closely to observed facts. According to them, India is the one and only cradle of the popular tales which are found all over the world;[8]* whatever one may like to assume about their original authors, the stories spread from India and became common property on as wide a scale as can be imagined. There is no need for us to attempt to decide the question here. It is enough to remember that, like seeds carried by wind across the ocean, they are for ever floating in the air and are found in all lands, without ever being definitively associated with a name or a place.

A *legend,* on the other hand, has of necessity an historical or topographical connexion. It refers imaginary events to a real person, associates fanciful stories with an existing place. Thus we speak of the legend of Alexander or of Julius Caesar, the legend of Drachenfels castle on the Rhine or of the Red Lake, Lough Derg, in Ireland.

Such, in accordance with approved usage, is the strict meaning of our terms. But it must be added that in practice the differences are less clear and classification less easy. As it flies from one people to another, one of our winged stories may settle for a moment on some famous building, or the nameless being who is its hero may be given a name of historical significance. Thus the tale is turned into a legend, which misleads you unless you come across some other version of the same story that shows the historical element to be a purely accidental accretion.[9]* In the same way a myth can easily take on the appearance of a legend.

Or again, if you take away from a legend the elements that tie it to reality, you make it look like a simple tale. This accounts for the difficulty of disentangling legend and tale in the famous collection of the *Thousand and One Nights* ("The Arabian Nights"), for in spite of their highly fanciful character parts of these stories appear to have an historical basis.[10] Contrariwise, it can happen that a seemingly clear example of legend suddenly turns up in the form of a folk tale. It was a long time before it was recognized that the legend of St Dympna[11] is an adaptation of the well-known tale of the donkey's skin, or that the theme of the moving story of Genevieve of Brabant had already been used by the epic poets of India.[12*]

So we see that a legend, considered as a connected narrative and as distinct from a myth or a tale, presupposes an historical fact which is its subject or occasion : that is the first essential element of this *genre*. The second is that the historical fact is embroidered or distorted by popular imagination. The two elements may be combined in very unequal proportions, and according as fact or fiction preponderates the narrative can be classed as history or as legend.

As it is the fictional element that determines the category of legend, it has quite naturally come about that the same name is applied to the fictional element itself, and so we find the term "legend" extended to every unconscious distortion of historical truth, whether a single or several matters be in question.

It can hardly be necessary to emphasize the considerable part played by legend (in all its meanings) in writings about the saints, a form of literature that is eminently of the people both in its origins and its aims. The very word has been borrowed from hagiography. Originally, the legend was the account of a saint to be read, *legenda,* on his feast-day, the passion of a martyr or the eulogy of a confessor, without reference to its worth as history.

"Legendarius vocatur liber ille ubi agitur de vita et obitu confessorum, qui legitur in eorum festis, martyrum autem in passionariis", wrote the twelfth-century liturgist John Beleth;[13*] he distinguishes between "passions" and "legends", contrary to the usage that soon prevailed, for from the thirteenth century the *Legenda Aurea* confirmed the wider meaning which includes in legends the acts of martyrs as well as the biographies of other saints. We could, then, conform with the old usage and give the name legend to all hagiographical narratives, including even those that have a recognized value as historical documents. But to do so would lead to confusion, and we will wholly refrain from it in the pages that follow; the word legend will be used only for a narrative or feature that is not historical.

Hagiographical literature has been formed under the influence of two quite distinct factors, which indeed are to be found when tracing back any literary stream. There is that anonymous creator called the people or, taking effect for cause, the legend : a hidden, collective worker, uncontrolled in his ways, quick and disorderly as the human imagination itself, always bringing forth something new, but not able to make it permanent by writing it down. By his side there is the scholar, the editor, whom we see burdened by a laborious task, compelled to follow a direction laid down for him, imprinting a stamp of reflection and lastingness on all that he produces. Together they have laboured at that huge work called The Lives of the Saints, and it is important that we should recognize the part taken by each in this undertaking, ages old but never ended.

We intend to confine ourselves almost wholly to the religious literature of the middle ages, seeking out how it was elaborated by the people on the one hand and by the hagiographers on the other. Some readers may think that the methods of both sides have not yet gone completely out of fashion. We shall not disagree with that opinion.

NOTES ON CHAPTER I

[1]The following are the titles of some relevant works; we give them without discussing the conclusions of their authors, who do not always agree with one another. J. F. L. George, *Mythus and Sage* (Berlin, 1837); J. Fiske, *Myths and Myth-makers* (London, 1873); H. Steinthal, "Mythos, Sage, Märchen, Legende, Erzählung, Fabel", in *Zeitschrift für Völkerpsychologie und Sprachwissenschaft,* vol xvii (1865), pp. 113-39; E. Bernheim, *Lehrbuch der historischen Methode,* 3rd edn (Leipzig, 1903) pp. 317, 349, 457-68; E. Siecke, *Mythologische Briefe* (Berlin, 1901); E. Betha, "Mythus, Sage, Märchen", in *Hessische Blätter für Volkskunde,* vol. iv (1905), pp. 97-142); F. Lanzoni, *Genesi, svolgimento e tramonto delle leggende storiche* (Rome, 1925; *Studi e Testi,* 43).

[2]S. J. Warren, *De Grieksche christelijke roman Barlaam en Joasaf en zijne parabels* (Rotterdam, 1899).

[3]There is an interesting account in E. von Dobschütz "Der Roman in der altchristlichen Literatur", in *Deutsche Rundschau,* April 1902, pp. 87-106.

[4]H. U. Mayboom, *De Clemens-Roman,* 2 vols (Groningen, 1904). On this work and other Clementine studies, see *Analecta Bollandiana,* vol. xxiv, pp. 138-41

[5]In the *Revue critique* of 3 June 1905, p. 425, S. Reinach questioned this definition of a myth. "A myth", he wrote, "is essentially a story which mankind has believed to be true at a particular stage of its intellectual development". This seems to us too vague to use as a definition. Reinach may be right when he goes on, "To attempt, as the author has done, to distinguish rigorously between myth and legend is to require of the words a precision which they have not got". The definition we have adopted is on the whole the one most commonly used by specialists, so we may perhaps be allowed to keep to it for the avoidance of confusion.

[6]This is almost word for word how Apuleius begins *Cupid and Psyche:* "Erant in quadam civitate rex et regina. Hi tres numero filias forma conspicuas habuere" (*Met.* iv, 28).

[7]E. Cosquin, *Contes populaires de Lorraine,* vol. 1 (Paris, 1886), pp. 1 —lxvii; *L'origine des contes populaires européens et les théories de M. (Andrew) Lang* (Paris, 1891); *Quelques observations sur les "Incidents communs aux contes orientaux"* (London, 1892); *Études folkloriques: Recherches sur les migrations des contes populaires et leur point de départ* (Paris, 1922); *Les contes indiens et l'Occident* (Paris, 1922). Cosquin was a decided supporter of the Eastern theory, which has been opposed notably by J. Bédier, *Les Fabliaux* (*Bibliothèque de l'École des Hautes Études,* fasc. 98, Paris, 1893), pp. 45-250. For other systems and their variations, see C. Martens, "L'origine des contes populaires", in *Revue néoscolastique,* vol. i (1894), pp. 234-262, 352-384; G. Huet, *Les contes populaires* (Paris, 1923).

[8]Among holders of the Eastern theory there are some who look on Egypt as the birthplace of popular tales. See, for instance, S. Reinach in the *Revue d'histoire et de littérature religieuses,* vol. ix (1904), pp. 319-320. It does not seem to us to be proved, but we cannot discuss the subject here.

[9]Sometimes it is quite easy to see through the disguises of persons, as in those stories in which Jesus Christ and St Peter appear. Here, for example, is a legend from the Basque country, recorded by Cerquand: "Christ and St Peter were out walking one day, when they came upon a man on his knees in the middle of the road; he was calling on God to get his cart out of the ditch into which it had fallen. As Jesus went on without taking any notice, Peter said to him, 'Lord, won't you help this poor man?' And Jesus replied, 'He does not deserve our help, because he is not trying to help himself.' A little further on they came upon another man in the same plight but doing his best, shouting and cursing the while. Jesus hurried to his assistance, saying, 'This one deserves our help, for he is doing what he can.' " Everyone knows this anecdote, told by the fabulist about Hercules. See R. Köhler, *Kleine Schriften,* vol. ii (Berlin, 1900), pp. 102-4; cf. the excellent apologue, "Why men no longer know when they are going to die", *ibid.,* pp. 100-2.

[10]M. J. de Goeje, "De arabische Nachtvertellingen", in *De Gids,* vol. iii (1886), pp. 385-413.

[11]*Acta Sanctorum,* May, vol. iii, pp. 479-486.

[12]On the variations and derivatives of this story, see H. Suchier, *Œuvres poétiques de Beaumanoir (Société des anciens textes français,* vol. i, 1884), pp. xxv-lxxxi, clx. Neither Genevieve of Brabant nor Mary of Brabant (whose story is identical) has been an object of ecclesiastical cultus. *Acta SS,* Jan., vol. ii, p. 180; April, vol. i, p. 57.

[13]"A book which relates the life and death of confessors, to be read on their feasts, is called a Legendary; in the case of martyrs it is a Passionary" (*De divinis officiis,* 60, in *P. L.,* vol. ccii, p. 66). Cf. E. von Dobschütz, art. "Legende", in *Realencyklopaedie für protestantische Theologie,* 3rd edn, vol. xi, p. 345.

CHAPTER II

THE PRODUCTION OF LEGEND

1.—Unconscious distortion of truth by the individual, —by the people. Low level of general understanding. Tendency to simplify. Lack of knowledge. Substitution of the abstract form for the individual type. Poverty of invention. Borrowing and spread of legendary themes. Examples. Great age of some themes. Artificial grouping of persons and happenings. Cycles.

THE PRODUCTION of legend is by definition the result of unconscious or unconsidered action working on historical material, the introduction of a subjective element into the realm of fact.

Suppose that on the day after a battle you were to collect eyewitnesses' accounts of it. The engagement would be described in a score of different ways, the same details related from very varying points of view, and all with the same appearance of truthfulness. Each account would be affected by the extent of the narrator's information, his impressions and feelings, the side he was on; his story would be neither wholly true nor wholly false. Each one would tell you his own legend. The combined result of these varying accounts would be a legend too, and if you tried to extract the pure historical truth from it you would have to be satisfied with two or three salient facts that seemed to be established with certainty. Were you to fill in the gaps by a series of deductions, you would be making your own history of the battle, in fact creating a new legend; and you would have to be content with that, or else resign yourself to ignorance.

Everyone realizes the peculiar difficulty of giving an exact account of an event that is too complex to be taken in at a glance. But it does not follow that, these exceptional cases apart, it is quite easy and common to describe something faithfully. The truth is that in our daily life we are continually taking part in the unconscious process that produces legends; every one of us has had occasion scores of times to notice how difficult it is to recount our observation of something with complete exactness, even if it be only slightly complex.

To begin with, we do not usually grasp a happening in all its details or see the connexion between all its parts; still more rarely do we clearly perceive the causes that are at work, in such a way as to leave no doubt about the motives of the persons concerned. And we instinctively fill the gaps. We reconstruct the continuity of what happened by means of a series of intuitive links, and impose our way of seeing things on the factors that produced this or that result. If we are under the influence of some emotion or opinion that has obscured the clear sight of things, if in our heart we want something that happened not to have happened or not to be known, or that something we did not notice should really have happened, if it suits us that people concerned should have been moved by some particular impulse, why then, almost without thinking about it, we leave one part of the picture in the background or heighten the effect of another part, according to our own requirements. So, unless we strictly control our mental processes and discipline our impressions, we are liable to inject a large subjective element into our account of things, and truth will suffer. To give exact expression to a complex reality calls for sound and practised abilities and considerable effort, and consequently for a stimulus proportioned to the end in view.

It will be agreed that, ordinarily speaking, the average man has not got the mental energy required for this purpose. It is the privilege of only a few to be in the habit of analysing their thoughts and feelings and controlling the least impulses of their hearts, to such a degree that they are always on their guard against that natural tendency to mix up what we imagine with what we know. Even those whose natural gifts and education are well above the average do not invariably bring these advantages into play.

Suppose yourself to have been the eye-witness of a criminal killing. In talking to your friends, you describe the horrifying things that you saw in the smallest detail, nothing about the murderer and his victim seems to have escaped your notice. But then you are called as a witness at the assizes; a man's life depends on your evidence, given under oath. What a difference between the two versions of the same story! Your description is much less clear and full, and has lost the exciting quality you gave to it in private. The reason is that in the serious circumstances of a trial one is much more careful to be exact, and is no longer inclined to give way to the trifling vanity of appearing as a well-informed and interesting person; for the most truthful and honest man may unconsciously start little legends by bringing his own impressions, ideas and feelings into what he reports, thus presenting the truth in a form which, according to the circumstances, is either embellished or distorted.

It need hardly be pointed out that opportunities for error increase in number with the number of intermediaries through whom a story passes. Each one understands it in a certain way and repeats it in his own way. Through not listening properly or through forgetfulness, someone fails to mention an important circumstance and the coherence of the story is thereby impaired. Somebody else, more careful, notices something is missing, and uses his imagination to try and repair the omission; he invents a new detail here, and suppresses another there, till the requirements of likelihood and logic appear to him to be satisfied. This is generally achieved at the expense of truth, the speaker or writer not realizing that he has substituted a quite different story for the primitive version. Sometimes again a story is transmitted through someone who finds it embarrassing, and he contributes seriously to its falsification by some twist of thought or expression.

This sort of thing is happening every day. Whether we are eyewitnesses or intermediaries, our shallow understanding, our carelessness, our emotions and, perhaps above all, our petty prejudices conspire together against the accuracy of a story when we make it our business to repeat one.

This commonplace process becomes much more interesting and fraught with consequences when it takes place on a large scale, when for the understanding and impressions of individuals there are substituted the understanding and impressions of a crowd or of a whole people. These collective and, in a sense, abstract faculties are of a very special kind, their activities governed by laws that have been much studied in recent times as a special department of psychology.[1] The laws that have been formulated are verified by thousands of examples taken from the popular literature of all lands, and hagiographical writings provide a large number that confirm them.

We will not complicate the subject by trying to decide the respective degrees of capacity shown at different social levels. Nothing is more difficult to do, and as regards the matters that concern us here the most diverse elements have to be considered. In the middle ages the whole people were interested in the saints; everybody invoked them, kept their feasts and loved to hear their praises sung. Their legends were developed within a society that was a very mixed one, and it did not lack some persons with certain literary pretensions—I hasten to add that this was of no benefit to the saints.

The intellectual capacity of people at large is manifestly very limited everywhere, and it would be a mistake to suppose that in general it is improved through the influence of the more gifted. On the contrary, it is the *élite* which is acted on by the others, and there would be little logic in attributing special value to a popular tradition because it had grown up in a society that was not without intelligent and able members. In any crowd the better elements are swamped, and the average of intelligence is well below middling; its level can best be gauged by comparing it with the intelligence of a child.

What it comes to is that the generality of human minds can take in only a very few ideas, and those of the simplest. Its deductions are equally simple, made through a few intuitive principles, and they are often no more than mere associations of ideas or images.

The exceeding simplicity of the general mind and disposition is clearly shown in the legends it creates. For instance, the number of people and events it remembers is usually very limited; and its heroes do not live in memory side by side but replace one another, the latest comer inheriting all the qualities and achievements of his predecessors.

Antiquity has bequeathed to us outstanding examples of such "absorption". The wars of many centuries are concentrated beneath the walls of Troy; a prolonged evolution of law-making in Athens and Sparta is put to the credit of Solon and Lycurgus.[2]* In later ages it is Alexander, Julius Caesar, Charlemagne[3] who, according to the country, haunt the people's imagination, and honour after honour is heaped on the head of the chosen hero. He it is who was responsible for every striking achievement, the country's welfare and prosperity is due to him, his name is associated with everything noteworthy in the land. Some old legends would have us believe that in all Alexandria there was not a stone that had not been put there by Alexander himself.[4] From the day that Tiberius made Capri the scene of his debaucheries he became as it were the tutelary spirit of the place, whose generous hand has left its mark all over the island.[5]

It is obvious that this habit of concentrating all the glories of the past in a single person seriously alters his real proportions. The glory of his apotheosis is sometimes such that the hero loses his true appearance in it and emerges completely disguised. Virgil, for example, when he became the hero of the Neapolitans, ceased to be the inspired poet and was transformed into the city governor.[6] The local tradition of Sulmona has made Ovid everything that in fact he was not : a skilful wizard, a captain of commerce, a prophet, a preacher, a sort of paladin, yes, and—would you believe it ?—a great saint.[7]

Historical truth does not come into the picture, since it is taken for granted of the really popular hero that he is concerned in all important events : the great man has wholly captured the people's imagination, and nothing that is fine, striking or advantageous can happen without his having a hand in it. In the religious sphere, this great man is the saint who is specially revered in the place concerned. Here it is St Martin's name that crops up at every step; there it is St Patrick's.[8] Popular enthusiasm exaggerates the scope of the hero's activities, making it include a mass of things pulled out of their historical setting, or he is credited with achievements of his superseded predecessors.

Above all, it is useless to expect the multitude to distinguish between persons of the same name. Great men are so uncommon! What chance is there that there should be two of the same name? It is reasoning of this kind that has convinced the inhabitants of Calabria that, returning from the First Crusade, St Louis stayed in several of their towns; whereas in fact he never set foot in the neighbourhood. The King Louis who marched through the Neapolitan provinces with the remnants of a crusading army was Louis VII. When the holiness of Louis IX had put the renown of all his predecessors in the shade, it was quite natural that he should take the place of the other Louis in people's minds[9] In the same way did Alexander the Great and Charlemagne absorb all their namesakes.[10*]

This shows us that people at large are not, as we are, bothered by chronology. They were not startled to hear it read out, for instance, that St Austremonius was sent to Auvergne by St Clement in the reign of the emperor Decius.[11] It seemed all right to them that there should have been dukes and counts during the same reign; and why should they have suspected that it was an anachronism to give the title of archdeacon to St Stephen and St Lawrence, who were certainly not deacons as that office was understood later?

Neither was geography any difficulty, and distances did not exist. No eyebrow was raised at stories which confused Caesarea Philippi with Caesarea in Palestine,[12] or spoke of a war between the last named city and Carthage.[13] The caravan of seventy camels sent into the desert by the prefect of Périgueux, Isquirinus, to relieve the seventy monks dying of hunger there, did not seem to the hearers any the less interesting because the desert was situated on the banks of the river Dordogne.[14] No doubt they would be more critical about the topography of their own neighbourhood, for there the facts were right under their eyes; but why trouble about places that are farther off?[15]

Popular understanding of history is no less unsophisticated. For example, its idea of the persecutions under the Roman empire. No distinction is made between the emperors who ordered or those who allowed proceedings against Christians; there is but one epithet for them, they are all *impiissimus,* whether it be Nero, Decius or Diocletian, Trajan, Marcus Aurelius or Alexander Severus. All are equally inspired by the same insane hatred of Christianity, none has any concern but to destroy it. Often it is the emperor in person who presides at the trial of Christians, involving long journeys for himself which history does not record—and for good reason.

It was obvious that the head of state could not be everywhere at once, but that is no obstacle to his rage; he is worthily represented by emissaries, who scour the whole empire. Christians are outlawed everywhere, searched out and dragged before ferocious judges, who contrive to invent frightful tortures, that in fact were never inflicted on even the worst criminals. The intervention from on high which prevents these ingenious torments from harming the martyrs throws their persecutors' cruelty into higher relief, and at the same time provides an adequate and perceptible explanation of the numerous conversions which atrocious cruelty could do nothing to stop.[16]

That is a miniature sketch of the persecutions as seen in popular legend. Variations in legislation and in enforcement of the laws, the very marked individuality of the great enemies of Christianity, the local character of some outbreaks in which Christians suffered, such things do not touch the mind of the people at all; they would much rather have a simple picture that is brightly coloured and strongly drawn than a product of all these complicated factors.

Need we add that for them there is no such thing as historical sequence? They do not notice if a martyr's passion is dated indifferently to the reign of the wicked Decius or Numerian or Diocletian.[17*] They do not care about the judge's name, and are not puzzled about how the cruel Dacianus could have been at work in both Spain and Italy at the same time. They are not familiar with the long roll of popes, and the part played by a Pope Cyriacus does not arouse suspicion of the legend of the eleven thousand virgins,[18] any more than they are surprised at the mention of a Pope Alexander in that of St Ouen (Audoenus).[19]*

Thus historical persons are deprived of their individuality, removed from their proper surroundings, and in a way isolated in time and space, so that their image in people's minds is an incongruous and unreal one. An idealized figure takes the place of history's sharply defined and living portrait, and this figure is no more than the personification of an abstraction : instead of an individual, the people see only a type. Alexander personifies the conqueror; Julius Caesar, the organizational genius of the Roman people; Constantine stands for the Empire regenerated by Christianity.

· In truly popular hagiographical legends it is not St Lawrence who is portrayed, but the typical figure of a martyr; later on, St Martin becomes the typical missionary bishop and worker of miracles. There is the typical persecutor too, Diocletian in particular, and certain judges are as it were incarnations of the cruelty of heathen magistrates. One of the most famous is the formidable Anullinus, who in reality was proconsul of Africa during the great persecution. His name has become a synonym for a slayer of martyrs, and many are the legends that call on him to have Christians put to death, at Lucca, Milan, Ancona, in the days of Nero, Valerian, Gallienus, Maximian, to say nothing of the accounts of what he was really responsible for.[20]

It is not surprising that the reading of some hagiographical documents is a monotonous business, and that there are striking likenesses to be found between the acts of many different martyrs. Historical documents, such as the acts of St Polycarp, of SS. Perpetua and Felicity or of St Cyprian, display notable variations on the one theme; but *legends* of the martyrs are always repeating themselves, for they have almost wholly got rid of the personal element and only an abstract figure is left. Generally speaking, the martyr is everywhere inspired in the same way, voices the same thoughts, undergoes the same ordeals; the holy confessor whose good life has brought him to Heaven must have had all the virtues befitting his state of life, and the hagiographer, faithfully echoing popular tradition, loves to catalogue them.

Look at this portrait of St Fursey: "Erat enim forma praecipuus, corpore castus, mente devotus, affabilis colloquio, amabilis adspectu, prudentia praeditus, temperantia clarus, interna fortitudine firmus, censura iustitiae stabilis, longanimitate assiduus, patientia robustus, humilitate mansuetus, caritate sollicitus, et ita in eo omnium virtutum decorem sapientia adornabat, ut secundum apostolum sermo illius semper in gratiae sale esset conditus".[21]* That is indeed a fine panegyric; but could not the same be said of every saint?

The biographer of St Aldegund describes her thus: "Erat namque moribus honesta, eloquio suavis, in pauperibus misericors, in lectione velox, in responsis citissima, mitis omnibus, inter nobiles humilis, iunioribus quasi aequalis, in parcitate cibi et potus ita dedita abstinentiae ut nulla sodalium sibi aequipararetur".[22]* A few facts illustrating how these virtues were manifested would be far more impressive than this conventional picture. But the people have only a simple, generalized idea of holiness, and the hagiographer is its interpreter. You ask for a living portrait, and he gives you a programme.

What is more, there is very little variety in this programme, for poverty of invention is another characteristic of the popular mind; it always develops along the same lines, and its combinations and permutations show little of interest. The creative faculties seem doomed to barrenness directly people have got a few themes that are sufficient in interest and number to be adaptable to most situations. The comparative study of folk tales has shown that the same stories recur among all peoples and in all lands, that they can be reduced to a small number of subjects that are the same everywhere, and that they appear to have spread over the world from a common stock.

In our day, as we all know, famous sayings are constantly coming out in "new editions" under fresh labels, an amusing anecdote is pinned now on this person, then on that;[23] a classic example is the absent-minded man of legend, whose misfortunes are always the same: what town or village is without a local specimen?

Ancient writers provide any number of examples of the passing on of legendary themes. We have only to read over the old historians' accounts of well-known military sieges to find that the results of famine, the steadfastness of the besieged, and their tricks to hide their bad state from the enemy are nearly always reported in the same way. When the Gauls laid siege to Rome, soldiers were reduced to soaking leather from their shields and sandals in water to try and extract a little nourishment in this way. If we may believe Livy, the same thing happened at the siege of Casilinum during the second Punic war, and also at the siege of Jerusalem, on the evidence of Josephus. During the same siege of Rome, women cut off their hair to twist it into ropes; the women of Carthage, Salona, Byzantium, Aquileia, Thasos, and yet other cities[24] made this sacrifice too (it may well be called heroic, seeing that contemporary fashion in hairdressing did not require it). Medieval chronicles also are full of ingenious dodges whose aim was to hoodwink the enemy, who are duly taken in and raise the siege.[25*] It is sufficient to put these curious stories side by side with others of the same kind to see how much they are worth as history.

Examples could be varied indefinitely, and strange cases adduced of bizarre legends becoming naturalized in the most disparate places. Who would believe that the Irish had thought fit to borrow his donkey's ears from King Midas[26] and to bestow them on at least two of their own kings?[27]

A systematic classification of legendary motifs supplied by hagiographical documents would lead to similar conclusions. Many of the striking episodes that an inexperienced reader takes for original contributions are simply reminiscences, wandering features that have got attached now to one saint, now to another.

The crucifix which miraculously appears to St Hubert[28] between the antlers of a stag is not peculiar to his legend. It is also found in those of St Meinulf[29] and of St Eustace,[30] without speaking of many others wherein differences of detail make the incident less plainly recognizable. Lists have been made of saints who overcame a dragon,[31] but they all need to be made more

complete before óne could hope to exhaust the subject in some degree. But I do not see any point in doing so. It is nearly always a
waste of time to try and find the historical fact which lies behind
the introduction of this epic incident into a saint's life : one might
just as well ask why a seed carried by the wind has fallen on this
spot here rather than that one there.

A critic has rightly expressed distrust of a detail in the acts of
SS. Sergius and Bacchus.[32] The body of the second martyr, having
been thrown onto the public highway, is protected from maraud-
ing dogs by birds of prey.[33] The bodies of St Vincent,[34] St Vitus,[35]
St Florian[36] and St Stanislaus of Cracow[37] are protected in the
same remarkable way; and we must not forget the eagle which
Solomon summoned to guard the body of David, and other parallels in Talmudic writings.[38] Talking of eagles, it is to be remembered that the miraculous bird who spread its wings to shield St
Servatius,[39] St Bertulf,[40] St Medard[41] and others from sun and
rain is also met in other than hagiographical contexts.

In the Life of St Elizabeth of Hungary we read that her husband, when leaving to go on a crusade, gave her a ring whose stone
had the property of breaking when any harm befell the donor.
This legend, probably introduced into the story because of some
historic happening, is found in a slightly different form in the life
of St Honorius of Buzançais. It is a popular feature which has not
only been used in the romance of *Flores and Blanchefleur,* but
also in the *Thousand and One Nights,* in a Kalmuk tale and in
more than one Indian tale.[42]

The dramatic adventure of St Elizabeth of Portugal's page is
a Christian adaptation of a story that originated in India;[43] and
according to some scholars the story of St Francis Xavier's crucifix, which fell into the sea and was recovered by a crab, is derived
from Japanese mythology.[44]

At Valencia in Spain there is kept in Saint Saviour's church an
image of Christ which arrived there miraculously by sea, floating
against the tide. At Santa Maria del Grao, the port of Valencia,
there is another image of Christ, together with the ladder used at
his crucifixion; these also came there by sea, in a ship empty alike

of crew and freight. The vessel stopped in mid-stream, and the inhabitants on either shore began to quarrel about who should have these holy relics. To settle the dispute, the ship was towed out to the open sea and there set adrift to go where it would; it at once returned to the river and took up its station near the Santa Maria bank.[45]

Pausanias gives a similar account of the coming of the statue of Hercules to Erythrae. It arrived from Tyre on a raft and stopped at the headland of Juno, called Cape Mesata because it is halfway between Erythrae and Khios. As soon as they saw the god, the inhabitants of each town did all they could to ensure possession of it; but the heavens decided in favour of Erythrae. A fisherman from there, named Phormio, was told in a dream that if the women made a tow-rope of their hair they would be able easily to pull the raft; accordingly the Thracian women living in the town sacrificed their locks, and thus won the miraculous statue for Erythrae.[46] The two legends are identical except for the final details.

There is no theme more hackneyed in popular hagiography than the miraculous arrival of the image or the body of a saint in a derelict vessel; nor anything more commonplace than the miraculous stopping of a ship, or the refusal of draught oxen to go on, in order to indicate the place mysteriously predestined to be the home of some sacred treasure or to confirm a church in the lawful ownership of a saint's relics.[47]* Think of the arrival of St James in Spain, of St Lubentius at Dietkirchen, of St Maternus at Rodenkirchen, of St Emmeramus at Regensburg, of our Lady's girdle at Prato, of the *Volto Santo* at Lucca.[48]

Research has shown that the miraculous travels of crucifixes, madonnas and images of saints are particularly numerous in Sicily.[49] Similar inquiries elsewhere would probably result in as many discoveries in other countries.[50] In Istria an occurrence of the same kind is associated with Constantine's foundation of the see of Pedena.[51] The panegyrist of St Theodore of Sykeon attributed power of speech to an animal in order to declare the saint's express approval of the resting-place chosen for him.[52] The oxen bringing St Cyril of Gortyna to execution stopped at the right place in consequence of a command from on high,[53] and then there is the part played by camels in the story of St Menas the Egyptian.[54*]

There would be no end to a list of the commonplaces of hagiography. The examples we have given show that some of them are very old indeed, and that is a point that cannot be emphasized too much. Many of the legendary motifs found all over the place in the Lives of the saints, in accounts of the foundation of famous shrines and in stories about the origin of some miraculous images, already occur in the classics of antiquity. The ancients themselves would have been hard put to it to tell us where they came from; for them, as for us, they were leaves floating in the air, brought by the wind from afar.

The picture or letter dropped from heaven, the *akheiropoietos* or image not made by human hands, is not an invention of Christian story-tellers. The legend of the Palladium of Troy, the statue of Pallas Athene that fell from the sky and many similar legends show how familiar these ideas were to the men of old.[55] Like ourselves, they knew of sacred images which shed tears,[56] of statues exuding sweat in calamitous times,[57] of voices speaking from marble lips.[58]

The Lives of St Ambrose of Cahors, St Maurilius,[59] St Maglorius,[60] St Kentigern[61] and others tell us of objects lost in the sea and recovered from a fish's belly; it is only a reminiscence of Polycrates' ring, a story known to Herodotus.[62] The bees that swarmed in the cradle of St Ambrose,[63] and also visited St Isidore,[64] had long ago deposited their honey in the mouths of Pindar[65] and of Plato.[66] The rock opening to receive St Thecla[67] and St Ariadne[68] to shelter them from their pursuers is an echo of the fable of Daphne, just as the story of St Barbara recalls that of Danae, whose father shut her up in a brazen tower.[69]

Suetonius relates how, once when he was still a boy, Augustus silenced the frogs that were croaking round his grandfather's country house, and he adds that it is said that since then the frogs there have always been silent.[70] This same marvel has been credited to more than one saint: St Rieul (Regulus) of Senlis, St Antony

of Padua, St Benno of Meissen, St George of Suelli, St Ouen, St
Harvey (Herveus), St James of the March, St Segnorina, St
Ulphia.[71]*

It will be remembered with what vigour, at the beginning of his
Life of St Paul [the Hermit], St Jerome describes the horrors of
the persecution under Decius and Valerian : the martyr smeared
with honey and exposed to the biting of insects, and that other one
who bit out his tongue and spat it in the face of a woman sent to
seduce him from virtue.[72] The charm and vividness of Jerome's
writing give these stories an appearance of authenticity which they
can hardly claim. Torture by insects appears to be a reminiscence
deriving from Apuleius[73] or some such writer;[74] while the biting
out of the tongue was related several times by the ancients, and
attributed variously to the Pythagorean Timycha, to the harlot
Leaena and to the philosopher Zeno of Elea.[75] In recording this
Christian adaptation of an ancient legend, St Jerome did not ensure its final attribution; it was later told of the martyr Nicetas,[76]
and Nicephorus Callistus told it yet again, this time of an ascetic
who lived in the time of Diocletian.[77]

It is hardly necessary to recall the story of the Seven Sleepers.
The theme of a long sleep is already found in the legend of Epi-
menides, and it has gone on being used in folk tales under numberless forms.[78]

The apparent complexity of certain legends, and the unlooked-
for impression made by certain apparently very well contrived
arrangements of material, must not deceive us into drawing hasty
conclusions in favour of the creative ability of the people's genius.
Historical elements which cannot be easily simplified are merely
juxtaposed, and held together by threads that are usually of the
flimsiest. The resulting narratives are often incoherent and nearly
always extremely unconvincing.

But the general effect is not always lacking in grandeur and
impressiveness. Here, for instance, is one version of the legend of
the wood of Christ's cross. When Adam was driven from paradise
he took with him a branch from the tree of knowledge, and used
it as a staff till the end of his days. This staff passed from hand to

hand to the patriarchs, and during the wars an angel hid it in a
cave, where it was found by Jethro when herding his flocks. In his
old age Jethro sent to Moses to come and fetch the staff, which at
Moses' approach miraculously sprang towards him. This was the
staff on which Moses set up the brazen serpent. Later on it belonged to Phineas, who hid it in a waste place; and at the time of
Christ's birth the exact spot was revealed to St Joseph, who recovered the staff at the time of the flight into Egypt. He handed it
on to his son Jacob, who in turn gave it to Judas, the betrayer, and
from him it came into the hands of Christ's executioners; from it
was made the cross on which the Saviour of the world died.[79]

It will be agreed that, reduced to these terms, the legend of the
wood of the cross does not display much inventiveness, though the
root idea of the underlying continuity of the two Dispensations
gives it a certain dignity.

The legend of Judas's thirty pieces of silver has a similar flavour.
The coins were minted by Abraham's father, and used by Abraham to buy a piece of land as a burial-place for himself and his
family. Later they came into the hands of Jacob's sons, being the
money paid them by the slave-dealers to whom they had sold
Joseph; Jacob's sons in turn paid the same coins over for the corn
that Joseph supplied them with in Egypt. When Jacob died they
were expended on spices for his burial, and thus reached the land
of Sheba, where they remained till the Queen of Sheba included
them amongst other gifts to Solomon's temple. From Jerusalem the
coins passed into Arabia to come back again with the Magi. The
Virgin Mary took them with her on the flight into Egypt, and
there lost them. They were found by a shepherd who kept them by
him until, stricken with leprosy, he went to Jerusalem to ask Christ
to cure him. In gratitude he gave the thirty coins to the Temple,
and from the hands of the priests they passed to Judas, the wages
of his betrayal. When Judas repented and gave back the price of
his crime to the priests, they gave half of it to the soldiers who
guarded Christ's tomb and the other half to the potter from whom
was bought a field wherein to bury strangers.[80]

A similar succession of events has been used to identify the stone in the coronation-chair of the sovereigns of England in West-minster Abbey with the stone used as a pillow by the patriarch Jacob.[81] Many examples could be quoted of such puerile linking up of historical memories to produce narratives that appear to be highly elaborated, but which in reality are childishly simple.

The fancies of popular imagination have not been at work only on the famous names and events of sacred history. That imagi-nation has often been given its head with reference to well-known saints, the presence of whose tombs and the existence of a living cultus of whom prevented their being overlooked or confused with one another. The obvious thing to do was to group them together, to contrive family relationships or an activity in common, to invent a story in which each one of them should have his own fixed part to play, without regard to whether the same saint might not be taking incompatible parts in two different groups. Thus whole cycles of legends have arisen that are purely imaginary, in spite of their historical names and a given topographical setting.

The best-known example is that of the Roman martyrs, whose legends form a series of cycles, each one comprising a number of saints, who frequently had nothing in common but their burial place.[82] Some of these legends are interesting and, in parts, not without poetry; others, and they form the majority, are trifling and irrelevant. All the same, taken as a whole, a picture emerges from these legends, one that was not designed but is nevertheless impressive: if only there had been a poet to work up the raw material of these shapeless stories, the result could have been an epic of Christian Rome from St Peter's foundation of the mother and mistress of the churches, through the bloody conflicts of the days of persecution, down to the victory under Silvester and Con-stantine. But the genius who might have been able to give us this masterpiece did not appear; and our sense of the subject's gran-deur enables us the more to appreciate the poverty of the legends that we have and the lack of inspiration and originality in the productions of the people at large.

II.—*Predominance of sense impressions over ideas. Localizations and identifications. Literary origin of some of these. Legends arising from pictures and statues. Popular etymology. Miracles. Crowd psychology. Vigour of expression. Intensity of feeling. Ambitions of particular churches. Mass morality. Local claims.*

The mass mind, then, is narrow, unable to deal with several ideas at once, or even with a single idea if it be at all complex, unable too to follow any chain of reasoning that is close or subtle; but all ready, on the other hand, to receive impressions through the senses. An idea is easily obliterated, but a picture remains; the people as a whole is attracted by the material side of things, its thoughts and feelings are all associated with objects of sense. In this its intellectual level is that of a child, for abstractions are meaningless to a child too and it turns instinctively to whatever is glittering and attractive to the senses; the thoughts and memories of a child are all indissolubly bound up with concrete material things.

And so great men live less in the people's memory than in the stones, rocks, buildings with which their names have become associated by popular whim. For the people's mind hankers after something definite. It is not satisfied with knowing that such-and-such a hero passed through the country—it points out the exact spot where he set foot, the tree beneath which he sheltered, the house in which he lodged. Alexander's oak, for instance, which in Plutarch's day was pointed out near the river Cephissus as the place where he pitched his tent at the battle of Chaeronea;[83] or Horace's house at Venosa, an ancient ruin which still bears his name, though no historical tradition associated it with him; or Virgil's house at Brindisi, a dilapidated relic of the sixteenth century.[84]

Then again, people always want to explain the origin or purpose of whatever strikes the eye, to give a name to everything that attracts attention. Like children, they are content with the first explanation that comes to hand, if that explanation satisfies their fancy and their desire to know, without any intrusion of thought—or of critical sense—to suggest the insufficiency or unlikelihood of what they are inventing. Images that lurk in the imagination, famous names that are remembered, are carried over to curiosities of nature or works of man without a moment's hesitation. The same psychological cause is at work which, all over the world, has attracted well-known names to strangely-shaped rocks or unusual-looking cavities.

In the religious field this instinct works powerfully under both its aspects.

From this point of view there is nothing more interesting than accounts of pilgrimages to famous shrines, and especially to the Holy Land. The oldest narratives of devout pilgrims[85]* are innocent of any trace of the hesitations and uncertainties that beset our most learned expositors where topography is concerned; with magnificent assurance these pilgrims identify the place where David composed the psalms, the rock which Moses struck, the cave in which Elias sheltered, to say nothing of the places mentioned in the gospels, of which not one is overlooked, not excluding the mansion of Dives and the tree which Zacchaeus climbed. The degree to which material things dominate the mind, the senses stifle thought, is shown by the fact that people claim to have seen the very stone "which the builders rejected", and to have acquired relics *e lignis trium tabernaculorum,* of the three arbours which St Peter in his excitement wanted to build on the hill of the Transfiguration.[86]

In the same way saints' names are often associated with old monuments or noteworthy places which have a popular appeal. It is natural enough that in Rome the Mamertine prison should have been taken to be the place of St Peter's imprisonment, and that people should believe themselves able to show the exact spot where Simon Magus fell: *Silex ubi cecidit Simon Magus.*[87] Nor is it surprising that so many places in Ireland are associated with the memory of St Patrick, in Naples with St Januarius, in Touraine and around Autun with St Martin.

It is no less a particular example of a universal phenomenon that slight hollows in rocks should be greeted as the print of the feet, the hands, the knees of St Peter, St George, St Martin, just as elsewhere the footmarks of Adam, of Abraham, of Moses, of Buddha are shown.[88] It is a matter of indifference that many of these attributions, especially where megalithic monuments are concerned, have been christianized and that the Blessed Virgin and other saints should have taken the places of the heroes of heathen legends; that St Cornelius, rather than somebody else, should turn King Adar's soldiers to stone, thus forming the avenues of Carnac and Erdeven in Brittany,[89] that a fairy, rather than St Frodoberta, should drop stones useless for building purposes near the Maillard pool in the *département* of Seine-et-Marne,[90*] does not affect the identity of popular tradition, still manifesting the intellectual level of childhood.

It must not be forgotten that very precise localizations often have an origin that is purely literary. Romeo and Juliet existed only in poetical imagination,[91] but the visitor to Verona is shown their dwellings and their tomb; two ruined castles on neighbouring hills have become the residences of the Capulets and Montagues.[92*] In Alsace are shown the forge which Schiller "immortalized" in his ballad of Fridolin, and the castle of the counts of Saverne, despite the fact that these gentlemen never existed.[93] And this example shows that traditions of this kind do not need much time in which to take root and grow. Until Schiller versified the old tale in 1797 it had never been localized in Alsace; the popularity of his telling of it was all that was needed to materialize the tale and settle it exactly in a particular place.

Hagiography provides plenty of examples of such topographical legends. At Sofia (Sardica) near the church of St Petka (Parasceve), there is to be seen an aged tree-trunk half buried in a wall and covered with notches. This is known as St Therapon's Tree, and the people believe that the saint was martyred close by it. On his feast-day, May 27, they come in pilgrimage, and make a point of taking away little pieces of the sacred wood, to which special powers are attributed. Now St Therapon did not die at

Sardica; he belonged to Sardis, and according to his legend a great oak-tree grew up there from the ground his blood had soaked. This oak, always in leaf, was, we read, still in place and curing every disease.[94] Sardis having once been confused with Sardica, the miraculous tree soon followed the name of the town and was "transplanted".[95]

In view of this sort of thing there is little need to insist on the fallaciousness of trying to follow a saint's movements by means of the landmarks offered by legend. Such attempts have sometimes been made, and history has not exactly reaped advantage from them.[96]

Popular fancy has not been at work only on buildings and natural stones. Pictures and statues wrongly interpreted have been the starting-point of a crowd of odd legends.[97] A poet is represented resting his foot on a big book; so he must have been the most learned of mankind, for he could read with his feet.[98] During the middle ages the two fine statues on Monte Cavallo in Rome gave currency to a curious story : they were said to represent two famous philosophers, named Phidias and Praxiteles, who came to Rome in the reign of Tiberius and had the peculiar habit of walking about the city stark naked, in order to teach the nothingness of earthly things.[99]

What has not been imagined to explain images of saints? St Lucy is sometimes represented carrying two eyes on a plate, to remind people that she is invoked for the cure of eye troubles. This gave rise to the story that, to rid herself of the attentions of a young man enamoured of the beauty of her eyes, Lucy plucked them from their sockets and threw them to the tiresome youth, imploring him to leave her alone.[100] The origin of the legend of St Nicholas and the three children is also generally attributed to a pictorial convention,[101] and a symbol taken materially led to a whole romance growing round a feature in the Life of St Julian the Hospitaller.[102] Later on we shall see that the extraordinary story of St Livrade (Liberata) merely transposes into popular terms the explanation of the peculiar features of a religious image.

Here is another example drawn from hagiography. An inscription, now in the museum at Marseilles, refers to a certain Eusebia, abbess of Saint Quiricus: *Hic requiescit in pace Eusebia religiosa magna ancella Dei,* without indication that any cultus was accorded to this worthy woman. But her body had been laid in an older stone coffin, which bore the carved image of the dead person for whom it had originally been intended; it was the head and shoulders of a clean-shaven man, which in the course of time had become worn and damaged. This was enough to give birth to a legend, which related that St Eusebia, abbess of a convent at Marseilles, together with her forty companions, cut off their noses to escape outrage by the Saracens. "Quam traditionem confirmat generosae illius heroinae effigies, dimidia facie et naso praeciso supra tumulum posita cum epigraphe", says a Benedictine monk quoted by Le Blant.[103*]

More than one legend owes its existence to names misunderstood, or to resemblances in sound. To the vagaries of popular etymology collected by several learned scholars,[104] there must be added a very numerous body of cases that are special to hagiography; but we must confine ourselves to a few brief examples.

The church of SS. Nereus and Achilleus in Rome, on the Appian Way near the Baths of Caracalla, was known in ancient times as the *Titulus de Fasciola.*[105] Opinions differ about the meaning of this term. Some think that Fasciola is the name of the foundress of the church; others regard it as a topographical expression whose origin is obscure. The scholars may hesitate, but legend knows nothing of hesitation. The name Fasciola, it tells us, is a reminiscence of St Peter. As he went by there on his way from prison, a bandage (*fasciola*) round his injured leg fell off, "Tunc beatissimus Petrus", says an old account, "dum tibiam demolitam haberet de compede ferri, cecidit ei fasciola ante Septisolium in via nova".[106*] Notice the unsophisticated mind of the people, which thinks that a famous man cannot drop his handkerchief without the spot being at once marked and remembered and honoured by the setting up of a memorial.

It is well known that a sound may influence people's idea of a saint, with the result that a pun is sometimes decisive in the choice of a patron. In France, for example, St Clare is invoked in cases of eye trouble, because she enables people to see clearly (*voir clair*); St Ouen cures the deaf, because he enables them to hear (*ouïr*); St Cloud cures boils (*clous*). In some parts of Germany it is St Augustine who heals bad eyes (*Auge*), in other parts he is invoked against a bad cough (*Husten*). Lists have been made of these plays on words;[107] they are not all of popular origin, scholars have amused themselves by adding to them. There is one of relatively recent date that had a surprising and regrettable success: thanks to his name, St Expeditus came to be regarded as the advocate in cases of pressing emergency.[108]

Owing to the working of phonetic laws, the names of some saints have become unrecognizable. Near Rome, on the way to Porto, there is a little country church, a dependency of the basilica of St Mary "in via Lata", which is known as Santa Passera. No such saint is to be found in the calendars. Who was she? Unbelievably enough, the chapel and its name are meant to commemorate the translation of the relics of SS. Cyrus and John, martyrs formerly honoured at Menuthis, near Alexandria. Saint Cyrus, ἀββὰ Κῦρος Abbacirus, was finally transformed into Passera.[109*] Did this metamorphosis end there, or has the new female saint acquired her own legend? I do not know, but it would not surprise me if she has. The least that could happen is that St Passera should be confused with St Praxedes—and that has come about.[110*]

Surely enough has now been said to show that, among the people at large, the senses govern the understanding, that there is a certain sluggishness of mind that stops short at what can be touched, seen, heard, unable to rise to a higher level. This mental insufficiency explains people's blind attraction towards what is marvellous, the supernatural made concrete. The thought of the invisible sovereignty of divine Providence is not enough; the inward working of grace does not offer anything that can be seen or taken hold of; and the soul's mysterious commerce with God has to be translated into concrete effects if it is to make any impression on the people's mind. The supernatural makes full appeal to it only if the supernatural is blended with the marvellous, and consequently popular legends are overflowing with wonders. Visions, prophecies and miracles are a necessary part of the lives of saints as recounted by the people.

There is no point in writing here about the marvels wrought through the intercession of wonder-working saints in favour of those who visit their shrines or touch their relics; these form a special class of event, which needs to be studied separately. But everything to do with the saint is, as it were, impregnated with miraculous elements. His greatness is heralded before he is yet born, and visible signs of Heaven's favour attend his cradle; angels watch over his every footstep, nature is at his command, wild beasts acknowledge his power; in direct peril he can always count on rescue from on high. Indeed, it would seem that God in a way defers to the whims of his friends, multiplying wonders without any observable reason. The staff of St Géry (Gaugericus) stood upright without support all the time its owner was praying,[111] and the same thing happened while St Julian talked with King Chlotar.[112] Several saints hung their cloaks on a sunbeam, or gave back life to fowls already turning on the spit. Bd Marianus Scotus needed no candle when he wrote after dark, for his fingers gave off the necessary light.[113] The same convenience was granted to a peasant, at the prayer of St Sebald, to enable him to find his straying kine.[114] St Ludwin was protected from the sun's rays by an eagle's outstretched wings,[115] and St Landoald's servant carried fire to his master in the skirt of his tunic.[116] Joshua's miracle was renewed in favour of St Ludwin to allow him to ordain priests at Rheims and at Laon, both on the same day.[117] This is a field in which popular imagination knew no limits; and it cannot be denied that, in certain environments, especially among people of poetic disposition, these bold and artless fictions sometimes attain a real beauty.

However, the fertility of these hagiographical "troubadours" must not be exaggerated. A methodical classification of the themes that they use shows that repetitions are frequent, and that the semblance of variety found in some groups of legends is principally due to new arrangements of old commonplaces. We must especially beware of supposing that from an artistic standpoint the level of the miracle-centred productions of popular hagiography is in general a high one. Apart from a few really happy finds and interesting *motifs* well marked out, we are confronted with nothing but platitudes and grotesque fancies that are frequently altogether fantastic. The feverish imagination thirsts for wonders, it is itching with ambition to outstrip extraordinary stories by others yet more extraordinary; and only too often it exceeds all propriety in a sphere wherein opportunities for ingenius fiction are endless.

The time came when the miracle of relics arriving in an abandoned ship[118] had been related so often that it appeared trite; so they were made to float on the water in a stone coffin. Thus did St Mamas come to Cyprus,[119] St Julian to Rimini,[120] St Liberius to Ancona.[121] For a child to stir in his mother's womb, as did St John the Baptist, was esteemed not to do justice to a holy man's greatness. St Fursey spoke before he was born,[122] and so did St Isaac, who made his voice heard three times in one day.[123] This hardly surpasses the prodigy of St Rumwold, an English baby who lived only three days; he not only pronounced his profession of faith in such a way as to be understood by all the bystanders, but also preached a long sermon to his parents and relatives before dying.[124]

In the *Acta Petri* we read of a seven-months-old child who, "in a manly voice", addressed passionate reproaches to Simon Magus;[125] and what is more, of a big dog which talked with St Peter, and was entrusted by him with a message for Simon.[126] Commodian has preserved the memory of a lion which spoke up in support of St Paul's preaching.[127] It is possible that these stories are reminiscences of Balaam's ass, unless indeed they were suggested by reading the fabulists.

Such wild excesses invite us to consider the emotions which beset the people at large, intense, unrestrained emotions which give
to everything they touch a stamp of exaggeration and sometimes
violence, as so many legends testify. The multitude is moved by
very strong feelings: it knows nothing of moderate opinions or
fine distinctions, which it can neither perceive nor express; when
it says what it thinks and feels it does so vigorously.

One example from among many, concerning St Catald of Tar-
anto. His holiness was manifested by some very remarkable happenings, and so an ecclesiatical inquiry was set on foot to decide
whether they were miraculous or not. This was too unexciting for
the public; and the legend tells us that the pope himself, with all
his cardinals, visited Catald's house and examined it from cellar
to attic.[128] We are reminded of those painters all whose skill consists in liveliness of expression.

It is hardly necessary to remark that the people's admiration
for its favourites is always unmeasured (and sometimes unjusti-
fied). Every good quality is attributed to them, and it is intoler-
able that other men should appear yet more worthy. Though it
has nothing to do with the history of the saints, there is a specially
instructive example of this in the legend of Saladin. His personal
qualities, in particular his moderation and humaneness, inspired
admiration and liking for him in those whom he conquered, and
gave rise to a wholly unconvincing story, which nevertheless
strongly emphasizes the high regard in which he was held: his
admirers could think of nothing better than to connect this Mos-
lem leader with a French family and to make a knight of him, and
almost a Christian.[129] Again, when people's imagination had been
stirred by the great expeditions to the Holy Land, it seemed impossible that such a warrior as Charlemagne had no part in them;
and so crusades were imported into the story of his life.

At a time when every saint was endowed with every virtue in
the highest degree, and when gentle birth added greatly to a
person's merits, it is not surprising that some saints were posthumously ennobled. But to have lived amongst the Saviour's immediate
following was yet more honourable than noble lineage, and

accordingly old patrons of churches were identified with certain persons referred to in the gospels or who were supposed to have had some part in Christ's life on earth. St Ignatius of Antioch became the little child whom our Lord showed to the people as an example of lowliness and simplicity;[130] St Syrus of Pavia was the boy with the five loaves;[131] St Martial carried the towel when Christ washed his disciples' feet;[132] and St Ursinus read a lesson at the Last Supper.[133]

It will readily be understood that legends associating the mission of the first bishops of important dioceses with Christ himself, or with St Peter, were not prompted solely by disinterested love for the bishops. The passion for exalted origins which made first the Romans and then the Franks connect themselves with the heroes of the *Iliad* found this new ground for self-esteem, and once the process was started churches vied with one another for the distinction of apostolic foundation.

In the East these claims seem to have originated in a literary fraud.[134] The forger who goes by the name of Dorotheus of Tyre drew up a list of the names of all the men in the New Testament, and assigned an episcopal see to each one. He went to work with such enthusiasm that he included several names of people who obviously never were bishops, such as Caesar, whom he got from St Paul's "Salutant te qui de Caesaris domo sunt" (Phil. 4 : 22), without realizing that this Caesar was no other than the emperor Nero.

In the churches of the West, particularly in France,[135] claims to apostolic foundation did not arise in one uniform way; but this is not the place to inquire into the relation between the popular and the literary elements in the development of these famous fictions. What must be said is that the inventors of pretentious stories could always count on popular co-operation in any enterprise that was calculated to flatter local pride.[136]

For as it is useless to expect a high degree of intelligence in a crowd, so it is to expect a high standard of morality. In the aggregate a crowd lacks that sense of responsibility which makes an individual person pause in face of a dishonest or unworthy course of action. It has no scruples, each man leaving it to his neighbour to examine their title to what is claimed for them; there is nothing easier than to set a crowd tingling with patriotism, self-importance or self-interest. So it does not matter much to know whether "apostolic" fantasies and such-like inventions are of literary origin, or whether they are products of the people's imagination which have been worked up by hagiographers, who simply arranged and polished them a little. They belong to the category of legendary productions, and are merely a normal development of popular ideas and aspirations concerning church origins.

Enjoying so complete a freedom, there is no limit to the people's ambitions, there is no difficulty that can restrain their audacity. Neither time nor space prevents them from claiming as their own special property any honoured saint whose reflected glory they covet.

Everybody has heard of the legend of the great St Katherine, whom her biographers connected with Alexandria, both by birth and martyrdom. That did not prevent the Cypriots from annexing her, a saint whose cultus[137]* and legend were amongst the most popular in the Greek as in the Latin church; and this was contrived by means of a device that was as obvious as it was little creditable.

Stephen of Lusignan asserted that he read at Famagusta the Greek text of a life of St Katherine, from which he learned that her father, the famous Costos, was not king of Egypt, but of Cyprus; in proof thereof he had given his name to the town of Salamis, henceforth known as Constantia. At some moment of difficulty Diocletian sent Costos to Alexandria, entrusting him with the government of Egypt. It was at this time that Katherine was born. She was very carefully brought up and became adept in all the liberal arts. After her father's death she went back to Cyprus, where her uncle, learning that she was a Christian, put her in prison at Salamis (the prison was still shown in Stephen's time). Later Katherine was sent back to Egypt, and there the emperor Maxentius, despairing of breaking down her resistance, had her put to death. She was martyred at Alexandria, which, the chronicler adds, accounts for its being said that she was a native of that city.[138]

The Seven Sleepers of Ephesus are so well known by that name, and their legend is so remarkably detailed, that one would have thought they were safe from any attempt at transference. But in fact the cave wherein they slept their three-hundred-years' sleep used to be shown close to Paphos. Stephen of Lusignan is a little surprised at this; but he tries to persuade himself that it might be a different group from the Ephesian one.[139]

St Savinus was a martyr whose veneration is attested in the sixth century[140] at Spoleto, where there was a basilica in his honour.[141] The inhabitants of Spoleto naturally look on him as their fellow citizen, but so do those of Fermo (who have some of his relics) and those of Monselice. At Monte San Savino he has been made a bishop of Chiusi, the near-by town; while at Faenza the citizens said that Savinus once stayed in their district and that, after his martyrdom at Spoleto, his relics were translated. Later on Faenza tried to pass him off as its first bishop.[142]

The connexions which the people endeavour to establish between themselves and their favourite saint are not always equally close. Often it is honour enough to have welcomed him, alive or dead, within their city walls, in which case they have only to invent a journey which does not affect the main lines of his history. It is by this simple device that the celebrated martyr St Nicephorus ("of Antioch")[143] became a local saint in Istria,[144] and that St Maurus has been claimed by so many places—Rome, Fondi, Fleury, Lavello and Gallipoli, without counting Parenzo.[145]

The author of legends is anonymous, and we have now seen him at work. As he himself does not hold the pen, we have usually been obliged to have recourse to the hagiographer, who records his stories and discoveries; but hitherto we have turned to the hagiographer only in so far as he echoes the voice of the people. In what follows, our principal object is to discover what is his own particular contribution and to lay bare the mysteries of his trade.

NOTES ON CHAPTER II

[1]Lazarus and Steinthal, *Zeitschrift für Völkerpsychologie und Sprachwissenschaft*, vols i—xix (Berlin, Leipzig, 1860-89). G. Le Bon's *Psychologie des foules* (Paris, 1895), treated from a very specialized standpoint, has some useful observations as well as some marked exaggerations.

[2]On this example and others like it, see Wachsmuth, "Ueber die Quellen der Geschichtsfälschung", in *Berichte über die Verhandlungen der K. Sächsischen Gesellschaft der Wissenschaften zu Leipzig*, Phil.-Hist. Cl., vol. viii (1856), pp. 121-53. It is worth remembering that legends of the same kind grow up still. "Legend has made of the Civil Code a 2,000-article digest of the Revolution, made by order of the First Consul. In this abridgement of history the Code ceases to be the fruit of centuries of effort on the part of king and *parlement* and of burgesses in their communes and corporations; only the emperor is remembered; it is the *Code Napoléon*" (H. Leroy, "Le centenaire du Code civil", in *Revue de Paris*, 1 Octr 1903).

[3]On the legend of Alexander, see P. Meyer, "Alexandre le Grand dans la littérature française du moyen âge", in *Bibliothèque française du moyen âge*, vol. iv (Paris, 1886); J. Darmesteter, "La légende d'Alexandre chez les Perses", in *Bibliothèque de l'École des Hautes Études*, fasc. 35 (Paris, 1878), pp. 83-99; I. Lévi, "La légende d'Alexandre dans le Talmud", in *Revue des études juives*, vol. ii (1881), p. 203; vol. vii, p. 78; *Mélusine*, vol. v, pp. 116-118; S. S. Hoogstra, *Proza-bewerkingen van het leven van Alexander den Groote in het Middlenederlandsch* (s'Gravenhage, 1898), pp. i-xxiii; F. Kampers, *Alexander der Grosse und die Idee des Weltimperiums in Prophetie und Sage* (Freiburg i. B., 1901). For the legend of Caesar see A. and G. Doutrepont, "La légende de César en Belgique", in *IIIᵉ Congrès des savants catholiques*, vol. v (Brussels, 1894), pp. 80-108. For Charlemagne, see G Paris, *Histoire poétique de Charlemagne* (Paris, 1865); E. Müntz, "La légende de Charlemagne dans l'art au moyen âge", in *Romania*, vol. xiv (1883), p. 320.

[4]G. Lumbroso, *L'Egitto dei Greci e dei Romani*, 2nd edn (Rome, 1895), p. 157.

[5]M. Du Camp, *Orient et Italie* (Paris, 1868), pp. 13, 60, 74.

[6]The subject has been exhaustively treated by D. Comparetti, *Virgilio nel medio evo*, 2nd edn, 2 vols (Florence, 1896); Eng. trans. *Virgil in the Middle Ages* (Stechert, 1929).

[7]A. De Nino, *Ovidio nella tradizione popolare di Sulmona* (Casalbardino, 1886), p. l.

[8]Bulliot, *La mission et le culte de saint Martin d'après les légendes et les monuments populaires dans le pays Éduen.* (Autun, 1892); Shearman, *Loca patriciana* (Dublin, 1879); W. G. Wood-Martin, *Traces of the Elder Faiths of Ireland* (London, 1902), vol. i, pp. 163, 245; ii, 20, 88.

[9]F. Leonormant, *À travers l'Apulie et la Lucanie* vol. i (Paris, 1883) p.323.

[10]It is well known that Alexander the Great has been credited with the foundations of Alexander Severus, and doings that history attributes to Charles Martel have been attached to the name of Charlemagne. P. Rajna, *Le origini dell' epopea francese* (Florence, 1884), p. 199.

[11]*Acta SS.,* Nov., vol. i, p. 49.

[12]*Passio S. Procopii,* no. 27 in *Acta SS.,* July, vol. ii. p. 564.

[13]"Saint Cassiodore", in *Mélanges Paul Fabre* (Paris, 1902), pp. 40-50.

[14]*Vita S. Frontonis a. Gauzberto.* Cf. L. Duchesne, *Fastes épiscopaux de l'ancienne Gaule,* vol. ii, p. 132.

[15]We have written of the value of topographical data in hagiographical legends in *Analecta Bollandiana,* vol. xvi, pp. 222-235, 243-244. For the people's tenacious memory where place-names are concerned, see M. J. Lagrange, *La méthode historique, surtout à propos de l'Ancien Testament* (Paris, 1903), pp. 188-192.

[16]There are many examples in *Les Passions des martyrs et les genres littéraires,* pp. 136-315.

[17]Among other examples, the martyrdom of St Cecily, which is dated sometimes *temporibus Alexandri imperatoris,* sometimes *Marci Aurelii et Commodi temporibus.* Cf. *Analecta Bollandiana,* vol. xxii, pp. 86-88.

[18]*Acta SS.,* Oct., vol. ix, pp. 100-104, 214, 276-278.

[19]*Analecta Bollandiana,* vol. xx, pp. 175-176.—According to the legend of SS Chrysanthus and Daria, they were martyred under Numerian in 283, and their acts were written by order of Pope Stephen, who died in 257 (*Acta SS.,* Oct., vol. xi, p. 484). As a pendant to this anachronism there is the legend of St Florian and his companions at Bologna: their martyrdom is dated in the twenty-seventh year of Heraclius (637), and the translation of their relics is put during the episcopate of St Petronius during the fifth century (*Analecta Bollandiana,* vol. xxiii, p. 298).

[20]See the quotations in Le Blant, *Les Actes des martyrs* (Paris, 1882), p. 27.

[21]["He was indeed a man of distinguished appearance, chaste in body, single-minded, affable of speech, of attractive presence, endowed with good sense and moderation, of resolute spirit, steadfast in right judgement, constant in long suffering, sturdily patient, quiet and humble, full of charity; and wisdom so adorned the beauty of all his virtues that, as the Apostle wrote, his discourse was at all times gracious, seasoned with salt."] *Acta SS.,* Jan. vol. ii, p. 37.

[22]["For her conduct was virtuous, her speech pleasant, she was kind to the poor, she could read easily and give an answer quickly, she was gentle towards everybody, modest among the high-born, like an equal to those below her, and so sparing in her use of food and drink that none of her companions could be compared with her."] *Acta SS.,* Jan., vol. ii, p. 1306.

[23]Some examples were collected by H. Gaidoz, "Légendes contemporaines", in *Mélusine,* vol. ix (1898-99), pp. 77, 118, 140, 187.

[24]The texts were collected by A. Schwegler, *Römische Geschichte,* vol. iii (Tübingen, 1858), p. 260.

[25]Well-fed domestic animals were driven into the besiegers' camp, or the enemy was pelted with loaves or, better still, cheeses (sometimes made from human milk), to make them think that the town was well victualled. See G. Pitrè, *Stratagemmi leggendarii da città assediate,* new ed. (Palermo, 1904), and also in *Archivio per lo studio della tradizioni popolari,* vol. xxii (1903-04), pp. 193-211. Cf. *Romania,* vol. xxxiii (1904), p. 459.

[26]Ovid, *Metam.,* xi, 180 ff; Hyginus, *Fabulae,* 191, 3.

[27]H. d'Arbois de Jubainville, in *Revue celtique,* vol. xxiv (1903), p. 215.

[28]*Acta SS.,* Nov. vol. i, p. 839.

[29]*Acta SS.,* Oct., vol. iii, pp. 188, 212.

[30]*Acta SS.,* Sep., vol. vi, p. 124; H. Delehaye, "La légende de S. Eustache" in *Bulletin de la classe des lettres de l'Académie Royale de Belgique* (1919), pp. 1-36.

[31]For instance, C. Cahier, *Caractéristiques des saints,* vol. i, pp. 315-22. See also M. Meyer, "Ueber die Verwandtschaft heidnischer und christlicher Drachentödter", in *Verhandlungen der XI Versammlung deutscher Philologen* (Leipzig, 1890). pp. 336 ff.

[32]Father Byaeus, in *Acta SS.,* Oct., vol. iii, p. 838.

[33]*Acta SS.,* Oct., vol. iii, p. 867.

[34]Prudentius, *Peristeph.,* v. 102 ff.

[35]*Acta SS.,* Jan., vol. ii, pp. 1025-1026.

[36]*Acta SS.,* May, vol. iv, p. 465.

[37]*Acta SS.,* May, vol. vii, pp. 202-231.

[38]S. Singer, "Salomosagen in Deutschland", in *Zeitschrift für deutsches Alterthum,* vol. xxxv (1891), p. 186; and "Sagen geschichtliche Parallelen aus dem Babylonischen Talmud", in *Zeitschrift des Vereins für Volkskunde,* vol. ii (1892), p 301.

[39]*Acta SS.,* May, vol. iii, p. 215.

[40]*Acta SS.,* Feb., vol. i, p. 679.

[41]*Acta SS.,* Jan., vol. ii, p. 87. Cf Singer, *Salomosagen,* l. c., p. 185.

[42]E. Cosquin, *Contes populaires de Lorraine,* vol. i, p. 71.

[43]E. Cosquin, "La légende du page de sainte Elisabeth de Portugal et le conte indien des 'Bons Conseils' ", in *Revue des Questions historiques,* vol. lxxiii (1903), pp. 3-42; ib., "La légende de sainte Elisabeth de Portugal et les contes orientaux", in the same, vol. lxxiv, pp. 207-217; ib., *Études folkloriques,* pp. 73-162; C. Formichi, "La leggenda del paggio di santa Elisabetta", in *Archivio delle tradizioni popolari,* vol. xxii (1903), pp. 9-30.

[44]Bouhours, *Vie de saint François-Xavier,* book iii. The Japanese legend is told by A. B. Mitford, *Tales of Old Japan* (London, 1871), pp. 40-43. The borrowing was pointed out in *Revue des traditions populaires,* 15 Aug. 1890. I am indebted to E. Cosquin for these references.

[45]See Fages, *Histoire de saint Vincent Ferrier,* vol. ii, pp. 46-47.

[46]Pausanias, vii, 5, 5-8.

[47]In Belgium it is not usually oxen that are used for the transport of sacred things. In the legend of The Christ of the White Ladies of Tirle-

mont it is the canons of Saint-Germain who find it impossible to carry their precious burden any farther. P. V. Bets, *Histoire de Tirlemont* (Louvain, 1861), vol. ii, p. 88. Similarly with the relics of St George in Gregory of Tours, *In gloria martyrum,* c. 101.

[48]The texts have been collected by H. Usener, *Die Sintflutsagen* (Bonn, 1899), pp. 136-137.

[49]G. Pitrè, "Feste patronali in Sicilia", in *Biblioteca delle tradizioni popolari Siciliane,* vol. xxi (Turin, Palermo, 1900), pp. xx-xxii.

[50]On the miraculous crucifix at Hoboken, near Antwerp, see P. D. Kuyl, *Hoboken en zijn wonderdadig kruisbeeld* (Antwerp, 1866), pp. 147-156; on the local legend of St Desiderius (Allier), J. Stramoy, "La légende de sainte Agathe", in *Revue des traditions populaires,* vol. xiii, p. 694; on the coming of St Thomas's relics to Ortona, A. De Nino, *Usi e costumi Abruzzesi,* vol. iv (Florence, 1887) p. 151. There may also be mentioned the legend of St Rainerius of Bagno, *ibid.,* pp. 162-163. See also F. de Mély, "L'image du Christ du Sancta Sanctorum et les reliques chrétiennes apportées par les flots", in *Mémoires de la Société des Antiquaires de France,* series 7, vol. iii (Paris, 1904), pp. 113-144.

[51]Manzuoli, *Vite e fatti de' santi e beati dell' Istria* (Venice, 1711), pp. 107-112.

[52]*Analecta Bollandiana,* vol. xx, p. 269.

[53]*Synaxarium ecclesiae Constantinopolitanae,* pp. 17, 750.

[54]*Bibl. hag. lat.,* n. 5921. The site for the church of St Auxentius in Cyprus also was pointed out by the oxen carrying his relics; C. Sathas, "Vies des saints allemands de Chypre", in *Archives de l'Orient latin,* vol. ii, p. 419.

[55]See the demonstration of this in E. von Dobschütz, "Christusbilder", in *Texte und Untersuchungen,* N.S., vol. iii (Leipzig, 1899).

[56]"Apollo triduum et tres noctes lacrimavit", Livy, xliii, 13.

[57]"Signa ad Iunonis Sospitae sudore manavere", Livy, xxiii, 31.

[58]"Fortunae item muliebris simulacrum, quod est in via Latina non semel sed bis locutum constitit, his paene verbis: 'Bene me matronae vidistis riteque dedicastis' ", Valerius Maximus, i, 8.

[59]Cf. A. Houtin, *Les origines de l'Église d'Angers* (Laval, 1901), pp. 54-55.

[60]*Acta SS.,* Oct., vol. x, p. 787.

[61]*Acta SS.,* Jan., vol. i, p. 820.

[62]Herodotus, *Hist.,* iii, 43. Other parallels are given in R. Köhler, *Kleinere Schriften,* vol. ii (Berlin, 1900), p. 209, n. I.

[63]*Vita a. Paulino,* no. 3.

[64]*Acta SS.,* April, vol. i, p. 331.

[65]Pausanias, ix, 23, 2.

[66]Cicero, *De divinatione,* i, 36; Olympiodorus, *Vita Platonis,* Westermann, p. 1.

[67]Lipsius, *Acta apostolorum apocrypha,* vol. i, p. 272.

[68]P. Franchi de' Cavalieri, "I martirii di santo Teodoto e di santa

Ariadne", in *Studi e Testi*, 6 (Rome, 1901), p. 132. The *Acta sanctae Mariae ancillae* (in *Acta SS.*, Nov., vol. i, pp. 201-206) must not be cited in this connexion as they are not distinct from those of St Ariadne.

[69]Papebroch had already noted the borrowing: *Acta SS. Bollandiana apologeticis libris in unum volumen nunc primum contractis vindicata* (Antwerp, 1755, p. 370).

[70]Suetonius, *Octavius*, xciv. Antigonus, Ἱστοριῶν παραδόξων συναγωγή, 2, relates the same thing of Hercules. Keller, p. I.

[71]The hagiographical texts are collected in *Caractéristiques des saints* by Cahier, who is not concerned with the early origin of the incident (vol. i, pp. 274-276). Many legends could be quoted in which other animals play a similar part, as of St Tygris, virgin, who silenced the sparrows who disturbed her prayers and were never heard again (*Acta SS.*, June, vol. v, p. 74, n. 9). For the same reason St Ursinus silenced the birds at Levroux; when he came that way St Martin restored their power of song (*Acta SS.*, Nov., vol. iv., p. 103). Wild boars attracted hordes of hunting men to the neighbourhood of the monastery of St Caesarius of Arles; at his prayer the animals disappeared (*Acta SS.*, Aug., vol. vi, p. 72, n. 36).

[72]These unnamed martyrs are referred to in the Roman Martyrology under July 28.

[73]*Metamorph.*, viii, 22.

[74]See P. Franchi de' Cavalieri, *Hagiographica*, p. 124; and there are the torments of Mark of Arethusa: Gregory Naz., *In Iulian.*, i, 89; Sozomen, *Hist. eccl.*, v. 10.

[75]The principal classical texts are given by Wachsmuth, *Berichte der k. Sächs. Gesellschaft der Wissenschaften*, Phil. Hist. Cl., vol. viii (1856), p. 132.

[76]*Acta. SS.*, Sep., vol. iv, p. 7.

[77]*Hist. eccl.*, vii, 13.

[78]H. Demoulin, "Epiménide de Crète", in *Bibliothèque de la Faculté de Philosophie et Lettres de l'Université de Liège*, fasc. xii (Brussels, 1901), pp. 96-100, where other versions of the legend of a long sleep are indicated.

[79]F. Kampers, *Mittelalterliche Sagen vom Paradiese und vom Holze des Kreuzes Christi* (Cologne, 1897), pp. 89-90. Cf. W. Meyer, "Die Geschichte des Kreuzholzes von Christus", in *Abhandlungen der k. Bayer. Akademie der Wissenschaften*, I Cl., vol. xvi (1881).

[80]See, for example, A. Graf, *Roma nella memoria e nelle immaginazioni del medio evo* (Turin, 1883), vol. ii, pp. 462-463; L. De Feis, "Le monete del prezzo di Giuda", in *Studi Religiosi*, vol. ii (1902), pp. 412-430, 506-521. In passing, notice the version of the legend of the thirty pieces of silver in Solomon of Basra, *The Book of the Bee*, ed. E. A. Wallis Budge (Oxford, 1886), pp. 94 ff.

[81]J. H. Rivett-Carnac, "La piedra de la coronación en la abadía de Westminster y su conexion legendaria con Santiago de Compostela", in *Boletín de la real academia de la Historia*, vol. xl (1902), pp. 430-438.

[82]*Analecta Bollandiana,* vol. xvi, pp. 217 ff.

[83]Plutarch, *Alexander,* ix, 2.

[84]F. Lenormant, *À travers l'Apulie et la Lucanie,* vol. i (Paris, 1883), pp. 202-203. In the same way the site of Ovid's house is still shown at Sulmona: A. De Nino, *Ovidio nella tradizione di Sulmona* (Casalbordino, 1886), p. 21.

[85]See especially the narratives of Antoninus, Theodosius and Adamnan: Geyer, *Itinera Hierosolymitana saec. IIII-VIII,* in *Corpus script. eccl. lat.,* vol. xxxix.

[86]*Angilberti abbatis de ecclesia Centulensi libellus,* M.G.H., Scr., vol. xv, p. 17.

[87]L. Duchesne, *Le Forum chrétien* (Rome, 1899), p. 17.

[88]S. Reinach, "Les monuments de pierre brute dans le langage et les croyances populaires", in *Revue archéologique,* 3rd series, vol. xxi, p. 224.

[89]S. Reinach, op. cit., p. 355.

[90]Id., p. 354. Many miraculous imprints in Italy have been remarked by scholars; their notes were printed in *Archivio per lo studio delle Tradizioni popolari,* vol. xxii (1903), p. 128, and the preceding years. A number of these imprints are attributed to various popular saints. There are other examples in F. Lanzoni, *Le fonti della leggenda di Sant' Apollinare di Ravenna* (Bologna, 1915), p. 57.

[91]L. Frankel, "Untersuchungen zur Entwickelungsgeschichte des Stoffes von Romeo und Julia", in *Zeitschrift für vergleichende Literaturgeschichte,* N.S., vol. iii (1890), pp. 171ff.; iv, 48ff.; G. Brognoligo, "La leggenda di Giulietta e Romeo", in *Giornale Ligustico,* vol. xix (1892), pp. 423-439.

[92]According to Dante the Cappelleti and the Montecchi were not historical people but types. R. Davidsohn, "Die Feindschaft der Montecchi und Cappelletti ein Irrtum", in *Deutsche Rundschau,* Dec., 1903, pp. 419-428. On 8 July 1905 the "historic" house called Juliet's was bought by the Verona municipality: see *The Times,* 10 July 1905.

[93]W. Herz, *Deutsche Sage im Elsass* (Stuttgart, 1872), pp. 278ff.

[94]*Synaxarium ecclesiae Constantinopolitanae,* p. 711.

[95]C. Jirecek, "Des christliche Element in der topographischen Nomenclatur der Balkanländer", in *Sitzungsberichte der k. Akademie,* vol. cxxxvi (1897), pp. 54-55. There are other examples of the same kind in this article.

[96]J. G. Bulliot and F. Thiollier, *La mission et le culte de saint Martin d'après les légendes et les monuments populaires dans le pays Éduen* (Autun-Paris, 1892), A similar attempt has been made concerning the life of St Radegund: see *Analecta Bollandiana,* vol. x, pp. 59-60.

[97]C. Kinkel, *Mosaik zur Kunstgeschichte* (Berlin, 1876), gives a whole chapter to this question: "Sagen aus Kunstwerken entstanden", pp. 161-243.

[98]A. De Nino, *Ovidio nella tradizione popolare di Sulmona,* p. 17.

[99]C. L. Urlichs, *Codex urbis Romae topographicus* (Würzburg, 1871), pp. 122-123.

[100]See *Anal. Boll.*, vol. xxxix, p. 162.

[101]Cahier, *Caractéristiques des saints*, vol. i, p. 304.

[102]A. Ledru, "Le premier miracle attribué à saint Julien", in *La province du Maine*, vol. x (1902), pp. 177-185. Cf. *Anal. Boll.*, vol. xxii, p. 351.

[103]Le Blant, *Inscriptions chrétiennes de la Gaule*, n. 545. ["Which tradition is confirmed by the effigy of that noble heroine, with mutilated face and severed nose, placed with an epitaph on the tomb".]

[104]A. F. Pott, "Etymologische Legenden bei den Alten", in *Philologus*, Supplementband, vol. ii, no. 3; O. Keller, *Lateinische Volksetymologie* (Leipzig, 1891); O. Weise, "Zur Charakteristik der Volksetymologie", in *Zeitschrift für Völkerpsychologie*, vol. xii (1880), pp. 203-223.

[105]On this title, see De Rossi, *Bullettino di archeologia cristiana*, 1875, pp. 49-56; J. P. Kirsch, *Die römischen Titelkirchen im Altertum* (Paderborn, 1918), pp. 909-994.

[106]*Acta SS. Processi et Martiniani*, BHL., N. 6947. ["At that time blessed Peter, his leg freed from the iron chain, let fall a bandage by Septisolium on the new road".]

[107]*Mélusine*, vol. iv, pp. 505-524; v, 152.

[108]See below, chap. iii, 2. Cf. *Anal. Boll.*, vol. xviii, p. 425; xxv, 90-98.

[109]*Abbacyrus, Abbacíro, Abbácíro, Pácero, Pacera, Passera* is the series of changes recorded by M. Tomassetti in *Archivio storico romano*, vol. xxii, p. 465. *Passera* and *Abuquir* are therefore strictly equivalent. Another instance is Sancta *Fumia* on the Appian Way; she is no other than St Euphemia (De Rossi, *Bullettino di archeologia cristiana*, 1869, p. 80). There is also St *Twosole*, in whom it is not easy to recognize St Oswald; J. Aubrey, *Remains of Gentilism and Judaism*, ed. J. Britten (London, 1881), p. 29.

[110]Tomassetti, op. cit., p. 466. The Venetian dialect has produced numerous transformations of saints' names, and very bewildering they are to foreigners. Thus the church of *San Marcuola* in Venice is really dedicated to *SS. Ermagora e Fortunato; San Trovaso* is the local version of *SS. Gervasio e Protasio; San Zanipolo of SS. Giovanni e Paolo; San Stae* of *S. Eustachio; San Zandegolà* of *S. Giovanni decollato; San Stin* of *S. Stefanin; San Boldo* of *S. Ubaldo; San Lio* of *S. Leone*, and so on. See G. Tassini, *Curiosità Veneziane*, 4th ed. (Venice, 1887), p. 428 ff. There are also some interesting examples of the phonetic corruption of saints' names in A. Longnon, *Les noms de lieu de la France* (Paris, 1920-23), pp. 400-446.

[111]*Acta SS.*, Aug., vol. ii, p. 674.

[112]*Acta SS.*, Aug., vol. iii, p. 41.

[113]*Acta SS.*, Feb., vol. ii, p. 367.

[114]*Acta SS.*, Aug., vol. iii, p. 772

[115]*Acta SS.*, Mar., vol. i, p. 319; see above, page 22.

[116]*Acta SS.*, Mar., vol. iii, p. 36.

[117]*Acta SS.*, Sep., vol. viii, p. 171

[118]See above, pages 22-23.

[119]Stefano Lusignano, *Raccolta di cinque discorsi intitolati corone* (Padua, 1577), cor. iv, p. 52.

[120]*Acta SS.*, June, vol. iv, p. 139.

[121]*Acta SS.*, May, vol. vi, p. 729.

[122]*Acta SS.*, Jan., vol. ii, p. 45.

[123]*Acta SS.*, June, vol. i, p. 325. The motif of a child speaking before its birth has not been used only by hagiographers: see *Mélusine*, vol. iv, pp. 228, 272-277, 297, 323, 405, 447; v, 36, 257; vi, 91; vii, 70, 141.

[124]*Acta SS.*, Nov., vol. i, p. 605.

[125]R. A. Lipsius, *Acta apostolorum apocrypha*, vol. i (Leipzig, 1891), pp. 61-62. In Commodian, *Carmen apologeticum*, v. 630, the baby is only five months old. Cf. C. Schmidt, "Die alten Petrusakten", in *Texte und Untersuchungen*, vol. xxiv (1903), pp. 106-107.

[126]Lipsius, op. cit., pp. 56-60.

[127]*Carmen apolog.*, vv. 57-58. Cf. Schmidt, op. cit., pp. 108-109.

[128]A. De Nino, *Usi e costumi abruzzesi*, vol. iv (Florence, 1887), p. 195.

[129]G. Paris, "La légende de Saladin", in *Journal des Savants*, 1893, pp. 284-299, 354-365, 428-438, 486-498.

[130]*Acta SS.*, Feb., vol. i, p. 18.

[131]Prelini, *San Siro primo vescovo di Pavia*, vol. i (Pavia, 1880), p. 312.

[132]*Vita S. Martialis a. Pseudo-Aureliano*, n. 2; Bourret, *Documents sur les origines chrétiennes du Rouergue* (Rodez, 1887-1902), p. 13.

[133]*Vita S. Ursini*, in *Acta SS.*, Nov., vol. iv, p. 109.

[134]L. Duchesne, "Les anciens recueils de légendes apostoliques," in *Compte rendu du troisième Congrès scientifique international des catholiques*, vol. v (Brussels, 1894), pp. 67 ff.

[135]Houtin, *La controverse de l'apostolicité de l'Église de France*, 3rd. ed. (Paris, 1903). Such legends are very flattering to national vanity, and they have been fabricated in other countries as well: see *Anal. Boll.*, vol. xii, pp. 458, 462; xviii, 402.

[136]The Greeks have been unable to refrain from crediting any holy bishop who was more or less contemporary with the Council of Nicaea with having been one of "the three hundred and eighteen fathers" present thereat. So we must be in no hurry to believe those biographers who attribute this distinction to their hero; *Anal. Boll.*, vol. xviii, p. 54.

[137]In a general sense the French word *culte* expresses the recognition of every kind of excellence or superiority, together with the marks of esteem and respect expressive of it. In this translation the word is used in its Latin form, *cultus*, to designate the veneration, inward and outward, accorded to saints and to their relics and images.—TR.

[138]Lusignan's text is quoted in J. Hackett, *A History of the Orthodox Church of Cyprus* (London, 1901), p. 395.

[139]"Nella città di Paffo è una spelonca: la qual dicono esser delli sette dormienti. Però, noi ritroviamo nelli leggendarii, che li sette dormienti erano in Epheso, niente di meno essi citadini di Paffo dicono ab antiquo esser chiamata quella spelonca di santi sette dormienti: et possono esser altri di quelli de Effeso"; quoted in Hackett, op. cit., p. 456. On the localization of the legend in the East, see J. de Goeje, *De legende der Zevenslapers van Efeze* (Amsterdam, 1900). The various groups to which the title of Seven Sleepers has been given are referred to in *Acta SS.*, July, vol. vi, pp. 375-376.

[140]Gregorii I *Reg.*, ix, 59; *M.G.H.* Epist, vol. ii, 3, p. 82.

[141]Paul the Deacon, *Hist. Langobard.*, bk iv; *M.G.H., Scr. rer. Langobard.*, p. 121.

[142]F. Lanzoni, "La passio S. Sabini o Savini", in *Römische Quartalschrift,* vol. xvii (1903), pp. 1-26.

[143]*Bibliotheca hagiographica latina,* n. 6085.

[144]Ib., n. 6086.

[145]*Anal. Boll.,* vol. xviii, pp. 370-380.

CHAPTER III

THE WORK OF THE HAGIOGRAPHER

I.—*Meaning of the term "hagiographer". Literary genres, Moralities. The ancients' idea of history. Particular objects of medieval hagiographers.*

WE HAVE shown that the unconscious working on stories of the saints by the mind of the people leads to the weakening and obscuring of the evidence of history, often to its almost complete suppression. Have hagiographers been better guardians of historical tradition?

At the outset we must state clearly that, under the term "hagiographers", we do not mean to include the whole class of writers who have concerned themselves with the lives of the saints. Some of them simply recorded what they saw with their own eyes and touched with their own hands, and their writings are no less authentic memoirs than they are works of edification. These honest witnesses, known to everyone and recognized to be the purest sources of hagiography, are excluded from this study.

So too are those well-informed and accomplished writers who devoted themselves to historical work, such men as Sulpicius Severus, Hilary of Arles, Fortunatus, Ennodius, Eugippius. They were the last representatives of classical antiquity, and their works, shot through with art and life, must not be confused with the artificial productions of later epochs which sometimes affect to be inspired by them. With those writers we class the conscientious biographers who, at various times in the middle ages, successfully took them as models and produced work whose value is not disputed. We have to give all our attention to those conventionalized and dressed-up writings that were set down long after the events alleged and without any observable relation to fact.

Were we mentally to remove from the passionaries and

49

lectionaries of the West, and from the Greek menologies, all those pieces which everyone accepts as historical documents, there would still be left a very considerable body of martyrs' passions and saints' lives of inferior quality : of these, some are unanimously rejected by the critics, others are regarded with suspicion. The authors of this residue (generally anonymous) are the hagiographers whose methods we propose to examine. The acts of the martyrs, composed long after the persecutions—I strongly emphasize that point—form the greater part of their literary stock-in-trade. What we shall have to say about these particular compositions the reader will be able easily to apply to others as well.

There is no need to make any distinction between Greek and Latin writers. From a purely literary point of view, the Greeks are usually better than the Latins; but for historical sense there is nothing to choose between them and they must be thought of as forming one single group.

When one wishes to judge an author's work, the first matter to be decided is what sort of thing, *genre littéraire,* he was setting out to write; for it would be unjust to condemn an author in the name of history if he only intended to write imaginative fiction. Some hagiographical documents are clearly of this kind; they are parables or stories designed to bring out some religious truth or moral principle. The author tells a story in order to drive home a lesson more effectively, and he does not pretend to be relating actual facts. Story-tellers among the ancients made great play with kings and princes; the Christian moralist naturally strengthened his lesson with the weighty name of a martyr or an ascetic. And even when it was not a question of teaching some truth, when the writer simply wanted to gratify the reader with an appealing tale, "something about a saint" provided a topic of interest that was not to be despised at a time when lives of the saints were the Christian's favourite reading.

It was not infrequent for a serious lesson to be conveyed to the faithful in the form of a tale about a saint. This was the intention

of the well-known *Passio S. Niceſori*,[1] and of the stories of Theo-
dulus the Stylite,[2] of St Martinian,[3] of Boniface of Tarsus,[4] of
Cyprian of Antioch; the theme of the last named can be found
again in the Faust legend.[5] There is the recurring story of the devout woman who retires to a monastery disguised as a man; there
she is accused of misconduct, and found to be innocent after her
death. What is this but a pious novelette? The heroine is sometimes called Marina, sometimes Pelagia, or Eugenia or Euphro-
syme or Theodora or Margaret or Apollinaria.[6] It emerges as a
favourite subject of the purveyors of edifying fiction. They often
did not trouble to improve on a model, but simply adapted it as it
stood. The story of Oedipus in all its sombre horror was applied to
others besides St Gregory;[7] it was used of an imaginary St Alban,[8]
of St. Julian the Hospitaller,[9] of a St Ursius[10] and others, and
was widely read in the middle ages disguised as a saint's biography.[11]* It is now common knowledge that the Life of SS. Barlaam and Joasaph is nothing but an adaptation of the Buddha
legend.[12] In the mind of the monk John, to whom we owe its
christianized form, it was simply a pleasant, lively story that
served as a vehicle for moral and religious instruction.

But fictions of this kind are not free from danger. So long as
they are read in the spirit in which they were written, they achieve
their object. But the time comes, and it may come quickly, when
that original object is forgotten. The true nature, *genre,* of a
writing is often far from obvious, and it may be that our great-
nephews and nieces will be very puzzled by some of the successful
novels of today. In similar circumstances our ancestors felt no hesitation : for them, the fine stories that delighted them were history,
and the heroes of them were true saints equally with those who
were traditionally venerated.

Sometimes, though less often than might be expected, it happened that, in favourable circumstances, these new saints came
out of the literary setting which gave them birth and became objects of public cultus. Wherever and however this happened, it was
deplorable. Yet is it not the outcome of a quite natural evolution,
to be expected whenever hagiographical texts are accepted

uncritically and without discrimination? And when it happens, it
is very unfair to blame the hagiographer, who might well turn
round and blame us. We ought first to find out what he tried to
do, and then to judge him on that alone.

More often than not the hagiographer would reply to this
question that his intention was to write history; and so it is important to have his ideas about historical writing and the duties
of an historian.[18*] Need it be said that they were not the same as
ours?

When we study and try to understand the way in which the
ancients themselves understood history, we are less surprised at the
ingenuous notions of it held by educated men in the middle ages.
With few exceptions—Polybius, for instance, and he was not to
the public taste—classical antiquity saw little difference between
history and rhetoric. The historian held as it were a place midway
between the rhetor and the poet; and when we consider the
rhetor's easy attitude to truthfulness, it is not difficult to estimate
the distance that separates us from antiquity in the assessment of
the historian's business and duties. What is merely accessory for
us, was of the first importance for them. Their historians were
concerned above all with literary effectiveness; they gave less consideration to factual truth, and hardly any to exactness; as for
critical spirit, they generally had no idea of it whatever. The main
thing was to please the reader by the interest of the narrative,
beauty of description and brilliance of style.

The middle ages were in a measure the heir of the ancient literary traditions, and they did not seek new paths in the field of
history. In particular they were not interested in criticism. When
he did not wish to confine himself to the work of the chronicler or
writer of memoirs, the historian became an undiscriminating compiler, much more preoccupied with what his readers wanted than
with the toilsome quest for truth. The men of old who could be
his models knew no more than he did of the complex methods by
which we endeavour to separate truth from falsehood and to reconstruct the features of a person or a time. Moreover, the simple
minds of these half-barbarian clerks lacked the first qualification

needed for the exercise of the most elementary degree of critical faculty: they were guileless, and never suspected that a piece of written evidence could be false, that a plausible tale is not necessarily true. It was the never-ending confusion between history and legend. In the middle ages, history meant everything that was told, everything that was read in books.

Obviously this elementary idea of history was shared by the hagiographers. Their work shows it no less than their own statements. Nothing is commoner in prefaces to saints' lives than apologies for literary defects and preoccupation with literary style; the author often bewails his lack of skill and professes anxiety lest he should bore the reader. But he is clearly unaware of the ticklish problems that constantly beset an historian and, except occasionally, the only recommendations of his work that he offers are these common-form protestations of sincerity, which leave the reader unmoved and may even make him suspicious.

Among the many hagiographers from whom we could learn about how the obligations of their work were regarded in their day, here is one—the author of the Passion of St Fortunata—who in his opening lines testifies to the discredit brought by his predecessors and competitors on the kind of work in which he was engaged: "Sanctorum martyrum passiones idcirco minoris habentur auctoritatis, quia scilicet in quibusdam illarum falsa inveniuntur mixta cum veris".[14*] Such a beginning is unusual, and one is curious to know how the writer proposes to bring the desired authority to the new passion that he has been asked to write. He hastens to let us into the secret: "Passionem sanctissimae virginis Fortunatae hac ratione stilo propriae locutionis expressi, superflua scilicet resecans, necessaria quaeque subrogans, vitiata emendans, inordinata corrigens atque incomposita componens."[15*]

Here is a man who is quite aware that all is not well with the writing of saints' lives; but he can find no more effective way of remedying the abuses he complains of than by touching up the editing and the style. The idea of doing some new research, of studying documents, of comparing and weighing the evidence, does not even occur to him.

There was no public demand for anything better. When the monk Theodoric came to Rome, the canons of St Peter's begged him to get to work on a life of Pope St Martin, of whom they had an account "in tantum rusticano stilo praevaricata atque falsata, quae doctas aures terrerent potius quam mulcerent".[16]* It was the classic complaint of everyone who wanted a writer to rewrite a biography or the passion of a martyr—they were shocked by its unpolished style. They were not interested in anything else.

The hagiographer, then, shares the ideas of history current in his day. But he writes history with a special, clearly defined object in view, and this is not without influence on the character of his work; for he writes not only to interest people, but above all to edify them, to "do them good". And so a new form of literature is born, part biography, part panegyric, part moral lesson.

Its inseparable drawbacks are too familiar to call for emphasizing. The aim of the panegyrist is such that he is not bound to draw a portrait whose smallest details are exact; it is an idealized picture that is expected of him, one from which he is free to leave out his subject's less attractive aspects. In the same way, the eulogy of a saint admits of no blameworthiness; and as saints are subject to human infirmities, the hagiographer who wishes to respect the truth is faced with a task of considerable delicacy.

His faithfulness in this matter depends largely on his state of mind. His concern is to edify : and if, for example, he can persuade himself that the saint's failings, before or even after his conversion, so far from tarnishing his glory actually enhance the triumph of God's grace, why, then, the hagiographer will not leave his subject's human side in the shade, and will avoid putting him on so high a peak that others are discouraged from emulating him. But there is a school of hagiographers who would gladly expunge St Peter's denial from the gospels, in order not to tarnish the halo of the leader of the apostles. They conform, more than we could wish, to the strict requirements of the kind of writing they are engaged on. But before condemning them as misleading historians, we ought to ask ourselves whether the term "history", as we understand it today, should be applied to their writings at all.

We must also bear in mind another factor which helps us to grasp the medieval hagiographer's attitude. He knew two kinds of books: those which one was bound to believe, namely, the Bible in all its parts; and those which one was free to disbelieve. And he was perfectly well aware that his own writings belonged to the second category, and that his readers were fully aware of it too. This conviction that some books contained absolute truth, while others sometimes departed from it, naturally gave him a quite easy mind with regard to historical accuracy. And it accounts for the feigned indignation, so often found amongst hagiographers, against those who do not put faith in what they have written, an indignation that betrays the man whose conscience is not wholly clear.

II—Sources. False attributions. Written tradition. Oral tradition. Pictorial tradition. Fragments of the past. Selection of sources. Interpretation of sources. Inscriptions. Use of various kinds of document.

We have seen how our pious writers generally understood their task when professing to write as historians. We must now examine how they carried it out, and what historical elements may be looked for in their work. As always, it is a matter of settling a two-fold question in each particular case: what were the sources at their disposal, and what use did they make of them?

In general, they did not trouble themselves to tell their readers where they got their information; indeed, they sometimes seem, like some classical authors, rather coyly to hide the sources of their knowledge. Sometimes, too, they do not hesitate to represent themselves as eye-witnesses of things which they have got from written documents,[17] or which they have themselves invented. Writers who are worthy of credence[18] have made apt use of the biblical phrase *Quod vidimus oculis nostris, quod perspeximus . . .*, "that which we have seen with our eyes, which we have looked upon" (1 John 1 : 1); but there have not been wanting deceivers to abuse it.[19] Others have appropriated the familiar words of Eusebius when speaking of Diocletian's persecution in Palestine, ὁ καθ' ἡμᾶς διωγμός, "the persecution in our own time,"[20] and so passed themselves off as contemporaries.[21] We must be quite especially wary of our authors when they claim to have discovered inscribed tablets.[22]

There are so many examples of it that we must suppose that hagiographers considered it legitimate to use the literary fiction of speaking in the name of a saint's personal disciple, in order to give more weight to the narrative. There are Eurippus, said to be a follower of St John the Baptist;[23] Pasicrates, St George's servant;[24] Augarus, St Theodore's secretary;[25] Athanasius, St Katherine's shorthand-writer;[26] Nilus, companion of St Theodotus,[27] and Theotimus, of St Margaret;[28] Evagrius, disciple of St Pancras of Taormina;[29] Florentius, servant of SS. Cassiodorus, Senator and Dominata;[30] Gordian, St Placid's servant;[31] and Enoch, who witnessed the doings of St Angelus.[32] This list is far from exhaustive.

A variation was to attribute the narrative to some well-known person, as the Passion of SS. Menas, Hermogenes and Eugraphus, which St Athanasius is supposed to have written,[33] and the account of the image of Camuliana, attributed to St Gregory of Nyssa,[34] and so on.

So it is no use trusting to the hagiographers; we must examine their works themselves if we are to discover the elements of which they are composed.

The classification of historical sources proposed by Droysen can be conveniently applied to hagiography. They fall into two broad categories : tradition and remains of the past.

Tradition comprises in the first place *written tradition:* narratives, annals, chronicles, memoirs, biographies, historical inscriptions and other writings of all sorts. It is unnecessary to point out that all these kinds of document have been, according to the circumstances, at the disposal of hagiographers; but it would be a mistake to suppose that scarcity of documents has commonly turned people from working as historians or discouraged them from writing saints' lives. On the other hand, if a writer gives his reader plenty of information it does not necessarily follow that he was himself well informed : we shall see later how hagiographers filled the gaps in their sources.

Another error, and a very common one, is to assume that during the first centuries of the Church there existed authentic accounts of all martyrs who were honoured with a public cultus, and to infer from this that accounts of them which are clearly later in date are derived from an original contemporary version.

Because of special circumstances, the church of Africa was particularly well off in this respect, but its resources must not be exaggerated. St Augustine, speaking of St Stephen, whose martyrdom is related in the Acts of the Apostles, uttered these significant words : "Cum aliorum martyrum vix gesta inveniamus, quae in solemnitatibus eorum recitare possimus, huius passio in canonico libro est".[35]* Still, it remains true that the average value of hagiographical narratives from Africa is much higher than that of extant accounts emanating from most other churches.

The exceptional situation in the African church has been altogether wrongly extended to include others. On the strength of a text which has since been reduced to its proper value, some scholars have stated that, during the period of persecution, the church at Rome had a body of notaries whose business it was to collect the acts of the martyrs;[36] this alleged college has been curiously misused to attribute to the stories in the Roman Legendary an historical authority which they cannot claim. It is certain that in the fourth century, when Damasus set up his famous inscriptions over the martyrs' tombs, the Romans no longer knew the history of the greater number of them.[37] When the need was felt for circumstantial accounts of them, hagiographers could not rely on written tradition, because it did not exist.

Another source of information is *oral tradition* : the evidence of eye-witnesses or other contemporaries, accounts from indirect witnesses, stories current among the people, in a word every unwritten historical or legendary report that might be of use to the editor of a saint's life. No doubt hagiographers sometimes were able to glean valuable information from the lips of reliable witnesses; but how much more often did they have to be content with a tradition deformed through long transmission! We have seen above how something retained in the people's memory can undergo unconscious falsification, and with what strange accretions a hero's history can sometimes be burdened. The hagiographer was always being confronted by fanciful stories, and they were very often the only ones that oral tradition could supply.

It is hardly necessary to say that it is not always easy to decide the exact source of the legendary features which a hagiographer has used. He is as likely to have got them from literary as from oral tradition; often, indeed, what we are tempted to regard as the outcome of folk elaboration may have been drawn from his own internal resources. What is eventually said by a whole people must first have been said by an individual, and why should not the hagiographer who wrote it down have been the first to add some legendary detail? Oral tradition in written documents must always be considered with this possibility in mind.

Pictorial tradition must not be neglected, for it plays an important part in hagiography. Artists as a rule find their inspiration in tradition, written or oral. But these two sources in their turn owe something to the work of painters and sculptors, who transform and give back to them the ideas they have borrowed. We know for certain that some writers of legends were directly prompted by paintings or mosaics which they had before their eyes; Prudentius, for instance, when he describes the martyrdom of St Hippolytus.[38] The panegyric of St Euphemia by Asterius of Amasea is simply a description of a series of painted pictures;[39] and in the panegyric of St Theodore attributed to Gregory of Nyssa, the speaker directs the attention of his hearers to the scenes depicted on the walls of the basilica.[40] We shall see that more than one legend had its origin in an artist's imagination, or in a wrong interpretation of some iconographic detail.

Some hagiographers made a rather unexpected use of pictorial tradition. In the Greek synaxaries a number of biographies of illustrious saints end with a detailed portrait, whose preciseness seems to reveal an eye-witness. But when studied closely it appears that these descriptions are borrowed from the manuals of painting in which Byzantine artists found set out the characteristics of the unchangeable physical appearance of their saints.[41] Were this origin not recognized, an exaggerated importance might be given to these verbal portraits.

There, then, is what tradition in its various forms can offer to the hagiographer : a more or less faithful picture of the past and an adumbration of personal characteristics. But at times the past has left us something of itself, a building, a record, an authentic document. In the same way we often possess something of the saints besides their memory, such as their relics, their shrines, sometimes their writings. The historian gets suggestions from all these; often enough the hagiographer has no documents other than these *fragments of the past*—here a hallowed body, a tomb visited by pilgrims, there a festival observed each year on the anniversary of the saint's death. But the writer knows that this is not enough to satisfy people's eager curiosity. If he feels obliged to gratify that curiosity, we can guess to what lengths he may go.

We have now gone over the hagiographer's ordinary sources of information. We will suppose him well supplied with material, and try to watch him at work. The bent of his mind will be shown by his choice of documents and pieces of information, in the interpretation he puts on them and in the way he combines them together.

In the first place, we must not expect a very judicious choice from our writer; he has to impose limits on himself and he is bound to be moved by his own preferences. He has never learned to weigh evidence, and all his sources seem to him of equal value. So he mixes the historical element indiscriminately with legendary items, and it is not these last which will most usually be discarded if there is not room for everything.

There are two medieval hagiographical collections which illustrate well the mind and methods of devout writers the nature of whose undertaking obliged them to keep their narratives short: the books of Gregory of Tours on the martyrs and confessors, which saw the light at the dawn of the middle ages, and the *Golden Legend* of James of Voragine, which appeared at their culminating point. We do not know exactly what materials the good Gregory had at his disposal; but there were plenty of them in existence, of all qualities, and one cannot help thinking that he neglected those that would have interested us more and preferred to concentrate on things that were sensational and out of the ordinary.[42*] As for James of Voragine, it is no secret that he summarized the legendaries, and these collections are well known to us. Certainly we should conceive the work he undertook in a different way from him, paying far less attention to what gives its particular character to his compilation.

Both these writers simply catered for popular taste, and that, as we have seen, was instinctively drawn towards all that is marvellous and appealing to the senses; it is perhaps to this tendency that there must be attributed the loss of the authentic acts of a number of saints, for whom a too great popularity has wrought this harm. Thus, without wishing to affirm that there ever existed written accounts of the death of the celebrated martyrs Theodore and Menas, whose cultus is exactly localized, it is quite natural that the fabulous stories about them that so attracted the crowds should have encouraged the hagiographers increasingly to ignore the more sober element in their acts, and even to get rid of it altogether. Study of the manuscripts consistently shows that, when the choice was between a purely historical piece and a version dressed up in fancies and fables, the medieval public did not hesitate. Nearly always it is the less simple form that is retained in most of the manuscripts, while often the primitive composition is to be found in only a single example.[43*]

The historical value of a work does not depend only on the selection of sources, but also on the interpretation of them and the way they are treated. Were it not for fear of being involved in too much detail, we could set out here what hagiographers and their helpers have sometimes been able to make of documents whose interpretation calls for no special skill. The clearest texts may be misunderstood, and made to give rise to the most unexpected deductions. A few examples will be sufficient.

The Scillitan martyrs were put to death on 17 July 180, at the beginning of the reign of Commodus; the text of their acts says so quite plainly at the outset: *Praesente bis et Condiano consulibus XVI kal. Augustas.* The first name was misunderstood, and someone or other took it for a participle. This participle was replaced by another, an equivalent or thought to be: *praesidente, praestante, existente,* Condianus became Claudianus, and then Claudius, who was identified with the consul of that name of the year 200. Now at that date there were two emperors reigning together. The *imperator* mentioned in the text was easily altered to the plural, *imperatores,* and there remained only to add the emperors' names, Severus and Caracalla.[44] This was done, naturally, without anyone suspecting what a disturbance was being introduced into the chronology of the persecutions by a correction that apparently was fully justified. That is what comes of not being able to tell a proper name from a participle!

The name of Amphibalus was given to the holy confessor who was saved by St Alban of Verulam, because Geoffrey of Monmouth mistook a chasuble for a man.[45]

In the passion of St Fructuosus and his companions there occurs this interesting passage between the judge, Aemilian, and the martyr: *Aemilianus dixit: "Episcopus es?"*
Fructuosus episcopus dixit: "Sum".
Aemilianus dixit: "Fuisti". Et jussit eos sua sententia vivos ardere.[46*]

A copyist, failing to notice the judge's sarcasm, read *fustibus* for *fuisti.* But this word means nothing by itself, so our hagiographer boldly added to it, *Fustibus eos sternite,* "Beat them with rods", thus adding a fresh torment to the martyr in order to get out of a bad reading.[47]

It was possibly also a copyist's slight error that turned a natural incident in the Acts of St Marciana into a miracle. A lion was let loose in the arena; it sprang at her fiercely, and stood over her with its paws on her chest; then, having sniffed at her, it left her unharmed : *martyris corpus odoratus eam ultra non contingit.*[48] The writer of a hymn in St Marciana's honour confused *odorare* with *adorare* (unless indeed he deliberately touched up the hagiographer's picture), and wrote :

> Leo percurrit percitus
> Adoraturus veniens
> Non comesturus virginem.[49*]

We must not fail to mention here a series of huge mistakes that were due to the carelessness of the editors of synaxaries and martyrologies, and to their summary methods of clearing up the difficulties they encountered in their work of compilation. Thus, what is more unlikely than the feast of St Babylas and the three children competing on the same date with another St Babylas and his eighty-four companions, and both having near enough the same history? The origin of this duplication was a two-letter contraction which was mistaken for a two-figure number. A moment's thought would have put this right; but our learned editors found it easier to prolong the list of saints.[50] They also concocted the three pairs of saints who were named Cosmas and Damian, without noticing the absurdities they were cheerfully accumulating.[51*] Set beside such enormities, the duplication of St Martin on the strength of a simple question of date seems a trifling fault.[52*] It is probable enough that a similar origin accounts for the two St Theodores of the Greeks, followed in this by the Latins.[53*] Two feasts would give rise to two legends, and educated men would seem to be to blame; for, as we have seen, the common people have their own way of simplifying things, and they are more likely to confound two persons into one than to make two where one was before.

We need not advert to the odd explanations which the people's imagination has sometimes conjured up to account for carvings and other images whose real significance was not understood. The hagiographers promptly accepted them and used them in their writings. The critics have not yet reached agreement about the origin of the cephalophores, that is, saints who are said to have carried their heads about after execution. Did the people invent this explanation for an iconographical feature? Or was it a writer who first put it into circulation? In any case it was the hagiographers who ensured its wide popularity, by giving it that authority which simple folk always accord to the written word.[54]

It has been said with reason that very probably the Passion of St Eleutherius was in part inspired by the sight of the paintings or mosaics that adorned his sanctuary. In particular, the scene in which Eleutherius sits on a hillock and preaches to the animals gathered around him is reminiscent of the well-known representation of Orpheus. And here is an interesting detail: the writer says that the listening beasts, not being able to praise God with the voice, all lifted up the right foot in worship. It seems clear that he had seen animals walking in line in mosaic.[55]

Our hagiographers have often had to pronounce on problems that they found more embarrassing, and we may ask ourselves whether their learned solutions—learning is a very relative term in this connexion—are always worth more than the interpretations of the unlettered multitude. But those of us who give ourselves headaches trying, with the help of the best manuscripts, to re-establish the primitive readings of the Hieronymian Martyrology (most of the time without success), why should we be surprised by the little blunders perpetrated by our forerunners in hagiographical documents?—as when they transformed the eighty-third mile on a Roman road, *LXXXIII mil* [*iario*], into eighty-three martyred soldiers, *LXXXIII mil* [*ites*].[56] Under the date June 12 there may be read without too much difficulty in the Hieronymian Martyrology the entry: *Romae via Aurelia miliario V Basilidis Tripoli Magdaletis*. This is a double entry, of a Roman martyr and of one in Phoenicia. In the middle ages they were looked on as a single group of the three persons, *Basilidis, Tripodis et Magdalis*: a new saint had been made out of the slightly distorted name of a town.[57*]

There is no difficulty in admitting that these hagiographers were poor interpreters of inscriptions. They succeeded in translating the classical B[onae] M[emoriae], "of happy memory", as B[eati] M[artyres], "blessed martyrs". [58*] Sometimes in an episcopal epitaph they came across the word *sanctus*, which in those days was an epithet of honour equivalent to "His Holiness", or "His Lordship" as we say; there was no one able to tell them that, at the time these inscriptions were cut, *sanctus* did not bear the significance they gave to it, which it only acquired later. Mistakes of this sort have given an easy canonization to a number of obscure people.[59] But such errors make no great impression, and would not always be avoided even in the age of the *Corpus inscriptionum*.

Only too often inscriptions offered hagiographers traps that are very obvious to us, but into which they fell headlong.[60*] They met the epitaph of a maiden which described her as *digna et merita*, a memorial formula in use for a time. Now there was a St Emerita, and so her name was identified with the second of the two epithets. The first naturally became the name of another saint, Digna, Emerita's companion, and a highly dramatic and circumstantial story was told about these two noble sisters.[61] The misunderstanding of the inscription of Pope Damasus in honour of SS. Felix and Adauctus gave rise to a hagiographical romance of unusual improbability, which supposed the existence of two martyred brothers, both named Felix.[62] The wrong interpretation of another inscription of Damasus[63] produced the legend of the men who came to Rome from the East to carry off the relics of SS. Peter and Paul. *Discipulos oriens misit*, wrote Damasus, meaning thereby simply Christ's disciples who came from the East to bring the Gospel to the Romans. The inscription to St Agnes, and doubtless several others,[64*] have also suggested new details to the imagination of hagiographers.[65]

An interesting example of a whole legend being suggested by

the words of an inscription is that of Abercius. The famous epitaph mentions his travels; the symbolic queen became the empress Faustina, and the object of his journey the healing of a princess possessed by an evil spirit.[66*] With the help of various episodes which are mostly reminiscences from other legends, the hagiographer produced a very detailed narrative which was highly successful.[67] But for all that there is no need to entertain serious doubts about the episcopacy of Abercius and the cultus traditionally accorded him at his native place.[68]

Unhappily it was not in the middle ages alone that the erroneous interpretation of inscriptions, of images and of other ancient remains gave rise to legends. Before the days of De Rossi most of the scholars who worked in the Roman catacombs had no really safe criteria for deciding what was evidence for ancient cultus and what was not, and they thought they had found saints' bodies in numerous tombs before which pilgrims of old had never thought of pausing.[69*] These relics, doubtful at best, were eagerly sought, and the people were often unwilling to be content with the name inscribed on the marble. Legends were composed on the model of the ancient passions; they seemed probable enough, and they were certainly calculated to satisfy the pious curiosity of the faithful. The best known example is that of St Philomena, whose insignificant epitaph suggested the most ingenious arrangements and provided the elements for a narrative so detailed that it includes the martyr's examination.[70*]

Wrong identification of geographical names has been responsible for a number of mistakes, but these are of less consequence since they do not lead to the invention of objects of cultus but only to their localization. The reading *Caeae Antonina* instead of *Nicaeae* enabled the Spanish town of Cea to claim a St Antonina for itself.[71] The inhabitants of Scilla in Calabria supposed that the Scillitan martyrs could only have got that name from their town. But the people of Squillace objected to this identification, claiming the Scillitans for themselves; and they pushed their claim with so much confidence that in 1740 the Congregation of Rites authorized celebration of the Mass and Office of St Speratus and his companions for Squillace.[72] Other places tried hard to prove that they had been visited by St Paul, as may be seen from the title of a book by Giorgi, published at Venice in 1730: *D. Paulus apostolus in mari quod nunc Venetus Sinus dicitur naufragus et Militae Dalmatensi insulae post naufragium hospes, sive de genuino significatu duorum locorum in Actibus apostolorum.* These examples are relatively recent, and they enable us the better to understand the proceedings of medieval hagiographers when confronted by problems that were insoluble for them.

We have now seen the hagiographer at grips with his historical sources. He has made his selection, and has considered what he can take from it. How does he use his materials?

This of course depends on his particular aptitudes and personal taste. When it is a matter of written sources we do not hesitate to prefer the hagiographer who has copied them slavishly and given them with the greatest fidelity, omitting as little as possible and adding of his own only what is absolutely necessary. There are cases where the hagiographer has been content with this modest part, and there is a curious instance of it in the collection of Metaphrastes: the famous Life of St Theoctista, whose author had written a slice of autobiography, was transcribed almost literally, and simply given a fresh preface. But as the new editor confined himself in this preface to high-sounding generalities, and did not trouble to warn the reader about what he had done, he succeeded in further complicating one of the most important questions in literary history, that of Metaphrastes himself.[73] Since he represented himself as the author of a writing that was full of personal details, all these details were naturally attributed to him, with the result of making him appear some fifty years older than he really was. Nowadays we give rude names to writers who casually appropriate other people's work, but in the middle ages a man did not mind being taken for a plagiarist.

We know that a hagiographer generally prepared, worked over and adapted his material, and thus in some measure gave it the mark of his own personality. He put it in good order and dressed it up in his best style; but he did not mind if he destroyed the character of his documents, and so would amplify them and combine them in various ways, thus producing a work which, if not original, was such that he became entitled to give it his own name.

Admittedly it is difficult to draw up general directions for a literature which is so vast and so varied. Use of sources and methods of composition may be studied in one author or in a group of closely related documents,[74] but not in the aggregate dispersed over the immense field tilled by hagiographers of all periods and all lands. Nevertheless it may be said, without doing them any injustice, that they often entered on that primrose path that leads to the embellishment of a story in order to make more impression on the reader. The historians of antiquity occasionally gave way to this temptation, which one would like to call innocent;[75] those of the middle ages succumbed to it often, and there are certain cases where comparison of texts enables us to catch them at it. Here are two examples from relatively recent lives;[76] it can easily be imagined what licence was taken in a less cultured age.

When St Bernard came to preach the crusade in the diocese of Constance, an archer in the service of the duke of Zähringen scoffed at the preacher and his preaching : "He can no more do miracles that I can," he said. When Bernard came forward to lay hands on the sick the mocker saw him, and straightway fell senseless, remaining unconscious for some time. "I was quite close to him when it happened . . ." adds Alexander of Cologne, "We called the abbot, and the poor man was unable to get up until Bernard came, prayed, and helped him to his feet". Not one of the eye-witnesses says a single word to suggest that the man had been dead. And yet a century later Herbert, author of a collection of St Bernard's miracles, Conrad, author of the *Exordium,* and Caesarius of Heisterbach all declare that the archer was dead and that Bernard brought him back to life.[77]

Everybody knows the touching incident in the life of St Elizabeth of Hungary when, in the very bed that she shared with her

husband, she laid a poor leper the sight of whom so sickened everybody that no one would look after him. The landgrave, her husband, vexed, hurried in to the room and pulled off the bedclothes,
"But," in the fine words of the historian, "at the same moment
the All-mighty opened the eyes of his soul and, instead of a leper,
he saw the figure of the crucified Christ stretched out on the bed."
Dietrich of Apolda's[78] moving narrative was accounted too commonplace by later biographers, and they altered the lofty vision
of faith into a material apparition. *Tunc aperuit Deus interiores
principis oculos,* "God opened the eyes of the prince's soul," wrote
the historian :[79] but modern hagiographers will tell you that in the
place where the leper had slept, "There lay a bleeding crucifix with
outstretched arms".

III.—*Dearth of material, and how it was supplemented. Amplification from stock. Acts of St Clement of Ancyra. Compilation
and adaptation. Life of St Vincent Madelgarius. An old proceeding. Forgeries.*

So far we have, almost exclusively, considered the case where the
editor of a saint's life follows the line set out for him by the materials at his disposal. But his undertaking is by no means always so
clearly delineated. He may know the saint's name, sometimes
that he was a martyr or a confessor or a bishop or otherwise, and
the holy place which is dedicated in his honour. But popular
tradition may have preserved nothing more; and in spite of this
the writer has got to satisfy the devout curiosity of pilgrims and
others, and supply edifying reading matter from such inadequate
data. While writing at some length about SS. Emeterius and
Chelidonius, Prudentius[80] nevertheless warns us that he lacked the
necessary documents; and the author of the passion of St Vincent
begins by declaring that *Probabile satis est ad gloriam Vincentii*

martyris quod de scriptis passionis ipsius gestis titulum invidit inimicus.[81*] This dearth of information, which by no means checked the fluency of his pen, has been a handicap common to a large number of hagiographers, and they were not embarrassed by it either. Since they had to write, and often, as they alleged, at the orders of a superior, they gallantly took the only course open to them and made liberal use of the method of development used in the schools, or else fell back on borrowing from other writers.

The first way is the easier, and it has given us an abundance of flat, colourless recitals. With greater or lesser degrees of fluency and imaginativeness, numberless hagiographers resigned themselves to the necessity of making up for deficient sources by writing what seemed to them likely to have happened : *omnia, quae in re praesenti accidisse credibile est,* as Quintilian says (vi, 2). Suppose a martyr is in question. The setting of what is to follow is clearly outlined, beginning with a more or less detailed account of the persecution. Christians are being everywhere hunted out; many of them fall into the soldiers' hands, among them the hero of the story; he is arrested and jailed. When brought before the judge he confesses his faith, and endures frightful tortures. He is put to death, and his tomb becomes a scene of miracles without number.[82*]

That, closely enough, is the pattern to which the editor has to work. Each part is capable of development, of which the elements are easily found in the historians who have related similar events, in other legends used as models, and by considering the relevant circumstances; these amplifications are for the most part full of the exaggerations which are the stock-in-trade of public speakers anxious to make the most of what they have to say. Thus the picture of the persecution is always made as black as possible;[88] the emperor or judge is generally presented as a monster in human form, thirsting for blood and interested only in wiping the new religion from the face of the earth. So much for the first of the stock themes.[84]

We must not let ourselves be taken in even when we are confronted with what appears to be an edict in correct form. Nothing is easier than to imitate an edict, just as in our day it is easy to imitate the jargon of an act of parliament or departmental regulation, especially if one is writing for a public that has never seen an encyclopaedia of forms and precedents.[85]

The interrogatory of a martyr is a favourite theme of the hagiographer, and it is on this part of his narrative that he principally relies for spinning it out to its required length. If he had used this dialogue as a means of making clear the martyr's own character or his noble attitude, the hagiographer would only have been doing what the writers of antiquity did, for they interspersed their historical works with conventional speeches, just as modern writers intersperse portraits. But it is only very rarely that we can detect some personal characteristic in this exchange of questions and answers. Instead, we are given dissertations on the absurdity of paganism and the beauty of Christianity, harangues of an unbelievable improbability, which would be more in place on the lips of a preacher in the pulpit than in the mouth of an accused person speaking in court during a brief hearing of his case. The martyr's triumphant eloquence is usually a foil for the ignorance and stupidity of the judge; but sometimes this official displays a knowledge of the Christian religion and its sacred books that is sufficient to call forth a learned rejoinder from the accused.

The hagiographer has not often gone to the trouble of composing the speech he puts into his hero's mouth; he finds it easier to copy a few paragraphs or a chapter out of some suitable treatise,[86] a proceeding similar to that which has preserved the Apology of Aristides in the Life of Barlaam and Joasaph. No one who has read the authentic acts of the martyrs needs to be told how hollow this rhetoric sounds, and what a difference there is between the short, moving answers of the martyrs, instinct with the wisdom of the divine Spirit, and these studied declamations that are like scholastic exercises.

With the interrogatory, it is the martyr's physical sufferings that lend themselves most readily to amplification. The simplicity of the last act of the tragedy in the authentic reports, such as the Passion of St Cyprian, is not acceptable to our pious rhetoricians,

who can conceive no other way of establishing a martyr's heroism
than by making him undergo torments long and crude. They
multiply these torments without pausing to consider the limitations of human endurance, for divine Providence is made to
intervene to prevent the holy man from succumbing to such
suffering, and to allow the writer to visit on him every torture that
imagination or memories from reading can suggest.

The masterpiece of this sort of thing is unquestionably the
martyrdom of SS. Clement of Ancyra and Agathangelus. The
scene of their contests moves successively from an unnamed town
in Galatia to Rome, to Nicomedia, to Ancyra, to Amisos, to Tarsus, and thence back to Ancyra. This itinerant martyrdom goes on
for no less than twenty-eight years, and is diversified by marvels
of very extraordinary kinds. The persecutors are the emperors
Diocletian and Maximian, and the prefects Domitian, Agrippinus,
Curicius, Domitius, Sacerdo, Maximus, Aphrodisius, Lucius and
Alexander. And these are the tortures that they inflict on
Clement and his companion, Agathangelus.

To start with, Clement is hung up, his flesh torn with iron
combs, and his lips and cheeks battered with stones; he is bound
to a wheel, beaten with sticks, and horribly slashed with knives;
spikes are thrust into his face, his jaws broken and his teeth pulled
out, and his feet are crushed in iron shackles. Then both martyrs
are scourged and suspended from a beam; their bodies are
scorched with burning torches and they are thrown to wild beasts.
Red-hot prongs are forced under their nails, and then they are
covered with quick-lime and left thus for two days; afterwards
strips are torn from their skin and they are whipped again. They
are laid on iron grids heated white-hot, and then cast into a fiery
furnace where they remain for a day and a night. Once more they
are rasped with metal hooks; then a sort of harrow is set up and
they are thrown against its tines. Agathangelus in addition has
molten lead poured over his head; he is dragged about the town
with a millstone round his neck, and stoned. Clement alone has
his ears pierced with red-hot needles, then is burned again with
torches, and beaten over the head with a stick. At last, having for

several days running received fifty lashes from a whip, he is beheaded, and Agathangelus with him.[87]

Only very occasionally have hagiographers carried their simplicity of mind, or rather their impudence, to such lengths; the
accounts of martyrs' sufferings do not ordinarily reach this degree
of incredibility. Nevertheless, taken separately, each chapter of
the passion of St Clement of Ancyra represents this kind of writing
well enough, and it is only when the writers have come to the end
of their own resources that they decide to make their heroes die.
After so many surprising torments St Clement simply had his head
cut off : this is so commonly the ending of a horrifying and miracle-
filled passion that some scholars have seriously inquired how it
comes about that the axe or the sword should have been the most
constantly effectual instrument of martyrdom when a succession
of other means had been reduced to powerlessness. "It has been
said that, the sword being the symbol of civil power in society,
God does not allow his providence to render it nugatory, for he
wills effective public order as the particular safeguard of numerous other interests. But might it not also be said that death by the
sword was as it were a reprobation from on high of the barbarous
inventions to which tyrants resorted, their hatred being such that
it was not satisfied simply by putting Christians to death?"[88]
The Roman penal code was relatively mild, but it cannot be denied that some of the persecutors were cruel. Yet has the problem
that has been raised been properly stated? Ought not the question
to be addressed to the hagiographers? It is they who have sooner
or later to bring their ramblings to an end and kill off their heroes.
The natural ending to the drama was the classical penalty—death
by the sword.

The composition of the life of a saint who was not a martyr
is governed by similar considerations whenever the author decides
to amplify. The narrative will necessarily be less dramatic and
enthralling, but the scope can be more easily extended. If com-
pleteness is aimed at, the biography will fall into three parts. Before birth : the saint's nationality and parentage, his future
greatness miraculously foretold; his lifetime : childhood and

youth, the most important things he did, his virtues and miracles; after death : his cultus and miracles. In numberless lives of saints at least one of the points in this programme is supplied "from stock", and at times the whole of it is no more than a string of such commonplaces. The saint's calling or rank is analysed. A bishop has not the same duties as a monk, different virtues are expected from an abbot than from a nun. Episodes vary accordingly. In the life of a holy bishop, for example, he never accepts election except under protest; for did he not resist, it would mean that he thought himself worthy of the episcopate, and if he took so complacent a view of himself how could he be held up as a model of humbleness? In the case of a holy monk, he must be exemplary in all the activities proper to his state, and there could be no risk in recording his fasts and watchings, his tirelessness in prayer and spiritual reading. And as it is above all through miracles that God shows forth the merits of his servants, we may be sure that any saint whatever gave sight to the blind, enabled the paralysed to walk, drove out evil spirits, and so on and so on.

The way of going to work that we have just described, simple and natural as it may appear, has not been used only by hagiographers who needed to fill the gaps in tradition. We have seen that the people's voice is ready and willing to attribute to its favourite heroes the qualities and distinctions of others, that certain noble deeds and striking happenings have become the common property of very diverse persons. Devout writers of the middle ages in their straits often imitated these legendary borrowings, and did not scruple to let themselves plunder for their saint stories that had nothing at all to do with him. I am not talking about the pretty frequent case where an identity of name has introduced absolutely foreign elements into a biography, as for example, the legend of St Fronto of Périgueux, where we find a highly exotic episode taken from an Egyptian legend about a man of the same name.[89] I am concerned with borrowings that are due neither to confusion nor heedlessness. Sometimes they are commonplaces about Christian virtues that the writer has copied word for word; sometimes they are matters which could at a stretch be repeated, and have been expressed in the same terms; sometimes again they are wholly characteristic passages which have been deliberately and unceremoniously incorporated in their entirety in another biography.

I agree that we must be in no hurry to raise a cry of plagiarism on the strength of mere resemblance. Occasionally a really disconcerting coincidence does occur, and I want to give one remarkable example. Were one to read that on the same day the Church keeps the feast of two saints, both of whom died in Italy, who in either case underwent a change of heart through reading the Lives of the Saints; that each founded a religious order under the same title; and that both orders were suppressed, by two popes of the same name; surely in that case one would feel justified in saying that a single individual had been made into two and entered in the martyrology twice over, under different names. And yet there *are* two perfectly historical saints, and relatively recent ones, of whom all these particulars are true. St John Colombini, who died near Siena on 31 July 1367, was brought to a Christian life by reading the life of a saint; he founded the order of Gesuati, and it was suppressed by Pope Clement IX.[90] St Ignatius of Loyola, who died at Rome on 31 July 1556, was touched by grace while reading saints' lives, which had been given him to while away the tedium of convalescence; he founded the order of Jesuits, and it was suppressed, as we all know, by another Pope Clement. I do not recall these facts in order to suggest that such coincidences can often be met: on the contrary, it would be very difficult to find another example like the one I have just given as a curiosity.

The artless hagiographers of the middle ages, compelled to make up for the deficiencies of primitive sources by more or less legitimate borrowings, rarely present us with a really tiresome problem. As a rule their methods are simple, and their secrets are easily prised open. The following example shows how a biographer of St Vincent Madelgarius set about honouring his patron by a piece of writing of adequate length.[91]

In the preface he begins by transcribing the prologue from the Life of St Ermin, to which he adds a sentence from Sulpicius Severus; there follows a second introduction, which is word for word the preface to Gregory of Tours' Life of St Patroclus. For the birth and early years of the saint he piles up reminiscences from the Life of St Ermin, not to speak of others from those of Vincent's relatives St Waudru (Waldetrudis) and St Aldegund, and the story of his marriage is straight out of the *Vita Leobardi* by Gregory of Tours. Vincent's son Landric enters the ranks of the clergy, and this is related according to the Life of St Gallus in Gregory of Tours. The same writer provides him with the main part of a vision (it fills one of the chapters of the Life of St Leobard). St Vincent becomes a monk and trains his followers : this is taken from the Lives of St Martius and St Quintianus, again by Gregory of Tours. He gives himself up to prayer and penance, and is a model of monastic virtue : from the Life of St Bavo. Feeling the approach of death, he entrusts his spiritual children to his son Landric : from the Life of St Ursmar. He is buried in his monastery, where those who invoke him experience his power : from the Life of St Bavo. A blind cleric has his sight restored at his tomb : this miracle is due in its entirety to Gregory of Tours, who tells it of St Martin. There must be added to our plagiarist's list of debts six chapters from the Life of St Waudru, which it is true he used as an historical source, but he copied it word for word, and a mass of other reminiscences, too many to enumerate.

Lives of saints filled with extracts from lives of other saints are very numerous, and some of them are no more than patchworks of such borrowings. It is certainly daunting for the critic when he finds the same things told in the same words about two different persons. What trust, he asks himself, can be put in the Lives of St Hubert, St Arnulf of Metz and St Lambert, which have several parts in common ?[92] What importance can be attached to the biography of St Remaclus, which is a close imitation of that of St Lambert ?[93]

Some editors were so badly off that they did not stop at the verbatim borrowing of passages expressed in general terms, or even of interesting incidents which seemed to fit nicely into their own writings; they were reduced to taking whole compositions and adapting them as best they could to their saint; sometimes only the names were altered. The Passion of St Martina, for instance, is simply that of St Tatiana; St Castissima has the same acts as St Euphrosyne, and St Caprasius the same as St Symphorian; SS. Florentius and Julian's group has an identical history with the group of SS. Secundian, Marcellian and Veranus, and many others. The list of these strange duplications is far longer than one would expect.[94]

A variation in the peculiar way of proceeding that has just been described is when the editor, keeping to the original hero and his history, nevertheless introduces a new character into it. Such is the case of St Florian, honoured at Bologna, who, in order to provide him with a history, has been introduced into the passion of the sixty martyrs of Eleutheropolis;[95] another is St Florent of Mont Glonne, whom it is very surprising to meet in the company of St Florian of Lorsch.[96]

Greek as well as Latin hagiographers have at times availed themselves of the convenient process of adaptation. This can be seen by comparing the story of St Barbara with that of SS. Irene and Cyriaena,[97] and that of St Onesimus with that of St Alexis.[98] There are parallel cases in Syrian hagiography : the Life of Mar Mikha does not differ from the Life of Mar Benjamin,[99] and St Azazaïl's story is an adaptation of that of St Pancras of Rome.[100]

This way of proceeding seems so childish and arbitrary that one is inclined to suppose that it was followed only at the darker periods of the middle ages, that such wretched plagiarisms were to be found only amid barbarous surroundings that had lost almost all literary culture. Unfortunately we have to recognize that from the fourth century open adaptations of foreign legends to national saints are found in Italy, and at Rome itself. In the Passion of St

Lawrence the gridiron torture, which it seems impossible to re-concile with the terms of Valerian's second edict,[101] is evidence of foreign influence; a legend about other martyrs current in the East is so like it as to exclude pure coincidence.[102] In the curious story of St Cassian of Imola more than one reminiscence can be detected :[103] that of the schoolmaster punished by Furius Cam-illus,[104] and a feature (the stabbing with iron pens) from the Passion of St Mark of Arethusa.[105] The martyrdom of St Euty-chius as given by Pope Damasus[106] is strangely like that of St Lucian,[107] and the same pope's version of St Agnes's passion has undeniable points of contact with that of St Eulalia.[108] These are not yet plagiarism in its crudest form, the almost word-for-word copying of a model, but legend has already come to be looked on as anybody's property; in a certain sense it constitutes part of the "common of saints", and transferences are made on a somewhat considerable scale.

Editors of saints' lives did not take their material from hagio-graphical literature alone. Thus the legend of St Vidian, a local martyr honoured at Martres-Tolosanes, is mixed up with the epic legend of Vivian, nephew of William of Orange, told in two of the *chansons de geste,* the *Enfances Vivien* and *Aliscans* :[109] the leg-end of St Dympna[110] is an adaptation of a very well-known tale, and so is that of St Olive, which has been popularized in Italy, not by the Church but by the stage.[111]

The writings of which we have just spoken are literary frauds, and we are inclined to judge them very severely. As a general rule I should not class them as forgeries, or look on their authors as more blameworthy than those who innocently believed themselves entitled to make up for the silence of tradition by means of narra-tives mainly produced from their own imagination. They were reduced to the extremity of imitating those stone-carvers who turned the statue of a consul into a saint by giving it another head or by putting into its hand a cross, a key, a lily or some other sym-bolical object.

But we must readily admit that hagiographical writing has been disgraced by a number of forgers who could not plead simplicity of mind as an excuse. Certain audacious fabrications, products of lying and ambition, have for long misled over-credulous minds and unwary critics. They include the Cypriot legend of St Barnabas,[112] the too-famous translation of St Denis to Regensburg,[113] the Life of St Maurus by the so-called Faustus, who was no other than Odo of Glanfeuil,[114] the Passion of St Placid by Peter the Deacon, under the name of Gordian.[115] The monk of Glastonbury who rewrote the legend of Joseph of Arimathea,[116] and the first authors of the apostolic legends of France, cannot plead their good faith before the judgement-seat of history. One can but turn from them with contempt, while marvelling at the simplicity of those whom they deceived.

NOTES ON CHAPTER III

[1]*Acta SS.*, Feb., vol. ii, pp. 894-895.

[2]*Acta SS.*, May, vol. vi, pp. 756-765. See H. Delehaye, *Les saints stylites* (Brussels, 1923), pp. cxviii-cxix.

[3]*Acta SS.*, Feb., vol. ii, p. 666: P. Rabbow, "Die Legende des Martinian", in *Wiener Studien*, 1895, pp. 253-293.

[4]Ruinart, *Acta mart. sincera*, pp. 289-291.

[5]*Cyprian von Antiochen und die deutsche Faustsage* (Erlangen, 1882).

[6]See below, Chapter VII. Cf. *Acta SS.*, Jan., vol. i, p. 258.

[7]*Bibliotheca hagiographica latina*, nn. 3649-3651.

[8]*Catalogus cod. hagiogr. lat biblioth. Regiae Bruxellensis*, vol. ii, pp. 444-456. Cf. *Anal. Boll.*, vol. xiv, p. 124.

[9]*Acta SS.*, Jan., vol. ii, p. 974.

[10]*Acta SS.*, May, vol. i, pp. 926-927.

[11]This legend has been applied also to Judas Iscariot; cf. *Legenda Aurea*, ch. xlv, De S. Mathia apostolo. See Creizenach, *Judas Ischarioth in Legende und Sage* ... (1875); V. Istrin, "Die griechische Version der Judas-Legende", in *Archiv für slavische Philologie*, vol. xx (1898), pp. 605-619.

[12]E. Cosquin, "La légende des saints Barlaam et Josaphat, son origine", in *Revue des Questions historiques*, October 1880, and in *Études folkloriques*, pp. 27-49. Kuhn, "Barlaam und Ioasaph", in *Abhandlungen der k. bayer. Akademie*, I. Cl., vol. xx (1893), pp. 1-88. G. Paris, *Poèmes et légendes du moyen âge*, pp. 181-215. On the cultus of these saints, see *Anal. Boll.*, vol. xxii, p. 131.

[13]The declamations of some of the ancients on the historian's ideals and duties are well known; to watch them at work shows how far practice was from theory. The study of sources and methods better enables us to grasp their idea of historical writing and how to carry it out. On all this see H. Peter, *Die geschichtliche Literatur über die römische Kaiserzeit bis Theodosius I*, vol. i (Leipzig, 1897), pp. 200-204; F. Norden, *Die antike Kunstprosa*, vol. I (Leipzig, 1898), pp. 81 ff.

[14]*Prologus ad passionem S. Fortunatae, v. et m.*, in A. Mai, *Spicilegium Romanum*, vol. iv, p. 289. ["The passions of the holy martyrs are held in less authority, for the reason that in some of them falsehood is mingled with truth."]

[15]["I have set forth the passion of the holy maiden Fortunata in my own words, leaving out whatever is superfluous, adding what is necessary, amending what is corrupt, correcting what is exaggerated and improving the arrangement."]

[16]*Thodorico monachi praefatio in vitam S. Martini papae*, in Mai, vol. cit., p. 294. On Theodoric the monk, see A. Poncelet in *Anal. Boll.*, vol. xxvii, pp. 5-27. [written in "so countrified a style, clumsy and

spurious, that educated ears are horrified rather than charmed."]

[17]An example is an author of the Carolingian age who, when working over the Life of St John of Réomé (d.c. 544), adds this sentence: "Et ne quis hoc fabulosum putet esse quod dicimus, referente viro venerabili Agrippino diacono, ipsius Agrestii filio, cognovimus". See *M.G.H., Scr. rer. Merov.*, vol. iii, p. 504.

[18]*Passio Perpetuae*, i. 5.

[19]*Passio S. Andreae*, n. 1. Bonnet, *Acta Apostolorum apocrypha*, vol. ii, I, p. 1; cf. *Acta Barnabae, n.* I, ib., vol. ii, 2, p. 292.

[20]*De martyribus Palaestinae*, 3, 6, 8.; cf. *Anal. Boll.*, vol. xvi, pp. 122-127.

[21]*Passio S. Sebastinae*, n. I, *Acta SS.*, June, vol. vi, p. 60.

[22]This proceeding was already familiar to early novelists: E. Rohde, *Der griechische Roman*, p. 271.

[23]A. Vassiliev, *Anecdota Graeco-Byzantina* (Moscow, 1893) p. I.

[24]*Bibliotheca hagiographica graeca*, p. 47, nn. 3, 6.

[25]*Anal. Boll.*, vol. ii, p. 359.

[26]Viteau, *Passion des saints Écatérine et Pierre d'Alexandrie* (Paris, 1897), p. 23.

[27]*Acta SS.*, May, vol. iv., p. 149; cf. *Anal. Boll.*, vol. xxii, pp. 320-328.

[28]*Acta SS.*, July, vol. v, pp. 31-32.

[29]*Catalogus cod. hagiogr. graec. biblioth. Vaticanae* (Brussels, 1899), p. 132.

[30]H. Delehaye, "Saint Cassiodore", in *Mélanges Paul Fabre* (Paris, 1902), p. 44.

[31]*Acta SS.*, Oct., vol. iii, pp. 114-138.

[32]*Acta SS.*, May, vol. ii, pp. 803-830.

[33]*Anal. Boll.*, vol. xviii, p. 405.

[34]E. von Dobschütz, *Christusbilder*, p. 12.

[35]Sermo 315, n. 1, *P.L.*, vol. xxxviii, p. 1426. ["We can hardly find enough particulars about other martyrs to read in public on their feast days, but this martyr's passion is set forth in a canonical book."]

[36]See Duchesne, *Le Liber pontificalis*, vol. i, pp. c-ci.

[37]*Anal. Boll.*, vol. xvi, p. 239; Dufourcq, *Les Gesta des martyrs romains*, pp.24ff.

[38]*Peristeph.*, xi.

[39]*P.G.*, vol. xl. p. 336.

[40]*P.G.*, vol. xlvi, p. 737.

[41]See *Synaxarium eccl. Constant., Propylaeum ad Acta SS., Novembris*, p. lxvi.

[42]The same preference appears very clearly in the Greek life of St Gregory the Great; we have attempted to show that this document was written by means of selected extracts sent to Constantinople by the Greek monks of the Caelian Hill at Rome (*Anal. Boll.*, vol. xxiii, pp. 449-454).

[43]This can be easily verified by means of the lists of Latin and Greek

hagiographical manuscripts published by the Bollandists in many volumes of *Analecta Bollandiana* following 1882, and separately.

[44]This sequence of alterations has been excellently set out by P. Monceaux, *Histoire littéraire de l'Afrique chrétienne*, vol. i (Paris, 1901), p. 62.

[45]J. Loth, "Saint Amphibalus", in *Revue Celtique*, vol. ii (1890), pp. 348-349.

[46][Aemilian asked: "Are you a bishop?"—Fructuosus the bishop replied: "I am."—Aemilian said: "You were." And he gave sentence that they were to be burnt alive.]

[47]*Acta SS.*, Jan., vol. ii, p. 340.

[48]*Acta SS.*, Jan., vol. i, p. 569.

[49]Ibid., p. 570. Cf. E. Le Blant, *Les Actes des martyrs*, p. 30. ["The lion eagerly bounds forward to adore the maiden, not to devour her."]

[50]"Les deux saints Babylas", in *Anal. Boll.*, vol. xix, pp. 5-8.

[51]"It should be known", say the synaxaries gravely, "that there are three groups of martyrs named Cosmas and Damian: those of Arabia, who were beheaded under Diocletian, those of Rome, stoned under Carinus, and Theodota's sons, who died in peace" (*Synax. eccl. Constant.*, 1 July, p. 791).

[52]St Martin, bishop of Terracina (of Tours), on Nov. 10; St Martin, bishop of France, on Nov. 12 (*Synaxarium,*) pp. 211, 217.

[53]The Greeks keep the feast of one St Theodore (Stratelates) on Feb. 8 and of another (Tiro) on Feb. 17. The Latins celebrate the two saints respectively on Feb. 7 and Nov. 9. *Acta SS.*, Nov., vol. iv, pp. 11-89; Delehaye, *Les légendes grecques des saints militaires* (Paris, 1909), pp. 11-43.

[54]E. A. Stückelberg, "Die Kephalophoren", in *Anzeiger für Schweizerische Altertumskunde*, 1916, p. 78, gives a long list of saints who were legendarily cephalophores; it could easily be made longer.

[55]P. Franchi de' Cavalieri, *I martirii di S. Teodoto e di S. Ariadne (Studi e Testi,* 6), p. 145; the Passion, pp. 149-161.

[56]*Anal. Boll.*, vol. xiii, p. 164.

[57]An account of the translation of the three martyrs, quoted by the priest Leo in the prologue to the Passion of SS. Trypho and Respicius, is lost; Mai, *Spicilegium Romanum*, vol. iv, p. 292. According to an old writer, Pope Honorius III gave the three bodies to the basilica of St Mary Transpontina: A. Mastelloni, *La Transpontina* (Naples, 1717), p. 93.

[58]See an example in G. Finazzi, *Delle iscrizioni cristiane anteriori al vii secolo appartenenti alla chiesa di Bergamo* (Florence, 1873), pp. 16, 30, 41; A. Mazzi, *I martiri della chiesa di Bergamo* (Bergamo, 1883), p. 14. We have given other examples of the same kind in the article on St Cassiodorus in *Mélanges Paul Fabre*, pp. 40-50. Several dozen inscriptions bearing the abbreviations B.M. before the name of the deceased have provided the scholars of Sardinia with as many martyrs. Thus they read *Hic iacet b.m. Speratus* as *Hic iacet beatus martyr Speratus*, and so on. The interesting collection of inscriptions compiled on these principles

may be seen in D. Bonfant, *Triumpho de los santos del regno de Cerdena* (En Caller, 1635).

[59]We have examined this question in *Anal. Boll.*, vol. xviii, pp. 407-411, and later in the volume called *Sanctus* (Brussels, 1927).

[60]Sometimes only a couple of words or less was needed to start the most extraordinary legends. In the inscription *C. Iulius. L. F. Caesar. Strabo. aed. cur. q. tr. mil. bis. X. vir. agr. dand. adtr. iud. pontif.* (*CIL*, vol. i, p. 278), the two last words were read as IVD(aeorum) PONTIF(ex), and this was referred to the treaty of friendship between the Jews and the Romans *quod rescripserunt in tabulis aereis* (I Mach. 8: 22). Hence this precise statement in the *Mirabilia* (see Jordan, *Topographie der Stadt Rom*, vol. ii, pp. 470-471): *In muro S. Basilii fuit magna tabula aenea, ubi fuit scripta amicitia in loco bono et notabili, quae fuit inter Romanos et Iudaeos tempore Iudae Machabaei.* Incidentally, the inscription in question was not engraved on bronze but on a marble tablet.

[61]*Anal. Boll.*, vol. xvi, pp. 30-40.

[62]Ibid., pp. 19-29.

[63]Ihm, *Damasi epigrammata*, n. 26.

[64]Some time ago Father Bonavenia tried to deduce from the inscription to SS. Protus and Hyacinth (Ihm, n. 49) proof that the Acts of St Eugenia contain "un fundo di vero da atti piu antichi e sinceri"; *Nuovo Bullettino di archeologia cristiana*, vol. iv, 1898, p. 80. Readers familiar with the phraseology of Damasus will not share his illusions.

[65]Ihm, op. cit., n. 40; and see P. Franchi de' Cavalieri, *S. Agnese nella tradizione e nella leggenda* (Rome, 1899), p. 35.

[66]In the Acts of St Marcellus the deacon Cyriacus is summoned to Rome for a like purpose. It is a commonplace, found also in the Acts of St Vitus, St Trypho, St Potitus, and in the Lives of St Maturinus and St Naamatius; *Anal. Boll.*, vol. xvi, p. 76.

[67]*Acta SS.*, Oct., vol. ix, pp. 485-493; L. Duchesne, "Saint Abercius", in *Revue des Questions historiques*, vol. xxxiv (1883), pp. 5-33; *Anal. Boll.*, vol. xvi, p. 76. A useful contribution to criticism of the Acts of St Abercius is F. C. Conybeare's "Talmudic elements in the Acts of Abercius", in *The Academy*, 6 June 1896, pp. 468-470.

[68]*Anal. Boll.*, vol. xv, p. 333.

[69]There is a decree of Pope Leo XIII concerning relics from the catacombs, 21 Dec. 1878. See Duchesne, "Les corps saints des catacombes", in *Bulletin critique*, vol. ii, pp. 198-202.

[70]*Anal. Boll.*, vol. xvii, p. 469. A discovery by M. Marucchi (*Osservazioni archelogiche sulla iscrizione di S. Filomena*, Rome, 1904) forces one to conclude that the famous epitaph *Pax tecum Filumena* was not that of the dead woman (or perhaps man) whose tomb the inscribed tiles closed at the time of the translation. See *Anal. Boll.*, vol. xxiv, pp. 119-120. [The feast of St Philomena was withdrawn by the Congregation of Rites in 1961.—*Tr.*]

[71]*Acta SS.*, Mar., vol. i, p. 26.

[72]Fiore, *Della Calabria illustrata* (Naples, 1743), vol. ii, pp. 27-28.

[73]We have referred to this in "La Vie de saint Paul le jeune et la chronologie de Métaphraste", in *Revue des Questions historiques,* July 1893. See also the bibliography given in *Bibliotheca hagiographica graeca,* 2nd ed., p. 269. The texts of the Life of St Theoctista have since appeared in *Acta SS.,* Nov., vol. iii, pp. 224-233.

[74]Here reference may be made to a good study by F. Lanzoni, "La Passio Sabini o Savini", in *Römische Quartalschrift,* vol. xvii (1903) pp. 1-26, where the close relations between a series of passions are brought to light: Passio Laurentii, Stephani p., Restituti, Marii et soc., Serapiae et Sabinae, Eusebii et Pontiani, Processi et Martiniani, Susannae, Callisti, Gordiani et Epimachi, Primi et Feliciani, Viti et Crescentiae, Marcelli p., Petri et Marcellini, Sabini.

[75]H. Peter, *Die geschichtliche Literatur über die römische Kaiserzeit bis Theodosius I,* vol. ii (Leipzig, 1897), p. 292.

[76]Noticed by E. Michael, *Geschichte des deutschen Volkes vom dreizehnten Jahrhundert bis zum Ausgang des Mittelalters,* vol. iii (Freiburg i. B., 1903), pp. 392-393.

[77]Cf. G. Hüffer, *Der heilige Bernard von Clairvaux,* vol. i (Münster, 1886), pp. 92, 182.

[78]*Bibliotheca hagiographica latina,* n. 2497.

[79]J. B. Menckenius, *Scriptores rerum germanicarum,* vol. ii, p. 1990.

[80]*Peristeph.,* i, 73-78.

[81]*Acta SS.,* Jan., vol. ii, p. 394. ["Doubtless it redounds enough to the glory of the martyred Vincent that the Enemy grudged him the splendour that a written passion would have added to his deeds."]

[82]The process of development "in accordance with the probabilities" has not been given up by hagiographers of our own time. It is due to this method that St Expeditus, whose name appears in the Hieronymian Martyrology on April 18 or 19 under the rubric *Melitinae in Armenia,* has become "the courageous leader of the Thundering Legion". See Dom Bérengier, "Saint Expédit, martyr en Arménie et patron des causes urgentes", in *Missions catholiques,* vol. xxviii. (1896), pp. 128-131. Cf. *Anal. Boll.,* vol. xviii, p. 425; xxv, 90-98.

[83]St Basil's rhetorical description of the persecution in his panegyric of St Gordius can serve as a model; Garnier, vol. ii, pp. 143-144.

[84]On all that follows, see Delehaye, *Les Passions des martyrs et les genres littéraires,* pp. 236-315.

[85]Edicts are common in hagiographical romances, and scholars have sometimes been at pains to investigate them. See, for example, that in the *Passio S. Procopii,* to which E. J. Goodspeed gives several pages in the *American Journal of Philology,* vol. xxiii (1902), pp. 68ff. Cf. *Anal. Boll.,* vol. xxii, p. 409. P. Franchi de' Cavalieri, *I martirii di S. Teodoto e di S. Ariadne,* p. 105 supplies other examples. Notice that the *Passio S. Ephysii* is imitated from that of St Procopius.

[86]There is no general work on this subject. But see G. Mercati, "Note

di letteratura biblica e cristiana antica", in *Studi e Testi*, vol. v (Rome, 1901), pp. 218-226; J. Bidez, "Sur diverses citations et notamment sur trois passages de Malalas retrouvés dans un texte hagiographique", in *Byzantinische Zeitschrift*, vol. xi (1902) pp. 388-394; J. Fuehrer, in *Mittheilungen des. k. d. archaeologischen Instituts*, Röm. Abth., vol. vii (1892), p. 159, has noted some borrowings from Clement of Alexandria by the author of the Passion of St Philip of Heraclea (*Bibl. hag. lat*, n. 6834). See also E. Klostermann and E. Seeberg, *Die Apologie der hl. Katharina* (Königsberg, 1926). Cf. *Anal. Boll.*, vol. xlv, p. 151.

[87]*Acta SS.*, Jan., vol. ii, pp. 459-460.

[88]Cahier, *Caractéristiques des saints*, vol. i, p. 307.

[89]See Duchesne, *Fastes épiscopaux de l'ancienne Gaule*, vol. ii, pp. 132-133.

[90]*Acta SS.*, July, vol. vii, pp. 333-354.

[91]There is a detailed study of this life by A. Poncelet in *Anal. Boll.*, vol. xii, pp. 422-440.

[92]*Acta SS.*, Nov., vol. i, pp. 760-763.

[93]G. Kurth, "Notice sur la plus ancienne biographie de saint Remacle", in *Bulletins de la Commission royale d'histoire*, fourth series, vol. iii (Brussels, 1876), pp. 355-368.

[94]Incomplete lists in *Hist. littéraire de la France*, vol. vii, p. 193; *Anal. Boll.*, vol. xvi, p. 496.

[95]*Anal. Boll.* vol. xxiii, pp. 292-295.

[96]*Acta SS.*, Sep., vol. vi, pp. 428-430. Cf. B. Krusch, in *M.G.H., Script. rer. merov.*, vol. iii, p. 67.

[97]*Acta SS.*, Nov., vol. i, p. 210.

[98]*Synaxarium eccl. Constant.*, p. 820.

[99]The Life of Mar Mikha has been published by Bedjan, *Acta martyrum et sanctorum*, vol. iii, pp. 513-532; that of Mar Benjamin by V. Scheil, "La vie de Mar Benjamin", in *Zeitschrift für Assyriologie*, vol. xii (1897), pp. 62-96. It was C. Brockelmann, "Zum Leben des Mar Benjamin", ibid., pp. 270-271, who pointed out this interesting case of a monk who appropriates a legend from a neighbouring monastery and does not hesitate to dedicate his plagiarism to the patriarch Simeon.

[100]F. Macler, "Histoire de saint Azazaïl", in *Bibliothèque de l'École des Hautes Études*, fasc. 141. Cf. *Anal. Boll.*, vol. xxiii, pp. 93-95.

[101]P. Franchi de' Cavalieri, in *Römische Quartalschrift*, vol. xiv, pp. 159-176.

[102]Cf. *Anal. Boll.*, vol. xix, pp. 452-453; xxxi, 264; P. Franchi de' Cavalieri, *Note agiografiche*, v, pp. 65-82.

[103]Livy, v, 27, 9.

[104]Gregory of Nazianzus, *In Iulian.*, c. 89 (*P.G.*, vol. xxxv, p. 620).

[105]P. Franchi de' Cavalieri, *Hagiographica*, pp. 131-132. The same episode has passed into the Passions of St Artemas of Pozzuoli (*Acta SS.*, Jan., vol. ii, p. 617) and of St Archippus (*Synax. eccl. Cp.*, pp. 248, 477).

[106]Ihm, *Damasi epigrammata*, n. 27.

[107]P. Franchi de' Cavalieri, *Nuove note agiografiche,* p. 58, n. 2.

[108]Id., *Santa Agnese nella tradizione e nelle leggenda* (Rome, 1899), p. 20.

[109]A. Thomas, "Viviens d'Aliscans et la légende de saint Vidian", in *Études romanes dédiées à Gaston Paris* (Paris, 1891), pp. 121-135; L. Saltet, "Saint Vidian de Martres-Tolosanes et la légende de Vivien des chansons de geste", in *Bulletin de littérature ecclésiastique,* Feb. 1902, pp. 44-56. It was Dom Lobineau's opinion that the author of the Life of S. Colledoc had "no other materials than the romance of Lancelot of the Lake and a bold and fertile imagination".

[110]See above, pages 7-8.

[111]A. d'Ancona, *Origini del teatro italiano,* (2nd ed. Turin, 1891), vol. i, pp. 436-437.

[112]*Acta SS.,* June, vol. ii, pp. 431-452. Cf. Duchesne, "Saint Barn-abé", in *Mélanges G. B. de Rossi,* pp. 45-49.

[113]*Neues Archiv für ältere deutsche Geschichtskunde,* vol. xv, pp. 340-358.

[114]*Acta SS.,* Jan., vol. i, pp. 1039-1052.

[115]*Acta SS.,* Oct., vol. iii, pp. 114-138.

[116]P. Paris, "De l'origine et du développement des romans de la Table ronde", in *Romania,* vol. i (1872), pp. 457-482. [J. Armitage Robinson, *Two Glastonbury Legends* (Cambridge, 1926).]

CHAPTER IV

THE CLASSIFICATION OF
HAGIOGRAPHICAL TEXTS

*Defective systems. Classification by subject, —by categories of
saints. System adopted; historical standpoint. Division into
six classes. These applied to Ruinart's* Acta sincera. *Le Blant's
"Supplement".*

IT WILL be useful to sum up the preceding pages by an attempt
to establish some principal categories into which we can group
most of the writings we call hagiographical documents.

We take no account of purely external divisions referring to the
subject of a piece of writing, such as Passions, Lives, Translations
[of relics], Miracles, or to the literary form, Lives in Verse, Rhyth-
mical Lives and the rest. Such a mechanical classification can
hardly provide the slightest clue to the historical value of a text.
It would be a mistake, for example, to conclude from the fact that
a hagiographer has written in verse that he has necessarily indulged
that licence which we recognize as the poet's prerogative. Medieval poets were often as skilful in turning their source text into
hexameters as they were lacking in poetical feeling and inventiveness.[1]

An apparently more logical system of grouping would be to
classify the documents according to the categories of the saints
themselves. Hagiographical literature bears on a very varied as-
sortment of people, and they have not all got equally certain rights
to public veneration. In the first place there are those whose cultus
is legitimately established in the Church and has received the
sanction of the centuries. No one will deny that St Lawrence in the
church of Rome, St Cyprian in the church of Africa, St Martin
in the church of Gaul belong in this class, and we have the *acta*
of each one of them.

They are followed by the real persons whose cultus has been
brought about irregularly, whatever consecration it may have

86

received through long custom. We have already remarked that the word *sanctus* has not always had the very precise meaning that it has nowadays, and that unless care be taken it may be misleading about more than one person who has no right to the honour of a tardy canonization.[2] The devout men and women whose virtues Pope St Gregory the Great recorded in his *Dialogues* all ended up by being given place amongst the saints of the Western church[3], and the solitaries of whom Theodoret wrote during their lifetime one day found themselves figuring in the annals of the Greek church through a whim of the hagiographers.[4] It has happened also that worthy men, on whom no halo of saintliness had been conferred by their contemporaries, were put among the martyrs or the blessed in some unusual circumstance : such a one was Cassiodorus, who became a martyr of the early centuries we know not quite how.[5] Sometimes it happened that the discovery of a grave, or of a series of burials of which the identity was not certainly established, gave rise to a local devotion, which might attain a long popularity. Most of these saints of questionable authenticity (though in varying degrees) have found hagiographers ready to stand up for them.

Then there is a third category that must not be overlooked, though it is relatively small : imaginary people to whom real existence has eventually been attributed. Some of them have a purely literary origin. We have already referred to several heroes of romance or of hagiographical tales who were transformed into historical characters, and at length became objects of religious veneration. There is the well-known *chanson de geste* of Amis and Amile, who were killed by Ogier the Dane near Mortara, in Montferrat. Their story was turned into a life of saints, and they had their chapel at Novara, at Milan and perhaps elsewhere.[6] The poem of Flore and Blanchefleur would have given birth to a St Rosana had not the authorities at Rome put a stop to it.[7] Other imaginary saints owe their origin to some iconographical peculiarity. One of the most celebrated was St Liberata or Wilgefortis (called Uncumber in England), who was represented as a bearded woman hanging on a cross; her legend was started by one of those crucifixes with the figure wearing a long tunic, of which the *Volto Santo* at Lucca is the best-known example.[8]

There is no need to emphasize the difficulties presented by a classification of texts exactly answering to these different categories of saints. It is obvious that there is no close relationship between the subject of a document and its historical value. It so happens that such famous and authentic saints as Lawrence and Agnes are known to us principally from legendary *acta,* while on the other hand some saints of the second category are properly documented. This lack of agreement, as frequent as it is regrettable, raises a crowd of troublesome problems that are often insoluble.

When historical Acts are lacking or defective it is often possible to supply for them from other documents, and to establish the fact of a traditional cultus from the martyrologies, itineraries and monuments. Elsewhere we have tried to show this by reference to a saint whose *acta* not only have no documentary value whatever but are clean contrary to good sense as well : namely, St George. If we set aside those extraordinary writings and concentrate on the history of this martyr's cultus, the result is notably more satisfactory, and relieves the mind about the origins of a devotion that hagiographers have made highly suspect.[9] Since then a very distinguished scholar has conducted a searching inquiry into all the texts concerning St George, after which all the versions of his Passion were published or analysed.[10] This inquiry has not succeeded in rehabilitating a single item in the martyr's vast legendary dossier; but the historical tradition, laboriously reconstituted, remains unshaken.

Similar research on the Acts of St Theodore, begun on a modest scale[11] and completed by a great publication of texts,[12] confirms this conclusion, that, if the stories be sacrificed, a very important historical element can be arrived at from the cultural records. The truth of this emerges no less clearly from the aggregate of texts relating to St Demetrius.[13]

But there are cases in which this means of control eludes us and it is found impossible to decide to which of the three classes of saints the name-saint of a legend belongs. If we had only his *acta* to enable us to decide about St Sebastian, we should be as hesitant about him as we are about St Martina, who seems to have been unknown to antiquity;[14] and it is probable that no decisive argument will ever be found enabling St Barbara and St Katherine of Alexandria to be included in either the first or the second category of saints.

We have, then, to fall back on the only principle that can ensure a strict classification of martyrs' Acts and hagiographical texts in general, namely, the degree of authenticity and historical reliability possessed by a given document. The following main divisions have been arrived at by applying this principle.

(1)   Theoretically, the first place belongs to the *official written reports* of the interrogation of martyrs. The existence of reports of this kind, deposited in the proconsular archives, is attested by more than one witness. The question is whether any of these reports have survived.

It may be objected that such authentic records do not belong in any category of hagiographical documents and that strictly speaking we ought to disregard them. But there is no substance in this objection, for it takes little research to show that these official reports from the age of persecution have hardly ever survived in a pure state : the pieces to which the name "proconsular acts" is given are generally compositions intended for the edification of the Christian faithful, in which the official text, scrupulously respected, forms the chief part of the narrative. One of the most famous of these documents, held up to us as the perfect model of "proconsular acts", the *Passio Cypriani,* is in fact a composite piece in which three separate documents are recognizable, strung together by a few sentences of the final editor. First there is the official text of a first interrogation, in the year 257, after which Cyprian was sent into exile; then the official report of his arrest and second interrogation, in 258; finally, an account of his martyrdom. In the Passion of the Martyrs of Scillium the hagiographer's handiwork is less apparent. The reader hears only the voices of the martyrs and their persecutor, and sees the sentence carried out. Was the interrogatory copied in the proconsul's registry, or was it taken down in shorthand by a Christian in court? This would be difficult to decide, but it is safe to say that the editor has added nothing of his own to the words attributed to the martyrs.

The genuine interrogatories are always most impressive, and the long passage of time has done nothing to lessen their effect on the reader. If anything could spoil the impression they make, it would be the clumsy imitations of them too often found in the passionaries. In the dramatic scenes fabricated by hagiographers to emphasize the heroism of his sacrifice, the martyr is made to posture like an actor and mouth academic speeches. Nothing is easier to recognize than genuine "proconsular acts"—but unhappily there are very few of them in existence.

(2) A second category of authentic Acts comprises the *accounts of reliable eye-witnesses* or of well-informed contemporaries reporting the recollections of other eye-witnesses. These narratives have a literary character, and they supply a good deal of the subjective element that is completely absent from the purely official records. It goes without saying that this category may be further analysed, subdividing it into three classes:

(*a*) Documents in which the witness simply gives his own first-hand evidence;

(*b*) Those in which a contemporary writer records the evidence of others;

(*c*) Those in which these two are combined, as in several chapters of Eusebius's *Martyrs of Palestine* and in the Life of Cyprian by the deacon Pontius.

All these kinds of Acts have this in common, that they give direct, living and contemporary testimony, without the intermediary of any written source.

(3) The third category is made up of *Acts of which the principal source is a written document* belonging to one of the two preceding series. It includes every degree of "working over", from simple editorial touching-up of details of arrangement and

development to a free recasting, in which a fresh editor uses his original as a quarry, pulls it about, amplifies it, and even interpolates new matter. We have so many as seven different redactions of the Passion of the Scillitan Martyrs, and the historical pieces which we have only in a worked-over form are very numerous. Some of the texts in the menology of Metaphrastes belong to the category of rearrangements whose sole source is an historical document, which has been freely abbreviated or paraphrased by the editor.

We naturally include in this class those second or third-hand versions whose authors did not work on a primitive document but on one that had already been retouched. This is the case of a good number of metaphrases.

(4)   The fourth category is made up of Acts whose basis is not a written source at all; they result from the arbitrary combination of a few real particulars within a purely imaginary framework, in other words they are *historical romances*. There is a good many of them, including, very importantly, the whole series of cycles of the Roman Legendary. These pieces are often a tissue of literary recollections, popular traditions and fictional situations, and the historical element is nearly always infinitesimal. In this sort of composition fancy is given full play, and ordinarily the only certainties that can be extracted therefrom are the saint's name, the existence of his shrine and the date of his feast.

Although their authors do not sin by excess of imagination, I would include in this class those Acts which are simply *adaptations*. Usually the historical residue in these plagiarisms is the same as in the laboriously elaborated romances just mentioned; for the minimum of alteration required to turn the history of one saint into that of another is necessarily concerned with his name, his shrine and his feast-day.

(5)   After the historical romances about a real person come the *imaginative romances*, wherein the hero himself is a poetical invention. The Passion of St Nicephorus and the story of Barlaam and Joasaph are typical examples.

(6)   It is desirable to make a separate category of *forgeries*

properly so called, that is, of hagiographical legends that are intended to deceive the reader. Here it is not always easy to find out the real author of the fraud, for the editor must often be only recording a version which was current before his own day; in that case the piece must be included under one of the previous headings.[15*]

We might refrain from going into fuller explanations, and leave it to the reader carefully to apply the principles we have set out to a number of particular examples. Endless research and the combined efforts of many workers would be required to make an exact classification into the categories we have established of all the hagiographical legends that are still in existence. But we can hardly excuse ourselves from examining briefly a rightly famous collection, which most scholars have for a long time looked on as the last word in critical hagiography, definitively marking off fable from history : the *Acta sincera* of Ruinart.

This fine work, well conceived, if somewhat summarily carried out, has been of the greatest service, and it would be sheer injustice to try to depreciate it. It is, however, not out of place to say that it no longer satisfies existing requirements. Everyone is agreed in asking for better texts, established in accordance with strict philological method. But the need to weed out or, to speak more exactly, to classify the pieces chosen by Ruinart seems to receive less attention.

It must be said that the title, Genuine Acts, easily lends itself to ambiguity nowadays. I do not question that all the acts collected by the learned Benedictine are genuine in the sense that he set out to exclude from his collection all pieces manufactured by forgers. But all his choices are not genuine in the sense that they can be looked on as pure historical sources, unalloyed by fantasy or fiction. Like many other poets, Prudentius is sincere, honest; but who would ever think of treating his poems as an historian's text? The frank, straightforward spirit of St John Chrysostom is reflected in his panegyrics no less than in his homilies; but must we for that reason neglect to take into account his preacher's temperament, and accord to his sermons the qualities proper to a law report? Obviously not. But what is admitted at once with regard to a poem or a sermon is too often forgotten when it is a question of writings whose authors are unknown, writings whose historical value has to be settled by internal criteria.

People have got into the way of putting all Ruinart's texts on practically the same level and of attributing an absolute authority to them *en bloc*. It would not be difficult to cite a whole series of works on the history of the primitive Church or on certain disciplinary matters in which the *Acta sincera* are quoted promiscuously, without any realization of the necessity to sift them in view of the special use being made of them. Except for Harnack's revision,[16] it can be said that lists of authentic Acts drawn up in recent times show little evidence of serious consideration : save for a few insignificant adjustments they simply repeat Ruinart's tables.[17] Sufficient attention has not been paid to the fact that Ruinart had only a rather hazy idea of the classification of hagiographical texts. Nowhere does he lay down any principles, and his only rule seems to have been to give the oldest and most respectable document for each martyr.

The *Acta sincera* consist of one hundred and seventeen pieces[18] of very unequal value, which it is manifestly impossible to subject to a uniform critical treatment; they must consequently be grouped in categories.

As regards a few saints (Irenaeus, Alexander of Jerusalem, Priscus, Malchus and Alexander, Mamas, Soteris), Ruinart had to confine himself to bringing together a number of scattered texts, in the style of those compilations that the Bollandists call *Sylloge*.

In the case of others he drew on historians, preachers, poets and others whose work is well enough known and its degree of credibility recognized. Thus he goes to Eusebius for James of Jerusalem, Simeon of Jerusalem, Ptolemy and Lucius, Apollonius, Leonides and companions, Dionysius of Alexandria, Maximus, the martyrs under Diocletian, the Palestinian martyrs, Romanus; to Prudentius for Hippolytus, Lawrence, Romanus,

Vincent, Eulalia, Agnes, the martyrs of Saragossa, Quirinus, Cassian : to St John Chrysostom for Domnina and companions, Lucian, Pelagia, Drosis, Julian; to St Gregory of Nyssa for the martyr Theodore; to St Basil for Barlaam, [19*] Gordius, Julitta, the Forty Martyrs; to St Asterius of Amasea for Euphemia, and Phocas; to St Ambrose for Lawrence, Vitalis and Agricola, Agnes, Theodora and Didymus; to Rufinus for Apollonius, and Theodore the confessor; to St Paulinus of Nola for Felix; to Socrates for Macedonius and his companions; to Sozomen for Eusebius and companions, and Basil of Ancyra; to Theodoret for Cyril and companions, Juventinus and Maximinus; to Palladius for Potamiaena; to St Augustine for the twenty African martyrs; and to St Vigilius for Sisinnius and his companions.

There remain isolated Passions to the number of seventy-four, and on these future critical effort will have to be concentrated. A certain number of them have already been finally classified. Others have been given provisional rank, and it can be foreseen that yet others will never emerge from the limbo to which the critics have been obliged to relegate them for lack of knowledge by which their merits or demerits could be judged.

There is general agreement about giving the place of honour (corresponding to the two first categories of our classification) to certain famous pieces. The list of them is unhappily far from long : Polycarp, Justin, the Martyrs of Lyons, the Scillitan Martyrs,[20] Perpetua, Cyprian, Fructuosus, James and Marian, Maximilian, Marcellus.[21] To these must be added Felix (when this document is rid of the serious interpolations it has undergone),[22] Pionius, Montanus and Lucius, Sabas the Goth,[23] Phileas and Philoromus.[24] If the setting be disregarded and only Ignatius's letter to the Christians at Rome, which is incorporated with them, be retained, the Acts of St Ignatius of Antioch must obviously be classed amongst the jewels of the collection.[25] Nor must the Passion of St Procopius be forgotten; the importance of this piece was not suspected at first because of a failure to recognize it as a fragment of the book of the Martyrs of Palestine, an authentic work of Eusebius.[26]

Let us at once go over to the other extreme. The *Passio Nicephori* and the *Passio Bonifatii* belong to the class of imaginative romances. Add to them the Acts of Didymus and Theodora,[27] of Genesius the Actor, and of Theodotus of Ancyra; the kernel of this last is a tale told by Herodotus,[28] and there is no historical evidence whatever for the existence of the hero of the narrative.[29]

The fourth category of hagiographical texts, historical romances, is pretty well represented in Ruinart. No one will object to including therein Symphorosa, Felicity and her seven sons, Cyricus and Julitta, Peter Balsam, Vincent, Firmus and Rusticus, Lucian and Marcian. I see no sufficient reason for giving a higher place to the Martyrs of Agaunum, to Donatian and Rogatian, Victor, Tarachus and Probus, Ferreolus, Arcadius, Leo and Paregorius, Trypho and Respicius.

The rest of the texts in the collection must for the present remain in the third category, that of Passions whose principal source is an historical document of the first or second class. This category of course is subdivided under several heads according to the quality of the original document and the capabilities of the editor. And it must be borne in mind that as yet there is no agreement about most of these texts, because they have not been studied deeply enough, and that the mixed character of some of them makes strict classification a difficult matter.

The most important pieces in this third class are undoubtedly the Passions of Maximus and of Crispina. It may be thought that these have not been put in good enough company; but I do not believe it is justifiable to give them a higher place. There can hardly be hesitation over joining with them the Passions of Afra, Peter, Andrew and companions, Saturninus, Dativus and companions, Agape and Chionia,[30] Irenaeus, Pollio, Euplus, Philip,[31] Quirinus, Julius, Marcian and Nicander.[32] The *Acta disputationis* of Achatius is still a puzzle.[33]

To these must be added the following Acts, to which much less attention has been given: Epipodius and Alexander, Cyril,

Claudius, Asterius and companions,[34] Serenus, Faustus and Januarius, Genesius of Arles, Patrick of Prusa, the martyrs of Egypt. It is not impossible that an exhaustive study of their sources and composition might lead to the reduction of some of these from the rank at present given them.

The Acts of the Persian martyrs, Simeon, Pherbuta, Sadoth, Bademus, form a separate group which might be included in the class under consideration.[35] But until the various recensions of the Passions in Armenian and Syriac have been published, it would be premature to pronounce on their original form and, consequently, on their documentary value.

Ruinart's collection can hardly be discussed without mentioning the work of Le Blant, who gave us a Supplement to the *Acta sincera*.[36] This learned man did not intend to enlarge Ruinart's volume by the addition of historical texts omitted therefrom or brought to light since its publication; Le Blant's object was to try to show that several pieces excluded from the *Acta sincera*, "although worked over and interpolated in varying degrees, have retained some sound passages derived from original documents".[37] He calls these pieces "Interpolated Acts" of fragmentary value,[38] and explains his method of detecting them : "In my opinion, the ready way to ascertain the degree of credibility to be accorded to hagiographical narratives is to subject them to a thorough comparison with the information provided by civil and criminal law, with the text of the most reliable Acts, and with the facts solidly established by ancient testimony. This is the method I shall endeavour to follow in searching for the grains of truth to be found here and there in certain documents which, in Tillemont's opinion, ought not to be rejected altogether simply because they have some disquieting features."[39]

I admire as much as anyone does Le Blant's great learning, and the exemplary patience with which he pursued the vestiges of antiquity, sometimes very elusive, through a mass of literature that is often flat and dull. But it must be said outright that the idea itself governing his work is wrong and of a kind to mislead investigators. The fact is that for an interpolated or paraphrased narrative to have any value it must be derived from an historical source whose traces are recognizable; purely literary borrowings may go back a long way without giving the slightest degree of authority to the document. Centos have been made from Virgil in every age. Think to what conclusions one could be led if one tried to make capital out of the age of the parts that compose them. The occurrence of correct legal phraseology in certain Passions may sometimes justify the conclusion that the author lived at a time when these ancient forms were still in use; but usually it means that he had read an old model from which he took felicitous expressions and technical phrases. It would be a great mistake to deduce from this one fact that he had worked from an historical source and that his narrative was derived from a contemporary record of events.

It is true that Le Blant was often able to find particulars disclosing a state of things going back to classical antiquity, in late or historically worthless texts; but he was wrong to draw the conclusion that "these writings have preserved features of the lost originals in more points than one".[40] Were we to follow him along these lines, we should have to infer from a few superficial signs that the Acts of St Agnes, St Agatha, St Urban, SS. Cosmas and Damian, St Cecily and others, in the form that we have them, are rearrangements of earlier acts which have undergone, as Le Blant puts it, "des retouches évidentes".[41] I could instance this or that contemporary novelist who has paraded a specialized knowledge of some technical matter in his writings. But will posterity have to conclude from this that his stories are founded on fact and that he made free use of original documents?

Le Blant did good service by showing that "often the information furnished by secondary texts agrees with that found in classical documents",[42] but he was mistaken in thinking that "if these last had never come into our hands, we should still have got useful information from the others about the chief aspects of the history of the persecutions". On the contrary; it is perfectly obvious that, if we had not got the check provided by the classical texts, we should have no means of discovering these ancient elements in *acta* that have no value of their own, and we should be reconstructing the history of the persecutions on a foundation of sand.

This is no reason for giving up all idea of supplementing Ruinart, after taking much away from him. But, as we have seen, it is necessary first to know what place to assign to each piece in the hierarchy of hagiographical documents. The new Ruinart that we should like to undertake would contain only the historical documents that belong to the first three categories set out at the beginning of this chapter.

NOTES ON CHAPTER IV

[1]There is a curious example in the *Versus domni Bertharii abbatis de miraculis almi patris Benedicti* (*M.G.H., Poet. lat. aevi carol.*, vol. iii, pp. 394-398) where the second book of St Gregory's *Dialogues* is summarized in verse chapter by chapter.

[2]*Anal. Boll.*, vol. xxviii, pp. 161-186. We have returned to the subject at greater length in *Sanctus* (Brussels, 1927).

[3]*Civiltà cattolica*, series xv, vol. vi (1894), pp. 292-305, 653-669.

[4]*Anal. Boll.*, vol. xiv, pp. 420-421.

[5]See above, pages 17, 56.

[6]*Acta SS.*, Oct., vol. vi, pp. 124-126.

[7]A. d'Ancona, *Origini del teatro italiano*, 2nd ed., vol. i, p. 437; ii, 60. Cf. H. Reusch, *Der Index der verbotenen Bücher*, vol. ii, I (1885), p. 227.

[8]*Acta SS.*, July, vol. v, pp. 50-70; A. Lütolf, "Sankt Kümmerniss und die Kümmernisse der Schweizer", in *Geschichtsfreund*, vol. xix (1863), pp. 183-205; G. Schnürer, "Die Kümmernisbilder als Kopien des Volto Santo von Lucca", in *Jahresbericht der Görres-Gesellschaft*, 1901, pp. 43-50; id., "Der Kultus des Volto Santo und der hl. Wilgefortis in Freiburg", in *Freiburger Geschichtsblaetter*, vol. ix (1902), pp. 74-105; "Ueber Alter und Herkunft des Volto Santo von Lucca", in *Römische Quartalschrift*, vol. xxxiv (1926), pp. 271-306. Cf. *Anal. Boll.*, vol. xxii, p. 482; xxiii, 128.

[9]See our *Légendes grecques des saints militaires*, pp. 45-76.

[10]K. Krumbacher, "Der heilige Georg", in *Abhandlungen der k. bayerischen Akademie*, Philos.-hist. cl., vol. xxv, 3.

[11]*Les légendes grecques des ss. militaires*, pp. 11-43, 127-201.

[12]*Acta SS.*, Nov. vol. iv, pp. 11-89.

[13]*Les légendes grecques des ss. militaires*, pp. 99-109. 259-263.

[14]P. Franchi de' Cavalieri, "S. Martina", in *Römische Quartalschrift*, vol. xvii (1903), pp. 222-235.

[15]A. Harnack, *Die Chronologie der altchristlichen Literatur bis Eusebius*, vol. ii (Leipzig, 1904), pp. 464-465, quotes our classification with approval. He suggests adding to it a seventh category, that of "Acts composed schematically and solely according to the pattern of famous Passions". From the historical point of view, which is ours, this group belongs to our fourth category.

[16]Ibid., vol. ii, pp. 463-482. Cf. *Anal. Boll.*, vol. xxiii, pp. 476-480. May we be allowed also to refer to the chapter "Les Passions historiques" in our *Les Passions des martyrs et les genres littéraires*, pp. 11-182.

[17]Preuschen, in Harnack, *Geschichte der altchristlichen Literatur bis Eusebius*, vol. i, pp. 807-834; G. Krueger, *Geschichte der altchristlichen Literatur in den ersten drei Jahrhunderten*, pp. 237-245; *Dictionnaire de théologie cath.*, vol. i, pp. 320-334; *Dict. d'archéologie chrét. et de liturgie*, vol. i, pp. 409-410.

[18]The *Acta Firmi et Rustici* was added by the Verona editor.

[19]The attribution to St Basil is false. See *Anal. Boll.*, vol. xxii, p. 132.

[20]The recension given by Ruinart, *Bibl. hag. lat.*, n. 7531, should be replaced by ib., n. 7527.

[21]*Anal. Boll.*, vol. xli, pp. 257-287.

[22]*Anal. Boll.*, vol. xxxix, pp. 241-276.

[23]See our *Saints de Thrace et de Mésie*, pp. 288-291.

[24]See our *Martyrs d'Égypte*, pp. 161-168.

[25]Vain efforts have been made to rehabilitate the Acts of Ignatius in their entirety; see *Anal. Boll.*, vol. xvii, p. 362; xix, 38.

[26]*Anal. Boll.*, vol. xvi, p. 115.

[27]To be compared with the Acts of Alexander and Antonina, *Acta SS.*, May, vol. i, pp. 744-746.

[28]On this tale see A. Schiefner, "De quelques versions orientales du conte du trésor de Rhampsinite", in *Bulletin de l'Académie de Saint-Pétersbourg,* vol. xiv (1869), pp. 299-316.

[29]*Anal. Boll.*, vol. xxii, pp. 320-328; xxiii, 478.

[30]P. Franchi de' Cavalieri, *Nuove note agiografiche,* pp. 3-19.

[31]J. Fuehrer, in *Mittheilungen des k. deutschen archaeologischen Instituts,* Röm. Abtheilung, vol. vii (1892), pp. 158-165. Harnack, *Die Chronologie,* p. 478.

[32]P. Franchi, in *Nuovo bullettino di archeologie cristiana,* vol. x (1904), pp. 22-26.

[33]*Les Passions des martyrs,* pp. 344-364.

[34]P. Franchi, in *Nuovo bullettino,* vol. cit., p. 17.

[35]J. Labourt, *Le Christianisme dans l'empire perse sous la dynastie Sassanide* (Paris, 1904), pp. 63-82; Delehaye, *Les versions grecques des Actes des martyrs persans sous Sapor II* (Paris, 1905), pp. 5-19.

[36]*Les Actes des martyrs: Supplément aux Acta sincera de Dom Ruinart;* extrait des *Mémoires de l'Académie des Inscriptions et Belles-Lettres,* vol. xxx, pt 2 (Paris, 1882).

[37]*Les persécuteurs et les martyrs aux premiers siècles de notre ère* (Paris, 1893), p. 1.

[38]*Les Actes des martyrs,* p. 5.

[39]Ibid., p. 4.

[40]Ibid., p. 127.

[41]*Les persécuteurs et les martyrs,* p. 1.

[42]*Les Actes des martyrs,* p. 279.

CHAPTER V

THE DOSSIER OF A SAINT

Documents concerning St Procopius of Caesarea. The account by Eusebius. Evidence of cultus. The three legends. Summaries of them. The synaxaries. Latin Acts of St Procopius. Adaptations to St Ephysius and to St John of Alexandria. Conclusions.

IT IS often a difficult task to establish the title of a saint of the earliest centuries to the honour of public veneration. Historical documents may be wholly lacking; even when they are not, they have sometimes been so altered by the combined efforts of legend and hagiographers that they can be used only with extreme caution. It is not all plain sailing even when, by a rare stroke of good fortune, a saint's cause is based on a comparatively adequate dossier. One must be able to classify the documents, to interpret them in accordance with their exact worth, to weigh the evidence, to estimate how much or little trust can be put in each one. It is often a long and extremely delicate job, and many a disappointment lies in wait for the novice at it.

A providential accident has preserved an exceptionally full series of documents about a saint of the persecution under Diocletian. Contemporary accounts, narratives derived from them and several times worked over, entries in martyrologies, historical proofs of the existence of a local cultus, distant echoes of legend— all that tradition commonly distributes with niggardly hand among several saints is here gathered around a single name : the name of St Procopius, who is honoured by the Greek church on July 8 as one of the Great Martyrs and entered in the Roman Martyrology on the same date. By following the evidences of his cultus step by step in the literary records we shall be able to gain a pretty exact appreciation of the value of the documents concerning him; and the conclusions to which we shall be led can easily be extended to analogous cases.

St Procopius was the first of the Palestinian martyrs whose courageous resistance and undaunted calmness in face of death was related by Eusebius, who was both eye-witness and historian of the great persecution. Two versions of Eusebius's work are in existence : one, the shorter and better known, is usually found between the eighth and ninth books of the author's *Ecclesiastical History;* the other, more developed, exists in its entirety only in a Syriac translation (only fragments and summaries remain of the Greek text).[1] The chapter about Procopius in the longer version, like several others of the same work, is not found in the Greek menologies; but Latin passionaries have preserved this fragment of Eusebius's book,[2] and so far as is known it is the only piece of it that penetrated to the West. It tells the history and martyrdom of Procopius as follows :

The first of the martyrs of Palestine was Procopius, a man filled with grace from on high, who had always ordered his life so well that from boyhood he was dedicated to chastity and the cultivation of every virtue. He so wore down his body that it seemed as it were to be dead; but he so invigorated his soul with the word of God that the body itself was fortified. He lived on bread and water, and ate this food only every two or three days; sometimes he fasted for a week on end. Meditation on God's word so engrossed his being that he was absorbed in it day and night without wearying. He was kind and gentle, regarding himself as the least of men, and all were edified by his discourses.[3] God's word was his sole study; of worldly knowledge he had little. He was born at Aelia, but had gone to live at Scythopolis, where he discharged three church offices : he was a reader, he interpreted in Syriac, and he cast out evil spirits by the laying on of hands.

He was sent with some companions from Scythopolis to Caesarea, and he had scarcely passed the city gate when he was haled before the governor; at once, before he had even experienced chains and imprisonment, he was urged by the judge Flavian to sacrifice to the gods. Whereupon Procopius declared in a loud voice that there are not many gods but One

God, the maker and creator of all things. This answer made a strong impression on the judge; knowing not what to reply, he tried to persuade Procopius at least to sacrifice to the emperors. But God's witness despised these entreaties. "Listen," he said, "to this line of Homer: 'It is not good to have several masters; let there be one chief, one king.' "

Οὐκ ἀγαθὸν πολυκοιρανίη· εἷς κοίρανος ἔστω,
εἷς βασιλεύς.   (Iliad ii, 204)

At these words, as if he had uttered imprecations against the emperors, the judge ordered him to be led to execution. They cut off his head, and he entered happily into everlasting life by the shortest road; it was the 7th of the month of Desius, the day that the Latins call the nones of July, in the first year of our persecution. This was the first martyrdom that took place at Caesarea.

Any comment would only weaken the effect of this impressive and sober narrative, and in these days no one would dream of putting it into what the middle ages called a better style. We shall see directly what success it had.

All the honours accorded to a martyr were soon being given to Procopius. It is perhaps not desirable to adduce as a proof the entry of his name in the Eastern martyrology, which has come down to us in the so-called Hieronymian compilation. It appears on July 8, in this form: *In Caesarea Cappadociae Procopi*. Its evidential value is not really lessened by the erroneous mention of Caesarea in Cappadocia instead of Caesàrea in Palestine: this is a mistake that runs through the Hieronymian Martyrology and is wholly due to the editor. But probably for all the Palestinian martyrs the Eastern chronicles depend on Eusebius's book, and so they do not in themselves testify to the existence of a living cultus.

Happily there are other proofs that establish the antiquity of the veneration for St Procopius. Pilgrims came to Caesarea to revere his sacred relics,[4] over which a basilica had been built; the emperor Zeno restored it in the year 484.[5] Scythopolis, the martyr's home, also built a shrine in his honour, the existence of which is attested in the sixth century.[6] Devotion to the saint must quickly have become popular, and it spread far beyond the borders of Palestine. This is proved by the crop of legends which soon grew up around the martyr's memory, legends whose chief stages we must examine.

There is a whole series of different versions of the legends of St Procopius, mostly unpublished, and this is not the place for a detailed study of them. Elsewhere we have discussed, from a technical standpoint, the relations of the texts to one another and tried to group them. The following are the results of this work of classification.

The legend takes three principal forms. The first and oldest is represented by the text of the Paris manuscript 1470[7] and by a Latin passion which we have in a manuscript at Monte Cassino.[8] The Latin version presupposes a Greek one somewhat different from that which we still possess. We shall confine ourselves to an analysis of this last, as from our point of view here the divergences have no importance. This group of two texts we will refer to as the *first legend* of St Procopius.

The *second legend* is found in a large number of manuscripts, in various more or less developed versions. A. Papadopoulos-Kerameus published the commonest one from a manuscript at the monastery of Vatopedi on Mount Athos.[9] Unfortunately this example is abridged, so I have used for our analysis the Greek manuscript Paris 897.

The *third legend* is represented by two closely related versions, one published in Greek by the Bollandists,[10] the other in Latin by Lippomano,[11] and afterwards by Surius.[12]

We may omit here the panegyrics of the saint, which are generally derived from one or other of the preceding categories.

The first legend of St Procopius is seven or eight times as long as Eusebius's account of him; as for their respective literary merits, the reader can judge for himself.

The narrative begins with an imaginary edict of Diocletian, a violent attack on Christians. Persecution is unloosed, and the judge Flavian, a monster of cruelty, arrives at Caesarea. The blessed man Procopius was a native of Aelia, and carried out the duties of a reader and exorcist. His ministry was so successful that it attracted the notice of Flavian, who sent for him.

The judge takes his seat in court, and Procopius is brought in. At the sight of him the people go wild and howl like brute beasts : "That is the man who scorns our religion and our gods, and wipes his feet on the emperor's decree!" Prompted by the Devil, Flavian asks the martyr, "What is your name?" And he replies, "I am a Christian. My name is Procopius". Then the judge addresses him : "Are you alone ignorant of the emperor's divine commands? He orders that those who do not sacrifice to the gods shall be tortured and put to death. I cannot express my amazement at seeing a man of your ripe years behave so madly. How can you teach others when you are yourself out of your mind? How dare you pretend that God was born of a woman and was crucified! Who would not laugh at such a tale? I warn you, then, to give up this empty superstition. Sacrifice to the gods, and worship the image of the emperor; if not, you will die in agony. May the sufferings of those who have preceded you at any rate teach you a little sense."

Flavian's harangue is followed by a long speech from Procopius, who exhorts him to acknowledge God the Creator. Among his arguments he puts forward the opinions of philosophers, Hermes Trismegistus, Homer, Plato, Aristotle, Socrates, Galen, Scamandrus, who all proclaim the oneness of God. After various considerations on behalf of Christianity, he is interrupted by the judge, who mingles appeals with threats.

Procopius goes on, but less calmly than before and without sparing of abuse. Invective trails away into a long dissertation, after which Flavian resorts to torture. The martyr is strung up and his flesh rasped; then salt is rubbed into the sores with a prickly cloth. The torturers tear his face with iron combs till he is unrecognizable, and break his bones.

The judge at length orders one Archelaus to behead the sufferer, but the man's hands are suddenly paralysed and he falls dead.

The exasperated Flavian sends Procopius to prison in chains. There he makes a long prayer. Christ appears to him in angel's form and heals his wounds. After three days there is another interrogation, during which Flavian accuses him of using magic to kill Archelaus and to get rid of all trace of his own hurts. Procopius is strung up again and lashed with thongs; burning coals are poured over his back and his wounds are reopened with red-hot nails. The holy man talks all the time, loading the judge with rebukes and insults; Flavian retorts with new torments. The dialogue is continued, while more hot spikes are thrust into the martyr's flesh.

Finally Flavian thinks of a new ordeal. He sends for a small altar. Procopius is made to stretch out his open hand; it is filled with burning embers, and incense is thrown on them. "If you spill this burning incense on the altar," says Flavian, "you have sacrificed to the gods." Procopius does not waver, and his hand does not shake. Tears fall from his eyes, tears not provoked by his sufferings but by Flavian's obstinacy. Staggered by such resolution, the judge gives sentence of death, and the blessed man Procopius is led outside the town. He asks for an hour's respite, and then at last receives the fatal stroke. Christians carry away the sacred body and give it fitting burial.

We have indeed come far from Eusebius's restrained simplicity and the religious feeling that permeates his narrative. The *Passio Procopii* we have just summarized is a piece of cold and clumsy rhetoric, depending for its effect on long speeches bloated with commonplaces and on descriptions of unbelievable tortures.

The hagiographer did not have to write in this way because he had no information about Procopius. He had in front of him, not the summary of Eusebius that is included in the *Ecclesiastical History*, but his amplified text. It was from that that he learned that Procopius was born in Aelia, that he lived a holy life, that he had ecclesiastical duties (as all mention of Scythopolis is suppressed the impression is given that this was at Jerusalem itself), that the judge's name was Flavianus, that the martyr died by the sword. All that has been added is sheer invention : for instance, the striking down of Archelaus at the moment when he was about to kill Procopius, his vision in prison and the instant healing of his wounds there, and the episode of the incense, which is taken from the story of St Barlaam.[13]

It is not easy to recognize beneath all these artificial decorations the martyr whom Eusebius eulogized, the simple man whose spirit was nourished on the sacred books, knowing nothing of rhetoric and dialectical subtleties. However, we can still recognize the reader, the exorcist and the ascetic. In later legends the transformation is carried much further : the austere figure of the cleric from Scythopolis disappears altogether, and instead we are shown an armoured warrior, his sword at his side and his spear at the ready.

We must now briefly summarize the second legend, which is considerably longer than the first.

Diocletian lets loose a terrible persecution of Christians. He sends out edicts in all directions, and we are told the terms of the one addressed to Aelia. The emperor goes to Egypt, where he defeats the usurper Achilles and then visits Antioch; there the senate presents him with a sort of profession of idolatrous faith.

Now there lived at Jerusalem (which at that time was called Aelia) a noble lady named Theodosia, who had a son, Neanias, a pagan as his mother was. Theodosia took him to Antioch in order to recommend him to the favourable notice of the emperor. Diocletian, pleased by his looks and bearing and also by his zeal for idol-worship, at once made Neanias duke of Alexandria; just as he was leaving to take up his duties the emperor urged him to seek out Christians and punish them severely. To show him how foolish these people were, Diocletian gave the young man a sketch of Christ's life, adding comments of his own.

So, like another Saul, Neanias went off breathing hatred and threats; but he too was to tread the road to Damascus. Upon leaving Apamea he encountered an earthquake and fierce lightning, and heard a voice from the sky saying, "Where are you going, Neanias?" Then he saw a cross like crystal, and heard the voice again: "I am Jesus who was crucified, the Son of God." Neanias raised objections to this, and yet again the voice spoke: "You are to be a chosen vessel to me," it said, "By this sign you will triumph."

Now completely overcome, Neanias goes on with his soldiers to Scythopolis, where he gets a certain Mark to make him a gold and silver cross, like the one he saw in his vision. When it is finished, three figures appear on it, with their names in Hebrew, Emmanuel, Michael and Gabriel. With the help of this miraculous cross, Neanias puts a band of Hagarenes to flight and kills six thousand of them. He then goes home to his mother and breaks up all the household gods, giving away their precious metal to the poor. The terrified Theodosia denounces him to the emperor, who consoles her by allowing her to choose a new son from among the senators. At the same time he sends a letter to the governor Oulcion, telling him to examine Neanias and, should he persist in his impiety, torture him to death. Neanias learns about the emperor's letter, tears it to pieces, and declares himself a Christian. The governor orders him to be taken to Caesarea in chains.

Oulcion presides at the trial, commanding that Neanias be strung up and tortured with iron combs. His bones are laid bare, and the torturers become exhausted, so he is taken off to prison. Here he is visited by angels and has a vision of Christ who baptizes him, changing his name to Procopius, and heals his injuries.

The next day there is another interrogation. The governor attributes the martyr's healing to the power of the gods. Procopius immediately asks to be taken to the temple. The wicked judge and the crowd suppose that his resistance has given way and that he will sacrifice to the gods, and he is therefore ceremoniously led to the temple. But instead of denying his Christian faith, Neanias breaks the idols in pieces by the power of the sign of the cross.

At this point two long episodes are inserted. The first is the conversion of some soldiers who visit Procopius in prison. The jailer lets him take them to the bishop, Leontius, who baptizes them. Procopius goes back to prison, and after he has strengthened the converts in the faith they are martyred before his eyes.

As a pendant to this there is the incident of the twelve matrons of senatorial rank who also become Christians, and die amid agonizing torments. The mother of Procopius is so moved by the sight of their constancy that she too is converted, and dies with them.

A little time later Oulcion, the governor, dies of a malignant fever, and Flavian takes his place at Caesarea. Procopius is brought before him, and there follow almost all the scenes related in the previous legend.

There is no need to adduce proof that this version is later than what we have called the first legend : it obviously is derived from it and marks a long step forward in legendary development. All the rhetoric and scenery of the first legend fail to alter entirely the martyr's characteristics; it at least retains the memory of his ecclesiastical duties. But now the reader and exorcist have disappeared completely, and we have instead a young heathen soldier and Roman magistrate who is converted to the Christian faith by a miracle. His very name is at first Neanias, and it takes a vision to give him the name of Procopius. This feature is enough by itself to show that a hagiographer has been at work. He has tacked two stories together, that of a Neanias in the time of Oulcion's governorship, and that of Procopius when Flavian was judge.

What is the origin of the Neanias legend? It is not known; and in any case there is no need to inquire into this before classifying it among the highly fantastic compositions : it is a medley of ready-made incidents and reminiscences. The editor has made use of material from St Paul's conversion, Constantine's vision, the Acts of St Polycarp and other sources which it would be tedious to detail. The introduction of Neanias into the story has completed the metamorphosis of St Procopius : nothing is left of him except his name, and of Eusebius's narrative there are only such vague reminiscences as the names Aelia, Scythopolis, Caesarea, Flavian.

This second legend is quite old. It was current in the eighth century, and was so trusted as to be produced before the Fathers of the second council of Nicaea. The episode of the miraculous cross was pointed to as evidence on behalf of the veneration of images, as can be read in the proceedings of the council.[14]

The third form of the legend achieved no less success. It was included in the collection of Metaphrastes, and through this was widespread in numerous copies.[15]

There are two recensions of this paraphrase, of which one (which seems to be the earlier in date) is still unpublished; but a sufficient idea of it can be gained from Lippomano's translation.[16] The other is the text in the *Acta Sanctorum*. The two forms of the third legend are not so different as to make it desirable that they should be examined separately here; it will be enough if we ignore the divergences and concentrate on the features common to both.

It must be said at the outset that there is no essential difference between the second legend and the third. The succession of events is the same in both, and the new editor has not deemed it necessary to modify the extravagances of his model. All his energies seem to have been concentrated on style, and all the old rhetorical tricks appear in these pretentious pages, which are supposed to tell the story of St Procopius's martyrdom in a more attractive way. I will quote one detail to illustrate a manner of writing about the saints which was very fashionable.

Whenever he comes upon an historical or geographical name, the editor uses it as a peg on which to hang an erudite little dissertation for the reader's benefit, bringing in whatever the name recalls to mind. When, for instance, he tells us that Diocletian came to Antioch, he remembers that there was once a famous shrine of Apollo near this city, at Daphne; and he hastens to add that the emperor went there to offer sacrifice to the god. Nor does he forget that Antioch was a renowned centre of the primitive Church, and he reminds us accordingly that it was here that the faithful were first called Christians.[17] A few lines further on reference is made to the dwelling-place of Procopius's mother, Theodosia, which is called Aelia in all previous texts. This is how he refers to it : "Theodosia belonged to the highest rank of society in the city. This city formerly had the name of Jerusalem and Zion; but after it had been captured by the Romans as a punishment for its crime against Christ, Hadrian, when he held the imperial sceptre, renamed it Aelia".[18]

The mention of Caesarea provides another opportunity for display of learning. But this time the editor's knowledge is at fault, for he confuses Caesarea Paneas or Philippi with Caesarea Stratonica or Palestinae, and he underlines his mistake heavily : "The judge ordered the saint to be brought to Caesarea, where he was busy building a temple. We mean that Caesarea which it is our custom to call 'of Philip', formerly called 'Tower of Strato'; the Phoenicians named it Paneas, after the neighbouring mountain of Paneos. And talking of this town, it would be a shame silently to pass over an interesting story associated with it . . .", and he goes on to tell, following Eusebius,[19] the well-known legend of the bronze group which was said to represent Christ and the woman who had an issue of blood.[20]

We need not further illustrate our author's pedantry. It did not prevent his story from being greatly enjoyed; the largest number of copies extant are of the third legend, and it fixed the traditional picture of St Procopius as a soldier who was martyred.

The inevitable consequence of the transformation of Procopius the cleric into Procopius the military officer has been to produce two persons. In certain synaxaries we read, on July 8, the passion of the great martyr Procopius, that is, of the officer of the second and third legends, followed by the entry of Procopius the exorcist, martyr at Caesarea.[21] The latter is further celebrated on November 22, and on this day a slightly shortened version of Eusebius's account is read.[22]

In some copies the commemoration of St Procopius occurs

again on the following day, November 23.[23] But there he is no longer called by his real name, Procopius of Palestine; he is called Procopius "who suffered in Persia". Where does this appellation come from? There is no known Persian martyr called Procopius. It is certainly a mistake; but it is impossible to find its precise origin, and we can only suppose that it is one of the many lapses for which the compilers of synaxaries are to blame. Those who are used to working with books of this kind will have no doubt whatever that it is always the one and only St Procopius who appears under different disguises.[24]

Synaxaries of recent date, and the *menaia* that have borrowed their historical parts, record only Procopius the officer; they add commemorations of his mother, Theodosia, of the twelve matrons martyred with her, and of the officers, Antiochus and Nicostratus, who according to the legend commanded the soldiers whom Procopius converted.

The Latins,[25] too, read the Acts of St Procopius, and we have seen that the original account by Eusebius has been preserved as a separate document in their passionaries alone. From it is derived the very exact entry in the historic Latin martyrologies.[26] We have also pointed out that the first legend of Procopius was known in the West, probably through a Latin version made in southern Italy. The part of the second legend read at the second council of Nicaea was translated by Anastasius the Librarian; but it is almost certain that there was a full translation of it as well.

We are able to conclude that this was so by a study of the Latin *adaptations* of the Acts of St Procopius. For this great martyr has not been spared a single one of the indignities to which blundering hagiographers have subjected those saints to whom they have given special attention. Not content with completely travestying facts and altering his character and qualities, they made his story into a sort of dummy biography, into which was fitted first one saint and then another, saints so obscure that no information at all was to be had about them.

The second legend of Procopius was used in the first place to provide Acts for St Ephysius of Cagliari.[27] Apart from some minor episodes, inserted clumsily enough, and a few place-names added to connect the saint with Sardinia, the legend was hardly altered; in particular, no attempt was made to render it more life-like.

In the narrative as applied to Ephysius there is no mention of his being sent to Alexandria; but the name of the city becomes the name of his mother (whereas Procopius's mother was called Theodosia). Both women are noble ladies of Jerusalem, married to a Christian named Christopher. Like Procopius, Ephysius is taken to Antioch by his mother and presented to Diocletian, who instructs him to persecute the Christians, not of Egypt, but of Italy. The vision happens at a place called Vrittania, and Ephysius has his cross made at Gaeta, by a goldsmith named John; by its power he routs the Saracens, and then he takes ship to Sardinia. He lands at Arborea, and soon makes himself master of the whole island. From Cagliari he writes to the emperor and to his mother to inform them of his conversion.

Diocletian sends out one of his officers, Julicus, who calls on Ephysius to apostatize. He refuses, and is cruelly tortured. Like Oulcion in the original legend, Julicus dies of a fever and is replaced by Flavian, whom we already know. This brutal judge does not forget to inflict the ordeal of St Barlaam on Ephysius, and then orders him to be beheaded. The sentence is carried out *apud Caralitanam civitatem, in loco qui dicitur Nuras.*

The narrative ends with a short reference to a St Juvenalis, archbishop of Cagliari, who is otherwise completely unknown,[28] and with the following declaration, which does not enable us for a moment to believe in the good faith of the biographer of St Ephysius: "Cuius passionem ego presbyter Marcus, dum a principio usque ad finem oculis meis vidissem, oratu ipsius beati martyris Ephysi fideliter veraciterque descripsi praesentibus atque posteris profuturam".[29*]

At the church of St Daniel in Venice there is preserved the body of a martyred St John (*sancti Iohannis ducis Alexandrini martyris*) which was brought there from Constantinople in 1215.[30] A history was needed for this unknown martyr and no better expedient was found than to plunder St Procopius for his benefit : the legend was applied to him in every detail and in its fullest and most fabulous form. John too was called Neanias before he became a Christian, and his mother was born at Aelia; it was the emperor Maximian who ordered him to exterminate the Christians of Alexandria. The two prefects who one after the other summoned him before their court were named Oulcion and Flavian; nor was the conversion of some soldiers, of twelve matrons and of his own mother overlooked. Leontius, instead of being bishop of Caesarea, appears as bishop of Alexandria, and it is in that city that John meets his end.[31]

It is time to summarize the preceding pages. The evidence of Eusebius fully guarantees the existence of the martyr Procopius and the main outlines of his life and how he died. Eusebius's account is not of itself sufficient to establish the fact of a traditional cultus, and the same is true, for the reason already given, of the entry of the saint's name in the Hieronymian Martyrology. But the existence of his shrines at Caesarea and Scythopolis provides completely certain proof of public veneration.

In the East, Eusebius's narrative was soon supplanted by legends. There is no trace of it in the Greek menologies; in them, the place which we should expect to see it occupy on July 8 is invariably filled by the legend in one or other of its forms. Of the three legends that we know, the one that is least far from its historical source is the one that has had least diffusion.

In the middle ages St Procopius was honoured under the guise that he assumes in the second legend, and today he still belongs to the category of soldier saints. It is important to remember that this type designates a number of famous saints—George, Theodore, Mercury, Menas and Demetrius among them—and for most of them the only relevant literary documents available are Acts of the same character as those which constitute the legend of Procopius.[32] How much can the historian accept or reject of this legend ?

The historical residue is this: a Christian named Procopius, originally from Jerusalem, was martyred by the judge Flavian under the emperor Diocletian, being put to death by the sword. We are in the happy position of being able to verify these particulars and confirm their accuracy by reference to the one historical source which tells us about St Procopius, a source available to us through a fortunate chance. On the other hand, comparison of the legends with Eusebius's testimony proves that everything else is pure invention.

The names of the saint's parents, his state of life, his characteristics, his career and adventures, his fellows, the interrogations he was subjected to and the speeches he made, the torments he endured, his imprisonment, the conversions he helped to bring about, the miracles, the visions—all these are simply made up. The impossible Oulcion must be banished from the list of Roman magistrates, and the names of Theodosia, the twelve matrons and the two officers[38] ought to be expunged from the Greek liturgical books, for hagiographers have invented them all.

And to think that the legends we have examined originate in an historical source of the first order! It shows what hagiographers are capable of producing even when they work on reliable documents. What then can be said about their productions when, for lack of material, they have given unbridled rein to the fancies of their imagination?

So his legend has the lowest possible place in St Procopius's dossier, and if we had nothing else to turn to, we should be able only to put a series of question-marks against the name of so famous a martyr. We see thus that the certainty we may be able to attain of a saint's historical existence and of the legitimacy of his cultus in no way depends on the popularity of his legend. A few lines written by a contemporary, an entry in a martyrology reflecting a church's liturgical tradition, a basilica going back to early times, it is such indications as these which are really valuable to the student; and it is a matter for thankfulness that they are not wholly absent from the dossiers of certain very famous saints whose credit has been seriously damaged by the goings-on of hagiographers.

Unfortunately such evidence is not found where St Ephysius of Cagliari and St John of Alexandria are concerned. The existence of Ephysius and the ancientness of his cultus are supported only by a document that is manifestly false, an ambiguous state of affairs that is found elsewhere in Sardinian hagiography. As for the martyr John, we know that his body was stolen from the church of a monastery at Constantinople, a monastery as little known as the saint himself.[34] His incompetent biographer has succeeded only in increasing our doubts about his identity.

NOTES ON CHAPTER V

[1]For all this, see *Analecta Bollandiana*, vol. xvi, pp. 113-122.

[2]*Bibliotheca hagiographica latina*, n. 6949.

[3]The state of the text makes this passage very difficult to elucidate. Our translation expresses only its general sense.

[4]*Antonini itinerarium*, 46, Geyer, p. 190.

[5]*Chronicon paschale*, Paris ed., p. 327.

[6]Cyrilli Scythopolitani, *Vita S. Sabae*, c. 75, Cotelier, p. 349.

[7]We have published this in *Les légendes grecques des saints militaires*, pp. 214-227.

[8]*Bibl. hag. lat.*, n. 6950.

[9]Ἀνάλεκτα ἱεροσολυμιτικῆς σταχυολογίας, vol. v (St Petersburg, 1898), pp. 1-27.

[10]*Acta SS.*, July, vol. ii, pp. 556-576.

[11]*Tomus sextus vitarum sanctorum patrum* (Rome, 1558), ff. 107-115^v.

[12]*De probatis sanctorum vitis*, at July 8.

[13]*Anal. Boll.*, vol. xxii, pp. 134-145.

[14]Hardouin, *Concilia*, vol. iv, pp. 229-232.

[15]*Anal. Boll.*, vol. xvi, pp. 311-329.

[16]See above, page 104.

[17]*Acta SS.*, July, vol. ii, p. 55, nn. 5, 6.

[18]Ibid., n. 7.

[19]*Hist. eccl.*, viii, 18.

[20]*Acta SS.*, July, vol. ii, pp. 563-564, nn. 27-29.

[21]*Synax. eccl. Constant.*, pp. 805, 808.

[22]Ibid., p. 245.

[23]Ibid., pp. 247, 249.

[24]The manuscript Vatican 679 contains an ἐγκώμιον εἰς τὸν ὅσιον μάρτυρα Προκόπιον τὸν Πέρσην, whose author is Hesychius, a priest of Jerusalem. There is nothing in this document enabling one to distinguish Procopius the Persian from Procopius of Caesarea. See *Anal. Boll.*, vol. xxiv, pp. 473-482.

[25]I will not here discuss the cultus of St Procopius in Slav lands. The literary remains all originate in Greek sources; the others are of relatively recent date. On the saint's cultus in Serbia, see C. Jirecek, "Das christliche Element in der topographischen Nomenclatur der Balkanländer", in *Sitzungsberichte der k. Akademie der Wissenschaften*, vol. cxxxvi (1897), n. xi, pp. 36-37.

[26]The following is Ado's text: "In Palaestina natalis sancti Procopii martyris, qui ab Scythopoli ductus Caesaream, ad primam responsionum eius confidentiam, irato iudice Fabiano (*read* Flaviano) capite caesus est." It is the same in Usuard, ed. Sollerius, pp. 388-389.

[27]*Anal. Boll.*, vol. iii, pp. 362-377.

[28]*Acta SS.*, May, vol. vi, p. 732.

[29]*Anal. Boll.*, vol. iii, p. 377. ["I, the priest **Mark**, having with my own eyes witnessed his passion from beginning to end, have at the request of the blessed martyr Ephysius himself described it exactly and truly for the benefit of our contemporaries and of those who will come after us."]

[30]Flaminius Cornelius, *Ecclesiae Venetae antiquis monumentis ... illustratae,* vol. iv (Venice, 1749), pp. 170-171.

[31]*Acta SS.*, May, vol. iv, pp. 304-307.

[32]See our *Légendes grecques des saints militaires,* pp. 1-119.

[33]*Acta SS.*, July, vol. ii, p. 576.

[34]Flaminius Cornelius, *Ecclesiae Venetae,* vol. iv, p. 171.

CHAPTER VI

PAGAN MEMORIES AND SURVIVALS

I.—*Rites and symbols common to Christianity and ancient relig-*
ions. Suspect practices. Incubation. Collections of miracles.
Literary borrowings from pagan sources. Inevitable analogies.
Superstitions.

THE SUBJECT we are entering on is full of surprises and—let us say
at once—of unfortunate confusions. It has given rise, and still
gives rise, to over-ingenious theorizing whose concern is to connect
certain religious phenomena specially relevant to hagiography
with pagan beliefs and customs. With the help of subtle argument,
often based on very wide learning, attempts are made to detect
remains of the old mythology and links with earlier religions beneath the surface of Christian legend; analogies or likenesses are
found between different religions, and it is claimed that they can
only be explained as borrowings.

Some people do not hesitate to assert that, in the conflict between Christianity and idolatry, victory has not always been on the
side that we suppose; and, as could be expected, it is the cultus of
saints in particular that provides arguments in favour of this paradox.

It would not be right to try to discredit the comparative study
of religion and religious observances by undue insistence on the
exaggerations of those who in these matters have transgressed by
being too ingenious or by not going deeply enough. Despite the
obscurity that surrounds it, the problem deserves to be examined
seriously.

A material but wholly external link between the new religion
and the old consists in the common possession of a number of
observances and symbols which we commonly regard as our own

particular property; consequently, we are surprised when we find them also in polytheism, and having a significance analagous to ours.

But it would have been very surprising if the Church, seeking to spread her faith amidst the Graeco-Roman civilization, had chosen to address the people in entirely novel terms, systematically rejecting everything that up till then had been used to give expression to religious feeling.

Within the limit of the customs imposed by the unity of a people or a culture, there is not an indefinite variety of ways in which the heart's impulses can be expressed; and it was natural that in the end the new religion should take over a whole ritual system which needed only to be soundly interpreted for it to become the language of the Christian soul aspiring to the true God. Any outward sign that did not involve an implicit acceptance of polytheism could find grace in the Church's eyes; some time passed before she formally adapted them to her use, but she made no objection when they reappeared as a way of expressing the people's religious instincts. Certain attitudes of prayer and reverence, the use of incense, lamps burning day and night in the holy place, votive offerings in acknowledgment of blessings received, these manifestations of piety and gratitude towards the divine power are too natural for them not to have their equivalent in every religion.

It is therefore not very judicious to fall back on the hypothesis of deliberate borrowing when all can be explained by human nature acting under the influence of religious feeling.[1*]

Nevertheless I know there are people who cannot see the faithful devoutly going up the steps of one of our shrines on their knees without at once thinking of the emperor Claudius, who went up the steps of the Capitol in the same way.[2] Others refer to the well-known fresco in the Naples museum which shows a priest of Isis standing before the *cella* of a temple and offering for the people's worship a sort of pyx containing water from the sacred Nile;[3] little change would be needed to make this represent a showing of or blessing with relics in accordance with present-day Christian custom. Cicero tells us[4] that at Agrigentum there was a

revered statue of Hercules, of which the mouth and chin were
worn away by the pressure of the lips of his devotees; the bronze
foot of St Peter's statue at Rome has not stood up to the kisses of
the faithful any better.

Yet these Christians of today owe nothing to the Sicilians who
were contemporary with Verres, any more than the pilgrims who
drag themselves on their knees in fulfilment of a vow or the priest
who blesses his congregation with a relic are carrying out rites
inherited from imperial Rome. What has happened is that one and
the same thought in analagous circumstances has, centuries later,
produced identical attitudes and actions. It seems to me that this
point does not call for any lengthy discussion.

On the other hand attention is sometimes drawn to certain observances of very pronounced pagan character the suspiciousness
of whose origins would be difficult to dispute. The odd ceremony
of plunging images of saints into water is too clearly like the sacred
bath of the mother of the gods[5] not to have some connexion with
that custom. In the same way it has been thought that the practice of incubation[6] lived on in the Church for centuries. This superstitious usage, practised especially in the sanctuaries of Aesculapius, Amphiaraus and Serapis, consisted essentially in sleeping in
the temple, after the prescribed preparation and ceremonies, with
the object of being granted a vision of the god in a dream, and of
receiving a revelation about the future or the healing of some
ailment.

A good deal is known about incubation, thanks chiefly to the
inscriptions at Epidaurus.[7] What was aimed at was the dream, in
which the god showed himself and bestowed good health or, more
often, indicated the treatment to be followed. The ritual of preparation, which could be rather complex, was simply to attract
the deity's favourable attention.

It is beyond question that several churches in the East were the
scene of practices that differed from incubation only in minor
details. SS. Cosmas and Damian in their church at Constantinople, SS. Cyrus and John at Menuthis in Egypt, St Artemius in
the church of St John the Baptist, ἐν τῇ Ὀξείᾳ, St Therapon

near the church of the Virgin τῆς Ἐλαίας, St Isaias in St Lawrence's church near Blakhernae, all cured their clients in the following circumstances, which are known to us from collections of saints' miracles.[8] The sick man had himself carried to the basilica, his bed was set up there, and he awaited the patron of the place to bring him relief while he slept. From the example of SS. Cosmas and Damian we learn that the sick were healed accordingly, or the remedy was indicated in the dream. The basilica is described as if it were a hospital : doctors made their rounds every night, visiting the beds, making diagnoses, prescribing treatment and writing prescriptions. And it was the same with the other healing saints we have mentioned.

Can it be said that in the East there were official attempts to christianize the old heathen rite ? Or was it simply that a considerable tolerance was extended to a practice introduced on the initiative of Christian converts not properly weaned from their old habits ? So far no liturgical text having any connexion with incubation has been produced, nor any ritual enactment to regulate it. It looks as if a preliminary offering of light was required at the tomb of St Artemius,[9] and it is evident that there were regulations to be observed in the sanctuaries organized for incubation. But we do not know what they were, just as we do not know the circumstances in which a form of devotion of so suspect an origin eventually disappeared.

The diffusion of the practice of incubation in the Christian world has certainly been exaggerated, especially as regards the Latin church. Most of the examples that are brought forward have no more to do with incubation than has this story about Bishop Redemptus of Ferentino, told by St Gregory : "Quadam die dum parochias suas ex more circuiret, pervenit ad ecclesiam beati Eutychii martyris. Advesperascente autem die, stratum fieri sibi iuxta sepulcrum martyris voluit, atque ibi post laborem quievit. Cum nocte media, ut asserebat, nec dormiebat, nec perfecte vigilare poterat, sed depressus, ut solet, somno, gravabatur quodam pondere vigilans animus; atque ante eum idem beatus martyr Eutychius adstitit, dicens, 'Redemte, vigilas ?' cui respondit,

'Vigilo'. Qui ait, 'Finis venit universae carnis, fins venit universae carnis, finis venit universae carnis'. Post quam trinam vocem,
visio martyris, quae mentis eius oculis apparebat, evanuit".[10*]

Notice that Redemptus was not expecting a vision, he simply
had his bed put up in the martyr's basilica. This was not a ritual
or religious observance. Except for the vision, which is quite
accidental, it was no more than what still commonly happens in
missionary lands, where bishop and priest are often obliged to
spend the night in the humble chapel of the village to which their
apostolic duties have taken them. In other instances we read of
sick people who do not leave the saint's tomb until their prayer is
granted; they sleep there, and they are cured, with or without a
vision, while they are sleeping. All of this has certain features in
common with incubation, but there is no sign of the institution
itself, with a body of observances.[11]

The books of miracles referred to above and the whole series of
old Greek collections call for a little more notice. We have analysed
them elsewhere,[12] and here it will be sufficient to say a few words
about one of the most celebrated of them, the Miracles of St Menas,
attributed to Timothy of Alexandria.[13] Tillemont knew them only
in an incomplete edition containing only five miracles,[14] and he
declared that "the first is thoroughly strange; the second a little
less so; the third and fourth are not bad; and the fifth is in the
highest degree scandalous". He was not the first to be scandalized;
the editors of the *menaia* (under date November 11) felt unable
to admit the story without considerable modification. Quite apart
from the buffoonery of its treatment, the governing idea of this
sham miracle is certainly not Christian. The story is called "The
Paralysed Man and the Dumb Woman", and it tells how the saint
told the man in a dream to share her bed with the woman; this
he did, and the consequent excitement and surprise caused the one
to recover the use of his limbs and the other her power of speech.

This anecdote is too reminiscent of certain comic cures by
Aesculapius not to have some connexion with the ἰάματα of

the god. Moreover, the fact that it also occurs among the miracles of SS. Cosmas and Damian,[15] with precisely similar details, suggests that it has nothing to do with St Menas. Some people are offended by the idea of any literary dependence of even Christian miracles on the records of wondrous cures wrought through the invocation of Aesculapius; to them it must be pointed out that there are several unquestionable examples of wonders identical on both sides and deriving from the same source. The miracle of the broken cup, attributed to St Lawrence by Gregory of Tours,[16] appears in practically the same form on one of the steles at Epidaurus.[17] The tale of the severed head, told on the same steles, is a version of an older one;[18] it too has been taken over by Christian story-tellers in spite of its utter absurdity.[19]

The editors of books of miracles made extensive use of borrowed matter and of adaptation, and these books can be used as historical documents only when a comprehensive inquiry has been made into the sources on which they depend. What is certain is that they are full of pagan reminiscences.[20]

The study of superstitious practices recorded at certain sanctuaries dedicated to very famous saints calls for more discrimination and critical sense than is generally found amongst students of folklore, who have undertaken the task of collecting data for the historian. The exactness of their information is often more apparent than real, and some of them practice the art of "forced resemblances" with masterly skill.

Take, for instance, the ritual of squeezing through an opening, such as a hole in a stone or a riven tree, regarded as an effective remedy for certain illnesses.[21] Some find a memory of this superstition in certain churches, where a saint's tomb is built up in such a way as to allow pilgrims to pass under it; there is an example at Gheel in Belgium, where the insane make the round of the choir, walking under the arcade that supports St Dympna's shrine. But surely it must be acknowledged that, supposing it to exist, the relationship between such rites is very remote, and that it is a far cry from a futile observance which sees a mysterious power in holed stones to a practice that is mainly based on a belief in the virtue of relics.

But some writers are obstinately bent on finding examples of suspect custom everywhere, right back to Christian antiquity, beneath the roofs of the oldest basilicas, St Peter's in Rome in the first place. In a well-known chapter, Gregory of Tours writes of the Apostle's tomb there: "Hoc enim sepulcrum sub altare collocatum valde rarum habetur. Sed qui orare desiderat, reseratis cancellis, quibus locus ille ambitur, accedit super sepulcrum, et sic fenestella parvula patefacta, immisso introrsum capite, quae necessitas promit efflagitat".[22*]

Archaeologists are quite familiar with the *fenestella confessionis,* and there is no need to explain how it is used, which depends on the arrangement and form of the *confessio* and not at all on any superstitious observance. The sepulchre of St Venerandus at Clermont[23] had a *fenestella,* and this too has been appealed to, with as little reason; and with even less the tomb of St Martin, which Gregory of Tours touched with his sore tongue *per lignum cancelli,* "through the wooden lattice".[24] Such devout actions at a saint's shrine do not recall paganism; on the contrary, they are prompted by the desire to get as close as possible to the sacred relics and they have a very marked flavour of early Christianity.

At the same time we do not deny the survival among Christian peoples of a number of usages, of very ancient origin, which are point-blank opposed to Christian beliefs or morality. Most of these superstitions are a legacy from our heathen ancestors,[25] and the Church has never ceased to fight against them, varying her tactics and with different degrees of success. Generally speaking, they have no connexion with public worship, and their accidental intermixture with properly approved religious practices or their association with the name of a saint does not confer any sort of approbation on them. The fact that in 1212 the count of Toulouse hurriedly left Montpellier, because he was terrified to see St Martin's bird flying about at his *left* hand,[26] has nothing to do with hagiography or with the history of religions: the incident belongs to the history of superstition, just as does the *sinistra cornix* of Moeris in Virgil. The same is true of astrological practices[27*] and formulas of incantation,[28*] in which it would be surprising to meet the names of saints did one not know that nonsense and inconsistency are characteristic of all manifestations of popular credulousness. But this aspect of the question need not detain us now. What we are concerned with is to inquire in which cases and to what extent hagiographical records reveal the existence of a real link between polytheism and a normal public manifestation of Christian piety.

II.—*Hero-worship, and the veneration of saints. The centre of hero-worship. Ceremonial translations. Relics. Fortuitous coincidences.*

The field of discussion now becomes very wide indeed, for it is the cultus of the saints itself that is called in question and accused of being a prolongation of idolatrous paganism. It is agreed that at its beginning the religion of Christ was kept free from all adulteration, that it rejected everything that could cloud the idea of the One God. But, we are told, when the faithful ceased to be an *élite* and the Church was as it were swamped by the mob, she had to relax her strictness, give way to the instincts of the multitude, and make concessions to the polytheistic ideas which still fermented in the people's mind.

It is said that, by introducing the cultus of the saints, the Church opened the way to a stream of clear paganism, that there is really no essential difference between the Church's saints and the heroes of Greek polytheism. It is unquestionable that the two cults are alike in their outward manifestations; but it goes deeper, and they are identical in their very spirit : we are in fact face to face with a

pagan survival.[29] Such is the thesis that these critics advance with
no little satisfaction.

We cannot disregard the details of the parallel. There is nothing
more instructive, if only because they enable us to appreciate the
exact significance of certain hagiographical legends.[30]

For the Greeks, the heroes were mortals set above the common
run of men by the gifts which the gods had bestowed on them.
They were privileged beings by their nature, half-way between
the divine and the human; they wielded some of the power of
the immortals, and they could intervene with effect in human
affairs.

These heroes, mortal sons of some god, great warriors, benefac-
tors of mankind and founders of nations, were specially honoured
in the cities with which they were connected by their origin or
history. They were their protectors or patrons. Every country,
every town, had its own heroes, to whom monuments were set up
and who were invoked in the people's prayers.

The centre of devotion to a hero was his tomb, sometimes to be
found in the *agora,* the centre of public life. It was generally
covered by a building, a sort of chapel, called a ἡρῷον.
There were many tombs of heroes in the great temples, just as
there are tombs of saints in Christian churches.[31]

When there were no mortal remains of a hero, a cenotaph was
built in his honour. But no effort was spared to have the substance
rather than the shadow : for the people had faith in the power of
a hero's bones and other remains, and whenever they thought they
had found the treasure that would protect their city they carried
it off with a pomp and ceremony that makes us think of our great
translations of relics.[32]

The best known account of one of these pagan translations is
that of the transferring of the relics of Theseus to Athens[33] during
the archonship of Apsephion (469 B.C.). The hero rested in the
island of Skyros, but his burial-place was carefully concealed by
the inhabitants. An oracle from Delphi told the Athenians to fetch
the bones of Theseus and cherish them in their city with all the
honour due to them. Cimon, son of Miltiades, led an expedition

against Skyros, seized the island, and searched for the tomb. A further prodigy revealed the exact spot: Cimon had only to dig at the place which an eagle pointed out to him with its beak and talons. In the coffin was found the skeleton of a tall man, together with a spear and a sword. Cimon loaded the precious cargo on to his trireme and the hero's relics entered Athens in triumph, amid loud rejoicing and the offering of sacrifices. Theseus was laid to rest in the centre of the city, near the gymnasium, and the tomb of him who in life had been kind and helpful to the lowly became an inviolable refuge for slaves and other poor people who sought to escape oppression by the mighty. A great sacrifice in his honour was instituted for the 8th of the month of Pyanepsion, to commemorate his return from Crete; it was also celebrated on the 8th of other months.

This page from Plutarch could be applied, without much alteration, to more than one medieval translation of relics. Those solemn transferences too are commonly preceded by instructions from Heaven; the sacred remains are discovered in miraculous circumstances; the people welcome them enthusiastically; magnificent shrines are made to contain them, and their presence is regarded as a protection for the country; and a yearly feast day is appointed in memory of the happy event.

The case of Theseus was not an isolated one: translations of the ashes of heroes were frequent in Greece.[34] Thebes recovered Hector's bones from Ilion, and gave to Athens those of Oedipus, to Lebadea those of Arcesilas and to Megara those of Aigialeus. These displacements were hardly ever undertaken without the approval or command of an oracle. But in spite of heavenly intervention it was often necessary to resort to a strategem in order to get possession of a sacred tomb; the seizure of Orestes' body by Lichas[35] is a curious footnote to some later expeditions in quest of a saint's relics.

Again, it sometimes happened, as in the middle ages, that a finding of bones led to a new cultus. Whenever these were of notably large size they were looked on as the remains of a hero, and an oracle might be consulted to find out his name. It was thus that

the Syrians learned from the god at Claros that the body of a big
man, found in the dry bed of the Orontes, was that of a hero of
the same name, Indian by origin.[36]

The analogy between pagan practices and the veneration given
to Christian relics does not stop at the honours paid to the mortal
remains of the heroes themselves. Just as in our churches things
that have belonged to saints or that particularly recall their
memory are displayed for the reverence of the faithful, so visitors
to heathen temples were shown objects of interest that the name
of a god or hero recommended to their respect. In Rome were to
be seen the bones of a whale, found at Jaffa and said to be those of
the monster to which Andromeda was exposed. In other places
there were the zither of Paris, the lyre of Orpheus, the ships of
Agamemnon and Aeneas. And since the avid curiosity of travellers
made the temple-servants and guides as ingenious as our vergers
and guides, there was eventually no relic too incredible to be
shown : the egg that Leda laid, the white sow with her thirty pig-
lets that Aeneas sacrificed on the site of Alba, the anvils which
Jupiter tied to Juno's feet, the remains of the clay out of which
Prometheus had made men.[37]

The parallel is complete when we add that the ancients, like
ourselves, were familiar with duplicate relics; they were surprised
when, for example, having seen at Coptos the hair that Isis had
torn from her head in despair at the death of Osiris, they found
the same again at Memphis. Still more when the tombs of certain
heroes were shown in several places : that of Aeneas at Bere-
cynthus in Phrygia, at Aenea in Macedonia and on the banks of
the Numicius near Lavinium.[38]

It may well be asked what more is needed now that it is clear that
the Greeks of old had a cultus which in every detail recalls that
of the saints, a cultus with shrines, translations, findings of relics,
apparitions, doubtful or obviously false relics. Is further evidence
required that the cultus of saints is nothing but a pagan survival?

The theory is plausible. But it does not stand up for a moment when brought to the bar of history. The cultus of the saints is not an outcome of hero-worship, but of reverence for the martyrs; and the honours given to them, from the beginning and by those first generations of Christians who knew baptism by blood, were a direct consequence of the high nobility of witnesses to Christ, nobility declared by Christ himself. From the respect with which their mortal remains were treated, together with the trust put in their intercession, arose the cultus of relics, with its various manifestations, with its natural, too natural, exaggerations and with—let us be frank—those excesses and extravagances which sometimes have harmed the memory of those whom it was intended to honour.[39]

There can be no need to emphasize that Greek hero-worship did not have the same theological basis and did not at all imply the same exact formulation as the religion which always sees an infinite distance between God and the man with whom God is well pleased. But it had an analagous starting-point, and it developed under the influence of general ideas that had some affinity with those which impelled hordes of Christians towards the tombs of the martyrs. And so similar practical consequences followed, and the history of the two cults shows us a logical parallel development, but without any interdependence. There was no need to remind oneself of the gods and heroes in order to invoke the martyrs trustingly, to beg for better health, safety on a long journey or success in some undertaking, to give them visible tokens of gratitude for benefits received. It was bound to follow that a martyr's tomb should be regarded not only as an honour but as a safeguard for the town that possessed it, and that the patron saint should be given all the titles of honour which had formerly belonged to tutelary heroes: Sosipolis, Sosipatris, Philopolis and the rest.[40]

In the same way, whatever the analogy of circumstances and likeness in particulars, there is no reason for the statement that the first accounts of the finding of relics were inspired by similar accounts of heathen translations. Christian narratives of this kind date from the fourth century, and they are neither forgeries nor imitations : they are the natural products of a similar state of mind in similar circumstances.

But we must not exaggerate. If we are told that the ideas disseminated by hero-worship disposed people's minds more readily to accept the *rôle* of the saints in Christianity, as intercessors before the throne of God, I do not see any reason for disputing the statement. The undoubtedly rapid spread of the cultus of martyrs and saints may well be explained by the fact that people were already prepared for it. Ancient ecclesiastical writers show no unwillingness to remark on the resemblances existing between the cultus of the martyrs and that of the heroes. Theodoret, indeed, made this the starting-point of his polemic against the pagans : "Although other people may take exception to what we do," he tells them, "you ought to be the last to complain, for you have heroes and demi-gods and divinized men."[41]

As for certain extravagances in this matter that from time to time did harm to the spirit of religion, I do not see that they must necessarily be attributed to unconscious reversions to paganism or to a secret attachment to the old religion. We have already said enough about the popular propensity for material and tangible things to account for these aberrations, which need to be continually kept in check and are found more especially among peoples whose imaginations are lively and passions strong. The body of a saint or his statue speaks to the eye, and makes far more impression than the mysteries, which speak only to faith. I would not then assimilate Neopolitan devotion[42] to heathenism—but that does not mean that I would hold it up as a model to be imitated.

III.—*Holy places. Christian transformations. Change of dedication. Ascertaining primitive titles. Holy wells.*

We hope enough examples have been given to show that we must not stop at external resemblances and fortuitous coincidences when we seek to discover what degree of continuity there may have been between certain Christian practices and Graeco-Roman religion. It is necessary to go further and deeper. Whenever in hagiographical matters there is question of getting back to the origins of a traditional cult, there are three essential elements to be studied in each case : place, date, legend. We will briefly examine the relevant questions.

It was not till the Christian faith had triumphed completely that it was possible to establish its sanctuaries on the same sites as the old temples that were now deserted or overthrown. But Christians did not wait for the definitive abandonment of pagan establishments before putting up impressive buildings that would serve all the needs of public worship. Often, indeed, they ventured to oppose the old religion on its own ground and to challenge its rights there.

We are pretty well informed about the methods the Church used to combat the superstitions associated with certain places. As a rule she did so by building a basilica or chapel and establishing a new cultus therein, with the object of diverting people's attention and giving a Christian satisfaction to their religious instincts.

We know, for instance, that the *caesar* Gallus in 351 conveyed the body of the martyr Babylas to Daphne, which was a centre both of idolatry and debauchery; to shelter it, he had a church built not far from the temple of Apollo, whose oracle was reduced to silence from that hour. The emperor Julian, annoyed at not receiving any response from the oracle, ordered the martyr's relics to be taken back to Antioch.[43]

In the time of St Cyril there was a little town called Menuthis, near Canopus, a dozen miles east of Alexandria; it was celebrated for its oracle, which the heathen came in crowds to consult, and many Christians too let themselves be led astray by it.[44] There was a Christian church at Menuthis, built by Theophilus of Alexandria and dedicated in honour of the apostles, but the den of superstition attracted more people than the house of God. Cyril put an end to these idolatrous gatherings by a ceremonial removal of the bodies of SS. Cyrus and John to Menuthis from their former resting-place in St Mark's church at Alexandria. This was the beginning of one of the most famous shrines of Christian Egypt.

Gregory of Tours[45] relates that in the Gévaudan country there was a large lake on a mountain called Helarius, and he says that the country folk used to make a sort of libation to the lake by throwing fabrics, cakes and other things into it. They came there every year, bringing food and drink in wagons, and after slaughtering beasts they gave themselves to feasting for three days. On the fourth day, just as they were leaving for home, a violent storm always broke. The bishop of Javols came to this place, and entreated the crowd to give up these observances, threatening them with divine wrath; but he preached in vain. Then God gave him an inspiration : on the edge of the lake be built a church in honour of St Hilary of Poitiers, enshrined some relics of the saint in it, and began his exhortations anew. This time they were listened to. The lake was deserted, the offerings formerly thrown into it were brought to the basilica instead, and storms ceased to rage at the time of the festival, which was henceforth dedicated to God.[46*]

In the cases just mentioned the Church did not take possession of the places of heathen worship, but sought to ruin them by successful competition. When the temples were finally deserted, she was careful not to let the sites, generally beautifully chosen, pass into profane use : whenever circumstances allowed, she consecrated them to the true God.

The story of the liquidation of the property of defeated paganism has often been told. In particular, it has been possible to make long lists of churches which were built on the foundations of heathen temples, or constructed with their materials, or simply established in the old building.[47] The classic examples of the last are the Pantheon at Rome and the Parthenon at Athens.

The memory of the original title of many other temples that were replaced by churches, temples less famous than the Pantheon and the Parthenon, has not been preserved with the same certainty. Some scholars have evolved an ingenious theory to make up for this frequent silence of history. Having noticed that there is sometimes a certain similarity between the Christian designation of a former temple and its earlier title, they have felt justified in attributing to the Church a system of christianizing these sanctuaries that would be evidence of a very accommodating policy towards the newly converted. According to this theory, the new churches were put under the patronage of saints whose name or legend recalled the divinity previously honoured at the same spot, and this in order to leave converts with the illusion that they had not completely broken with their past.

At Eleusis we find a church of St Demetrius on the site of the temple of Demeter : it is the name of the goddess, scarcely altered. It is true there was also a church of St George there : but this is Demeter again, the goddess of agriculture hidden under the name of the "holy husbandman", *Georgios*.[48] Elsewhere St George replaced Theseus or Hercules, but then it is as the vanquisher of monsters that he is substituted for the destroyer of the Minotaur or of the Lernean hydra.[49] Thus, whether the analogy be phonetic or symbolic, archaeologists can always turn it to use and find little difficulty in pointing out some similarity between the new patron and the old.

But it is not so easy for them to prove that these resemblances have usually been deliberately sought, and this has to be proved when one seeks to connect a saint's name with that of the god he displaced. Were it possible to demonstrate that a rule was followed in these matters, then valuable topographical information could obviously be attained by a very simple process. But a system cannot be deduced from a few examples. In order to get rid of the superstitious associations of a sacred lake on Mount Helarius or Hilarius, the bishop dedicated a basilica to St Hilary, evidently because of the similarity of name. It is less certain, however, that it was for the same reason that at Menuthis, Cyril of Alexandria chose the martyr St Cyrus (*Kuros*) with his companion St John, to oppose the cult of Isis (*Kura*), "the lady"; but he could hardly refrain from pointing out that henceforward *Kuros* must be invoked, a more powerful personage than the *Kura*.[50] At Antioch the martyred bishop Babylas was set over against Apollo without there being the slightest connexion between the name or legend of the saint and the name of the supplanted god. So the value of the criterion drawn from the resemblance of names is illusory; and if some critics have misused it strangely, others have treated it with well-deserved suspicion.

I am far from denying that popular devotion here and there may sometimes have become contaminated by the still-living memory of old superstitions, and that it often seriously altered the "appearance" of certain saints; that, for example, SS. Cyrus and John ended up by becoming types of holy healers, generous physicians, like Cosmas and Damian; or that in the people's imagination this group (whose origin and true history will probably always defy research) took a new and final form as kindly spirits well-disposed towards mankind, on the pattern of the Dioscuri.[51*] But, if we keep to facts, there is no justification for saying that the Church systematically used these transpositions of names which left the thing itself unaltered : it is indeed highly improbable that she should have lent herself to such dangerous equivocations.

A few examples must be given, to put the reader on his guard against the tempting theory just referred to. Take St Elias, dedicated under whose name numerous chapels are found in Greece, on the tops of mountains and hills. Some writers have stated that at these Elias has ordinarily taken the place of his namesake Helios, the god of the sun.[52] The assimilation is specious, the facts do not support it. The heights of Greece were not the places where shrines of Helios were especially numerous. Furthermore, sun-worship was eventually almost completely absorbed by the cult of Apollo, and this fact upsets the play on names which is supposed to account for so many chapels of St Elias. The prophet's history as related in the Bible, his going up to Heaven in a chariot of fire, his appearing at Christ's side at the Transfiguration, "made him the natural patron of high places".[53] It is quite probable that in many places the invocation of St Elias has been substituted for that of a heathen deity, but there is nothing to prove that this deity was Helios.

Moreover, if evidence is to be drawn from these dedications, they must be very early ones, going back to the time when the religion of the sanctuaries was changed. But some of them are known to be of more recent date.

At Athens, for instance, the church of St Paraskeve stands on the site of the Pompeion, a building intended for the organization of religious processions, as Pausanias says: ἐς παρασκευήν ἐστι τῶν πομπῶν.[54] Must there not have been connexion between *Paraskeve*, titular saint of the church, and the preparation, *paraskeve*, of processions that used to happen at the same place? And yet it can be stated without fear of error that there is no such connexion, and that it is simply a coincidence whose importance some archaeologists have exaggerated.

The fact is that St Paraskeve can have given her name to the chapel only at a relatively recent date, for she was unknown to the ancients; liturgical evidence of the tenth and eleventh centuries proves that her cultus, and still more her popularity, are later than that time. Need we add that, even had she been honoured in very remote ages, no one would have thought of giving her name to the little building of which Pausanias speaks? He uses the word παρασκευή in this connexion, but it was certainly not the name by which people knew the building.

Some scholars, starting from vague likenesses in names and combining them with topographical data, have built up full-blown romances on some hagiographical text. Unquestionably one of these is that essay in mythology[55] which sets out to demonstrate that St Donatus (of Euroea) took the place of Pluto, or, what comes to the same thing, Aidoneus, king of the Molossi, whose name admittedly is reminiscent of *Aios Donatos*. I should be the first to agree that we have no really authentic information about St Donatus, and that scraps of mythology were used in concocting a biography for him; but the erudite legend which tries to identify him with the god of the underworld is worth no more than the traditional story.

This idea can be found at the bottom of more than one learned dissertation on the origins of the cultus of saints, the idea that the great martyrs and wonderworkers of the ancient world, especially those who were regarded as the patrons of cities at an early date, were the direct heirs of a tutelary god whose altars attracted the multitude. The age-old fame of the place, it is said, easily explains the concourse of pilgrims; the tide of popular devotion had only to be slightly deflected from its former direction for it to forsake the idol in the temple and flow into the Christian basilica.[56]

The examples we have given of a sort of Christian canalization of a very strong religious movement do not stand alone in history. And it can be admitted that this sometimes came about spontaneously, without any intervention by the leaders of the Church. But this does not justify the formulation of a general law, one which, were it true, would be of considerable importance in the comparative study of religions. With the help of documents and monuments, it is not difficult to give the name of a specially honoured pagan god or hero in every Greek town which later became a place of Christian pilgrimage. This only amounts to saying that one local cultus succeeded another, just as one religion succeeded another everywhere. But we look in vain for any connecting link between them.

On the Capitoline hill at Rome there stood a temple dedicated to the ruler of gods and men, who for centuries was worshipped there by kings and peoples. Later on, pilgrims from all over the world flocked to Rome to the tomb of the leader of the apostles. Does anyone seriously suggest that St Peter is the direct heir of Jupiter Capitolinus?

The passage from Gregory of Tours referred to above draws attention to a particular aspect of popular hagiography connected with the christianization of centres of superstition by the introduction of the cultus of saints. Water-worship is particularly difficult to uproot, as the object of it cannot be destroyed or removed at will. The number of springs and wells put under the patronage of a saint is very large, and the conclusions drawn from this fact by students of local history are not all equally well-founded and exact.[57] To attempt a synthesis of the ample material available, very disparate and ill-classified, would be a long task, and we shall not undertake it. But it is worth asking whether the majority of the wells and springs bearing the name of a saint witness to the Church's war on heathenism.

Clearly they do not. It would be very difficult to prove that all these waters were once the object of superstitious reverence, and it is certainly not true to say that the memory of a saint could be associated with them only by an act of ecclesiastical authority. We have seen that people are never backward in "baptizing" note-worthy places in their neighbourhood, and quite naturally they give them the names that are uppermost in their minds. A St Martin's Well is not necessarily a holy well : the name simply testifies to the popularity of St Martin. Careful distinction must therefore be made between wells whose name alone attracts the attention of the hagiographer and those which are a centre of devotion or superstition. To this second category belong all those to which pagans brought their gifts and prayers.

IV.—*Dates of festivals. Change of object. Coincidences difficult to prove. Fallacious dating of pagan festivals. Examples.*

Correspondence of dates is a consideration of the highest import-ance in the search for the remote origins of a cultus. Celebrations that bring together a large number of people are necessarily kept on fixed days, and everybody knows that nothing is more difficult to change than the date of a fair or a pilgrimage; the tenacity of popular custom is nowhere more in evidence than in the faithful observance of holidays. We may then be quite sure that when a

Christian people has retained something from a heathen festival it
will at least include its date.

Usually when it was a matter of compensating converts for the
loss of pagan merrymaking in general, they were urged to keep
the feasts of martyrs, celebrated on the anniversary of their day of
death. Thus St Gregory the Wonderworker instituted annual
gatherings of his people in honour of the martyrs, and thereby
helped on the transition from secular amusements to purely religious rejoicings.[58] But it was different when bishops had to combat
a specific idolatrous festival and uproot an age-long observance.
When, as must often have happened, it was impossible to prevent
the people meeting together, all they could do was to change the
purpose of the occasion and so to sanctify the day.[59]* The bishop of
Javols would not have overcome the superstitions in his diocese
if he had done no more than celebrate the feast of St Hilary on
Mount Helarius on its liturgical date. He celebrated that feast on
the day of the heathen festival, which was thus definitely consecrated to the worship of the true God : *in hac solemnitate quae
Dei erat,* says Gregory of Tours (see above, page 133). Coincidence of dates is then of the first importance to those seeking an
unbroken link between a saint's feast and paganism.

But while all agree on the importance of this kind of evidence,
they do not all see so clearly the difficulty of verifying it. Absolute
accuracy is required, and one may well ask whether it is obtain-
able. Differences in calendars, the difficulty of establishing concordance between them, the numerous festivals in honour of the
same divinity, local liturgical divergences, all these complicate the
question of date so much as to make assimilation nearly always
impossible.

When it is a question of establishing a parallel between a Christian solemnity and an old Roman festival, the problem is relatively
easy, and results can be obtained with certainty. For example, it
can be agreed that the Greater Litanies on St Mark's day are a
Christian continuation of the *Robigalia* observed on April 25.[60]
The date, the similarity of the rites and the identity of the objects
of the observances leave no room for doubt.

But the solution is not alway so easy. The number of pagan feasts being very considerable, the chances of fortuitous coincidence are increased correspondingly; and it seems likely that the *Natalis invicti* celebrated on December 25 had nothing to do with the choice of this day for the feast of Christ's birth. The date would appear to have been determined by a calculation whose starting-point was March 25, that being supposed to be the date of our Lord's death.[61] This theory, which makes the cycle of feasts of Christ's childhood depend on Easter, which was certainly the earlier celebration, is more probable than the other, which rests only on an ingenious suggestion arising out of identity of date. Some have seen in the feast of the Purification of our Lady a Christian transformation of the pagan *Lupercalia* : but this was celebrated on February 15, not on the 2nd.[62]

Coincidences are far more difficult to verify when we have to compare our calendars with those of the Greeks or Asiatics and with totally different systems of festivals. Thus, at Athens the festival of the gods and heroes was not only celebrated on a fixed date, the corresponding date in each month was sacred to them as well.[63] Naturally, such multiple commemorations increase the likelihood of coincidences, and it is clear that we must be in no hurry to assert a connexion between two observances which happen to fall on the same day.

In the previous section of this chapter we have pointed out that it is an illusion to try to find the name of the original tutelary god of an old sanctuary concealed in the Christian dedication of the same place. It is equally dangerous to try to find the unknown date of a pagan festival from Christian particulars which are supposed to have some connexion with it.[64] The efforts of this kind which have been made always strike me as being particularly unfortunate, if the authors who have exercised such remarkable ingenuity will forgive my saying so. I will give an outstanding example. A series of deductions drawn from the survival of the cultus of the Dioscuri provides a proof of the existence, from extremely early times, of a monthly festival of the two heroes; customarily it fell on the same date in each month, the 18th or

19th. The following sums up the argument which leads to this unexpected discovery : [65]

It begins by the assertion that a series of saints are simply Castor and Pollux in a Christian disguise; then the dates of their feasts are brought together in a table, thus :

April 19 :   St Dioscurus.
May 19 :   St Polyeuctus.
June 18 :   SS. Mark and Marcellian.
June 19 :   St Judas Thomas and SS. Gervase and Protease.
August 18 : SS. Florus and Laurus.
September 18 : St Castor.
December 18 : St Castulus.
December 19 : St Polyeuctus.

Elsewhere I have done my best to show that not one of these saints has anything in common with the Dioscuri.[66] Nearly all of them are well-identified historical persons, whose cultus is properly established and rests on a traditional basis. There may be added that no Dioscurus figures on April 19 in the martyrologies; May 18 must be meant, the day on which the memory of St Dioscurus, reader, was kept in Egypt. May 19 is not the day of St Polyeuctus' martyrdom; he is the second of the group Timothy and Polyeuctus, entered in the Syriac martyrology on May 20. By a common copyist's mistake they have slipped in as well amongst the martyrs on the 19th.

But putting aside all these difficulties, and assuming there may have been some sort of connexion (which in fact there was not) between the Dioscuri and the saints named, let us suppose that they were all celebrated on the same day of the month, say the 18th. Should we then be justified in concluding that the Dioscuri probably had a festival on the 18th of each month? Certainly not; for it leaps to the eye that the date of the 18th by the Julian calendar does not at all correspond with the 18th in Greek, Syrian and Asiatic calendars, in accordance with which the festival of Castor and Pollux, supposedly monthly, would have been originally fixed.

A further example showing the necessity of not depending

merely on a coincidence of dates :[67] One of the arguments offered
in proof that SS. Florus and Laurus are no other than the Dioscuri
is the date of their feast, August 18; for St Helen is celebrated on
the same day and, according to the fable, Helen was the name of
the sister of Castor and Pollux. Give Florus and Laurus their real
names, and you have in the martyrology an authentic feast of the
Dioscuri and their sister.

But it is not all so simple as that. The truth is that the collocation
of Florus and Laurus with Helen is purely accidental. No old
Latin martyrology even mentions Florus and Laurus, who are
known in Greek tradition alone; and no Greek synaxary names
Helen on August 18 : she is invariably associated with Constantine on May 11, and nowhere else. It took a compilation from
Greek and Latin sources to bring Helen and the Greek martyrs
together on the same day in a martyrology, and this accidental
association did not happen until the sixteenth century. I think
this simple fact is enough to exclude from the ancient calendar a
feast of the Dioscuri corresponding to August 18.

We shall have something to say later on about how the festival
of the Epiphany of Dionysos in Bithynia came to be credited to
January 7.

In order to show the relationship of St Pelagia, specially honoured on October 8, to Aphrodite, much has been made,[68] among
other arguments, of the date of this festival, relying on the text
of an inscription at Aegae in Cilicia, which runs : Θεῷ Σεβαστῷ
Καίσαρι καὶ Ποσειδῶνι ἀσφαλείῳ καὶ ᾿Αφροδείτῃ Εὐπλοίᾳ.[69*]
Euploia is the title of Aphrodite of Cnidus. It might be expected
that the first thing to be proved would be that the goddess was
honoured on October 8. Nothing of the sort. Only a single date
has been verified concerning the worship of Venus Pelagia,[70]
and that is of a local festival, the dedication of a temple and statue
of the goddess at Nigra Corcyra (Curzola) on May 1 of the year
193 of the Christian era. But Poseidon is named in the votive inscription, and the 8th of each month was sacred to Poseidon. I
confess that the conclusion of the argument makes a poor impres-

sion on me, and would still do so even were it proved that the sea-god's day was on the 8th of the month in Cilicia as well as at Athens.

V.—Pagan legends. Christian adaptations. Three kinds of case. Examples: the legend of St Lucian of Antioch. The legend of St Pelagia and its fellows. St Liberata or Wilgefortis, etc.

The more obviously promising legends, those which as a whole or in part seem to reflect pagan traditions, have attracted most of the attention of critics, and it is principally by means of the legends that they have tried to establish a connexion between paganism and some of the saints (and these not the least well-known). We must follow them onto this ground, and attempt to clarify the method which should be adopted in research of this kind.

If no more be claimed than that, in a given series of legends, there can be found elements that were already in circulation among the peoples of classical antiquity, no contradiction is called for; when outlining the sources of hagiographical narratives we have given enough examples of such borrowings to put the matter beyond doubt (cf. above, pages 22-25). The more we make a comparative study of relevant writings, the more parallels are unearthed, and it is surprising to find how many remains of antiquity there are in medieval legendaries.[71]*

But, whether such material was used in its raw state or whether it had previously been given a Christian colouring, there is generally no need to talk about pagan infiltration or survival. It is not the religious element that is at work in such cases, it is the literary stream carrying along the bits and pieces of the ages.

The problem to be resolved is whether a given Christian legend in some way perpetuates something that is religious and pagan, in other words, whether the legend is the expression of an ancient cultus surviving under a Christian guise.

In the first place, therefore, all legends that are independent of any "cultual" element must be put aside. In such hagiographical collections as menologies and passionaries, and in such compilations as synaxaries and martyrologies, there are many names and passages which represent only a literary tradition. This tradition may go back to classical times, but that does not mean that we have to consider a possible influence from paganism.

Our business is with saints whose cultus is proved by a church built in their honour, by a feast regularly observed, or by their relics being offered for the veneration of the faithful. There are three sorts of case to be considered.

First, it sometimes happened that legends which had a purely literary dependence on pagan antiquity eventually gave birth to a cultus. The story of the Seven Sleepers began as a pious romance, but it imperceptibly passed from the realm of literature into the field of liturgy;[72] the heroes of a wholly imaginative tale were honoured as saints, their burial-place was shown and their relics sought. Barlaam and Joasaph, chief characters in a Buddhist romance, very gradually attained like honours. But their cultus was an artificial creation, it had no roots in the distant past of Buddhism, any more than the cultus of the Seven Sleepers was the continuation of a religious feature of Greek polytheism.

Second, a legend with a pagan flavour may have an authentic saint for its subject, one whose cultus was established before the legend arose and quite independently of it. The resulting question is not always easy to answer. It may be that the fabulous element has got mixed up with the saint's history simply in accordance with the inevitable process by which famous people acquire legendary traits that have no particular religious bearing. But it is also possible that the saint has inherited some attribute of the local god together with the honours given him. Nothing is less easy to decide at a single glance.

It must not be forgotten that very many customs, turns of speech and themes, whose origin is undoubtedly religious, implying, if pressed, clearly polytheistic doctrines, have gradually lost their original meaning and become either simple flourishes or conventional formulas devoid of objectionable significance. The charming godlings clambering among the garlands and vine-branches of pictures and carvings are merely decorative motifs, and *Dis Manibus Sacrum* was innocently written above Christian inscriptions on tombs, with no more significance than that of being the conventional beginning of an epitaph.[78]

The history of the saints itself provides examples which enable us to gauge the exact value of certain facts which at first sight depend on religion and worship, but which really are connected with them only by very slender threads.

The Byzantines sometimes named stars after the saints whose feasts corresponded with their rising. The star of October 26 was the star of St Demetrius, that of November 11, of St Menas, that of November 14, of St Philip.[74] It is difficult to see anything but a method of dating in this, and I should not care to assert that the Byzantines believed that the saints watched over the stars, attributing to them functions in the heavens of which the gods had been dispossessed.[75] It is obvious to me that, certain superstitious customs apart (cf. above, page 125), the star of St Nicholas was referred to in the same way as we speak of the Michaelmas term. When sailors gave the name "Cyprianic winds" to the gales at the autumn equinox, the expression[76] testified to the popularity of the cult of St Cyprian, but it did not in any way imply a religious act.

So, because something belongs both to mythology and to a saint's legend, it does not follow that the saint must be regarded as a god in disguise. It would not be logical to raise doubts about the existence of St George simply because of his legend, and it is going much too far to declare positively that in his person "the Church has converted and baptized the pagan hero Perseus".[77] It would be hard to demonstrate that the cultus of St George is the continuation of a heathen devotion. It was widespread in early times, and its centre is certain : it was at Lydda in Palestine, where the saint's tomb was shown, and everything seems to point to his cultus having originated in a perfectly regular way.[78] It is amusing to recall that the episode of the dragon, of which so much has been made in the efforts to reduce the saint to a myth, does not appear in any of the earlier legends of St George, either as a main feature or incidentally.[79]

The majority of hagiographical legends that are adorned with mythological odds and ends appear to belong to saints who have nothing else in common with the pagan gods. But there are exceptions. Some saints, well-authenticated ones too, acquired such special features at certain shrines that it is difficult to deny the survival of pagan belief and ritual in the cultus accorded them. Whatever the original history of SS. Cosmas and Damian may have been, they were soon looked on as the successors of the Dioscuri, and the honours given them at some of their sanctuaries had points of contact with pre-existing cults.[80] Seamen, too, for a long time had their own ways of honouring St Nicholas and St Phocas,[81*] attributing functions to them which make us think of the ancient heroes. If you like, you can describe them as the successors of Poseidon. The idea of protector saints gradually took the place of that of the sea-god; but the phenomenon is due to accidental circumstances, and the saint, even if heir to a heathen god, none the less keeps his own individuality.[82]

The third case is that of the legend which reveals purely and simply the continuity of a religious tradition, idolatrous or superstitious yesterday, Christian today. Here it is no longer a matter of deciding whether or not an authentic saint has acquired some characteristics or even the general appearance of a pagan god, but of studying the relevant sources to find out if a given saint be not himself a god or hero who has penetrated into the Christian sanctuary after an appropriate transformation.

The distinctions just made may seem a little over-subtle; but they surely are absolutely necessary if we wish to go beyond superficial resemblances and far-fetched associations. In order to realize the difficulty of mythological studies based on an examination of hagiographical legends, one has only to examine thoroughly a few particular cases on which scholars have worked, and to weigh the results of their critical efforts, which are as searching as they are well conceived. We will confine ourselves to two, the legends of St Lucian and of St Pelagia;[83] the interpretation which we shall suggest is very different from that which was current not so long ago.

St Lucian was a very celebrated martyr of the fourth century, who died at Nicomedia on 7 January 312. His body was taken to Drepanum, a town on the Bithynian coast which Constantine renamed Helenopolis in his mother's honour. Lucian's martyrdom is fully authenticated, and so is his cultus, attested by a basilica at Helenopolis as well as by written documents. Among the chief testimonies to St Lucian's history we have that of Eusebius,[84] a panegyric by St John Chrysostom,[85] and a celebrated legend,[86] incorporated in the menology of Metaphrastes but certainly dating from a much earlier period.

It is not necessary for us to consider the *acta* of St Lucian as a whole,[87] but we must refer to certain details in his legend which have been used in support of the theory we are going to examine.

First of all, the author of the passion relates that Lucian was denied all food for fourteen days on end : τέσσαρες καὶ δέκὰ τας πάσας ἡμέρας. [88] After a few days of suffering thus, he told his disciples he would keep the feast of the Theophany (Epiphany) with them and on the next day he would die. This prohecy came true : in the presence of envoys from the emperor, who were astonished at his surviving so long, Lucian repeated three times "I am a Christian", and died.[89]

Others state, adds the narrator, that he was thrown into the sea whilst still alive, the emperor Maximian, exasperated by his firmness, having ordered that he should be drowned, with a heavy stone tied to his arm so that he should be forever deprived of honourable burial. And he remained in the sea fourteen days, the same time that he had been in prison : τέσσαρες καὶ δέκα τὰ ὅλας ἡμέρας. On the fifteenth day a dolphin brought the martyr's body to land, and then itself died on the spot.[90]

One of the most widespread legendary themes of the classical age can be recognized in this remarkable happening. The dolphin, the friend of man, who carries him, living or dead, on his back, is the subject of more than one charming fable and of numerous pictorial representations.[91] Melicertes, Hesiod, Arion (the dolphin which brought the last-named to land also died on the beach), were the popular types, and it is not surprising that their poetical legend should have crept into hagiography: a dolphin appears in the stories of St Martinian,[92] St Callistratus,[93] St Arian[94] and yet others. This fact is sufficient to prove that the episode of the dolphin is purely adventitious, its connexion with St Lucian's story being accidental and in no sense mysterious, even though we are unable to discover the circumstances in which this reminiscence of a classical myth became associated with him.

It has been suggested that dolphins were carved on the martyr's sarcophagus, and that this was enough to set the people's imagination going.[95] This explanation, combined with the mythical tradition, which was not yet forgotten and could be brought to mind by the sight of the carved dolphins, need not be wholly rejected; but it has the disadvantage of being no more than an hypothesis produced to fit the case. The fact is that there is no information about how St Lucian's sarcophagus was decorated.

Another explanation has been offered, one that has the merit of resting on a fact.[96] St Lucian was martyred at Nicomedia; his basilica was not there but at Helenopolis, at the other end of the gulf. The people probably had no recollection of the translation of his body, and so later on they explained the anomaly by the familiar expedient of a miraculous intervention, for which tradition provided them with examples.

But the dolphin's presence in the Nicomedia legend has led the mythological school into much deeper waters.

Notice, they say, the persistence with which the number 15 recurs in connexion with St Lucian's name. Putting aside the fact (though it is worth noting) that the Greeks transferred his feast to October 15, look at the legend itself. Lucian died after suffering for fifteen days; the dophin brought back his body on the fifteenth

day; he died on the day after Epiphany, which is the 15th of the
month of Dionysos; and observe that at Heliopolis (Helenopolis)
his feast is celebrated on the eve which is precisely the 15th of the
month of Tishri.[97]

And what is the significance of the dolphin? It is one of the
attributes of Dionysos. Why is it then associated with the memory
of St Lucian? Because his feast coincided with the feast of Dionysos, which in Bithynia was kept on the 15th of the month of Dionysos. There you have a pagan festival which the people had not
forgotten and which they associated with a Christian anniversary.
The dolphin of St Lucian's legend is evidence of the new converts'
attachment to their old superstitions.

Those, in brief, are the learned deductions that are made.

Conclusions of such importance would of course have to be
carefully discussed, if only we knew that in fact the great solemnity in honour of Dionysos was observed on the 15th of the month,
coinciding with January 7, and that a legend of Dionysos, current
in Bithynia, was one of the numerous replicas of the story of the
dolphin bringing back the body of Melicertes. But we do not know
these things. For evidence of them we are simply referred to the
legend of St Lucius itself.[98]

It is difficult to say anything about this elaborate structure of
arguments except that it has no sound basis; not only do we fail to
see any link between St Lucian and Dionysos, but when we look
more closely Dionysos disappears altogether, leaving us only with
one of the commonest phenomena found in the folklore of every
land. It seems superfluous to lay stress on the weakness of the
argument—or rather the suggestion—drawn from the number
15, which is itself not even beyond doubt. The Arian commentary
on the book of Job, which seems to echo some of the same traditions as the Passion of St Lucian, gives another number: *Hic
namque beatus duodecim diebus supra testas pollinas extensus,
tertia decima die est consummatus.*[99*]

So the legend of St Lucian in no way discredits the Bithynian
Christians. It cannot be used as evidence against the integrity of
their faith or to show that they found it more difficult than other

people to forget Dionysos. And it still remains to be proved that
the great festival of this god coincided with the day after the
Christian Epiphany, the day of St Lucian's martyrdom; for so far
neither his own legend nor any historical text has offered proof of
it.

The legend of St Pelagia has been the starting-point of a far
more laborious inquiry, conducted according to the same principles; its results have been accepted by plenty of scholars who have
not been moved to look into them further, but they are very surprising. It is asserted that, admittedly under a purified form, the
Church continued to give homage to Aphrodite, Venus, the goddess of erotic pleasure and animal fertility.

Pelagia, also called Margarito because of the magnificence of
her pearls and other jewels, was the best known and also the most
licentious of the dancing-girls of Antioch. One day she went into a
church while Bishop Nonnus was preaching. Touched by grace,
she begged that she might be baptized; and when she had laid
aside the white gown of the neophyte, she put on a hair shirt and a
man's tunic, and withdrew to the Mount of Olives at Jerusalem.
There she lived for three years in a small hut, under the name of
Pelagius, until she went to receive the reward of her repentance.
The Greek church keeps her feast on October 8.

In this form and taken by itself there is nothing very improbable
about Pelagia's story, and it would indeed be difficult to find
traces of mythological survival in it. But its critics compare it with
other legends, with which it forms a whole and whose pagan origin
and character are manifest, or so they tell us.

On the same date of October 8 another Pelagia of Antioch is
commemorated, a virgin described by St John Chrysostom in a
panegyric preached in her honour.

And again on that day there is recalled the martyrdom of a
third Pelagia, of Tarsus, who preferred death by roasting alive in
a brazen bull to the love of the emperor's son.[100] Under the name
of Anthusa, Pelagia of Tarsus appears again on August 22 at

Seleucia, with a story[101] which, apart from its ending, recalls the previous one.

On July 17 among the Greeks, St Marina of Antioch in Pisidia,[102] and on July 20 among the Latins, St Margaret of Antioch,[103] suffered death like Pelagia of Tarsus for rejecting the advances of a judge, the prefect Olybrius.

There is no difficulty in recognizing a connexion between all the above and another group.

St Margaret, honoured on October 8, runs away on her wedding night, disguised as a man. She takes refuge in a monastery and lives there under the name of Pelagius. She is accused of seducing a nun, and is punished for the crime she could not have committed. Her innocence is discovered only when she dies. She is given the name of Reparata.[104]

Maria, or Marina (February 12), also enters a monastery disguised as a man. While the pretended monk is on a journey, the daughter of an innkeeper accuses "him" of being the father of her baby. Marina is driven from the monastery and made to support the child. Having done her penance, she is readmitted to the monastery, and at her death it is found that she has been slandered.[105]

St Eugenia (December 24) governs a house of monks as their abbot. A woman accuses her falsely in her father's court, he being prefect of Egypt.[106] In Egypt again we meet St Apollinaria (January 5), who hides herself under the name of Dorotheus and suffers a like misfortune.[107]

Euphrosyne of Alexandria (September 25) calls herself Smaragdos and lives undisturbed in a community of monks until she is recognized by her father.[108]

Theodora of Alexandria (September 11), being guilty of adultery, goes into a monastery of men to do penance; she is accused of misbehaviour, and cleared of it after her death.[109]*

Clearly there is kinship between all these legends, evidenced partly by the identity of names, Pelagia, Marina, Pelagius, Margaret (reminiscent of the nickname Margarito given to the Antiochene dancer), partly by the theme, a woman disguised as a monk, keeping her sex secret until her death. Sometimes this theme is amplified by the element of slander, which on the whole is a logical development of it.

Before looking at the deductions by means of which Venus or Aphrodite has been detected under the guise of St Pelagia, we must try to determine the starting-point of the whole series of legends just outlined.

The church of Antioch in the fourth century observed on October 8 the feast of a quite historical St Pelagia,[110] about whom we learn from St John Chrysostom and St Ambrose.[111] But her history bears no resemblance whatever to the story of the penitent harlot and it contains no hint of a rather romantic disguise. Pelagia was a fifteen-year-old girl, whose home was overrun by unruly soldiers. To escape outrage, she asked to be allowed to put on better clothes; and while the men awaited her she threw herself from the house-top, thus saving her honour by a voluntary death.

Ought we then to admit the existence of a second St Pelagia of Antioch, the penitent sinner? The identity of date, October 8, gives food for thought. And here we must turn to another passage from St John Chrysostom.

In his 67th homily on St Matthew's gospel he tells the story of a renowned actress, but without mentioning her name. She came to Antioch from one of the most dissolute of Phoenician cities, and her infamous life made her talked about so far away as Cilicia and Cappadocia. She ruined the good name and fortunes of many, the emperor's sister herself falling a victim to her allurements. All of a sudden she resolved on a change of life, and with the help of grace turned her back on Satan. She was admitted to the holy mysteries, and after baptism she lived austerely for long years, wearing a hair shirt and shutting herself up as in a prison cell, allowing no one to call on her.

There is no justification for assuming that this anonymous penitent became the object of an ecclesiastical cultus after she died; the very way Chrysostom speaks of her suggests the contrary. But it is quite certain that the work known as "Pelagia's Repentance" has Chrysostom's narration for its *mise-en-scène*. The editor, who calls himself James, found it too simple and added the element of a disguise, which could be suggested to him by more than one existing tale.

It is very difficult to decide whether the original intention of the self-styled James was to write an edifying romance in which a Pelagia would play the principal part, or whether he intended, with the help of new material, to compose a legend for the saint venerated at Antioch. We know from outstanding examples that historical tradition about local saints soon disappears when a legend begins to develop, and that hagiographers are not afraid of making alterations which render their subjects practically unrecognizable. Even if his heroine and St Pelagia of Antioch were not one and the same in "James's" mind, it was inevitable that their identity should become taken for granted.[112*]

The legend of Pelagia of Tarsus in Cilicia seems to be a result of the double tradition associated with the name Pelagia. In some respects she recalls the courtesan at Antioch, whose ill-repute, as Chrysostom tells us, was known in Cilicia and who also had been in touch with the imperial family; but Pelagia of Tarsus was a virgin and a martyr, and this confuses her with the original Pelagia, whose cultus was established from the fourth century.

The story of St Pelagia in its double form had a great success, and it produced a harvest of very complicated legend, as has happened elsewhere in the literature of the saints. "James's" version, easily the most interesting and highly coloured, was the most popular one. The personality of the Antiochene saint, shadowy from the start, was soon effaced by the interest taken in the legend, which by degrees shed all contact with history. Even the account of the conversion disappeared, and the wholly legendary residue took on, under various names, the primitive form of a tale in the strict sense of that word. So we have Saints Maria or Marina, Apollinaria, Euphrosyne and Theodora, who are nothing but literary replicas of "James's" Pelagia; or else, as in the case of St

Eugenia, the theme of a woman hiding her sex has been intruded into a narrative about some historical person.

We regard the long process of development that has just been set out as a rather commonplace phenomenon, explainable by the normal effect of legend-making ferment. If it contains anything of religious interest, it is the fact of a traditional cultus being gradually smothered by legend. But the cultus in question was Christian in origin, and the legend was Christian too, though mixed with elements drawn from general literature. There is nothing whatever in it to suggest any pagan influence.

That, of course, is not the conclusion reached by those who profess to identify Pelagia with Aphrodite.

After having gone through the train of narratives which we have summarized, a scholar wrote that "this bird's-eye view must give rise in the most prejudiced mind to the conviction that one and the same divinity, like a trunk lopped of its branches, is continually reviving throughout these varied legends; and so the image that was deeply printed in the soul of the people, having disappeared from the temples, continued to draw from hidden roots power to put forth new shoots on every side. . . . In the Hellenism of the imperial age there was only one idea which could have produced all these forms of a legend : the idea of Aphrodite. This dangerous image personifying physical loveliness had to be eradicated from the hearts of the faithful; it was taken just as it was, but cleansed in the fire of repentance and penance that it might be fit for Heaven".[113]

All that now remains to be done then is to prove that the heroine of the legends is in fact Aphrodite or Venus.

Nothing, apparently, is easier to do. Aphrodite was the goddess of the sea, and was known under a number of appropriate titles : Aigaia, Epipontia, Thalassaia, Pontia, Euploia and — *Pelagia,* of which Marina is a translation.

This is the kernel of the demonstration; and, since there is nothing to be elicited from the date of the feasts (cf. above, page

140), it is the whole of the argument. Need I say that I find it a weak one ?

If at any rate the name Pelagia had been a very rare or unusual one amongst women; if it had been less well known, especially at Antioch, the common source of all forms of the legend; or if the epithet "Pelagia" was one commonly applied to Aphrodite. ... But one example of Venus Pelagia[114] and two of Venus Marina (both provided by Horace[115]) are all that have been found, whereas there is every reason to believe that Pelagia was a common woman's name in other places besides Antioch.[116]

We may be excused from dwelling on other comparisons that are advanced in support of the thesis. *Anthusa* of Seleucia is paired with the Aphrodite *Anthera* of Knossos; *Porphyria* of Tyre with the Venus *Purpurina* of Rome; *Margarita* with Venus *Gene-trix,* because Julius Caesar dedicated to her a pearl-studded breast-plate.[117] What a waste of painstaking scholarship!

We cannot however omit one other consideration produced on behalf of the theory we are opposing : it is a very ingenious one, intended to show that, within Christianity itself, there is an un-ambiguous trace of the Aphrodite cult in one of its most mon-strous developments. Emphasis is put on the contrasts found in the Pelagia legends between pleasure and penance, sensuality and chastity, and on the recurrent theme of "change" of sex. This is to draw attention to the goddess of Amathus in Cyprus, who could be regarded at will as Aphrodite or Aphroditos and was represented in woman's clothes but bearded like a man. At the sacrifices offered to this deity men dressed as women and women as men.[118] It is the cultus of the hermaphrodite; and, we are told, the Pelagia legend bears its mark and it continues formally in the Church, there are bearded women among the saints : at Rome it is St Galla,[119] in Spain it is St Paula,[120] elsewhere it is St Liberata, Wilgefortis, Kümmernis, Livrade, Ontkommer and the rest.[121]

I have already remarked that sex-dissimulation is a common-place theme, found in all literatures. As for the supposed herma-phrodites, they could hardly have been worse chosen. How can anyone seriously point to Galla? Her story (told by St Gregory) is of the crudest kind : to induce her to marry again, the physicians told her that if she did not she would grow a beard; and so it happened.[122] Paula is an obscure saint of Avila, and her story is a repetition of that of Wilgefortis, whose grotesque legend is very far from having the mysterious origins that have been attributed to it. It took its rise from the diffusion of the *Volto Santo* image at Lucca, and is nothing but an uncouth misinterpretation of this unusual iconographic type (cf. above, pages 87-88).

VI.—*Mythological names. Other suspicious names. Iconographic parallels. The Blessed Virgin. Saints on horseback.*

It is clear from what has been said above that saints' names have their part in the researches of mythologists and that real importance is sometimes given to them in the question of heathen survivals. We are told, for instance, that "the continental Greeks and those of the islands and Asia Minor turned with enthusiasm to the old gods of the Hellenes, to whom they merely gave new names, often very transparent ones; Pelagia, Marina, Porphyria, Tychon, Achilleios, Mercurios, etc".[123] It is easy to show that, in this connexion, evidence drawn from names is particularly misleading.

At an early date the Romans gave the names of Greek gods, especially to slaves and to newly enfranchised persons; later on, the names of Roman gods were equally allowed. The Greeks had the same custom, and it became more prevalent as polytheism decayed. Hence the frequency of the names of gods and heroes, such as Hermes, Mercury, Apollo, Aphrodite, Pallas, Phoebus,[124] and the derivatives of mythological names, such as Apollonios, Pegasios, Dionysios.[125] Several of these are the names of unquestionably authentic saints, and this fact alone is sufficient to show that in general a pagan name throws no suspicion on the saint who bears it. And there are other names that are mythological only in appearance, such as that of St Venera, which makes us think of Venus: she was, in fact, St Paraskeve ("Friday") in a Latin or Italian form of the name.[126]

This is not to say that there are no strange names among the saints which may arouse legitimate suspicion. In Corfu (Corcyra) an obscure saint is honoured called Corcyra, Κέρκυρα, who plays a part in the legend of the evangelists of the island, Jason and Sosipater.[127] One is bound to think that this St Corcyra is to Corcyra what Nauplius is to Nauplia,[128] Romulus to Rome, Byzas to Byzantium, Sardus to Sardinia,[129] that she is in fact solely the brainchild of a hagiographer. Reading the Acts of SS. Jason and Sosipater[130] amply confirms this impression.

There is another class of names of a kind to excite distrust, namely, those which express a quality or function, as Therapon, Sosandros, Panteleemon and others. Names of this kind nearly always belong to saints with a strong reputation as wonder-workers, and this must not always be attributed to chance. I know, of course, that protests have been made, and rightly made, against the mania for dismissing as "myths" people whose names correspond with the activity attributed to them. "Considering that nearly all the names of the ancients had a meaning", writes Boeckh, "it would be easy to explain most of them as myths: and it would be difficult to know how the Greeks could have named their children in such a way as to avoid the danger of their losing their real existence and seeing themselves reduced to being myths. Socrates' father, Sophroniscos, would fall under grave suspicion, for it is Socrates who makes men wise, σώφρονας; his mother Phaenarete, has in fact been suspected by Buttman, for Socrates is indeed ὁ φαίνων τὴν ἀρετήν".[131]

This could not be put better. But, in the case we are considering, the existence of saints who seem to be personifications of attributes often has no better guarantee than some strange legend; moreover, we know that the people are quick to give the saints they invoke names that accord with their supposed characteristics. St

Liberata, Ontkommer or Kümmernis is an example. The homage paid to her was really addressed to Christ, since at first it was the crucifix of Lucca that was venerated, before it was transformed in accordance with the legend. The cultus of other saints of a similar sort perhaps concealed some cultus of a very different character, difficult to specify and connected with some pagan superstition by indeterminate links. Such an hypothesis is not excluded, but it cannot be put forward as a general principle. It is very unlikely, for example, in the case of St Panteleemon,[132] who had some celebrated shrines in the time of Justinian.[133]

This chapter cannot be concluded without brief reference to a point that in some measure illustrates what we have been saying. Just as, where legend is concerned, certain scholars have been eager to plot the stages of a kind of Christian metamorphosis beginning in pure paganism, so they regard certain Christian pictures and statues as christianized interpretations of idolatrous models. Here can be seen in all its clearness the danger of postulating a real dependence from certain outward resemblances, a way of proceeding which is especially risky in a matter in which the means of expression are of necessity very limited.

The few cautious attempts made in this direction have been notably unfortunate; and in almost every one of them the mere consideration of proved historical facts would have shattered all the conclusions drawn from a vague similarity between certain Christian motifs and images of pagan provenance. An outstanding example is the extraordinary claim of a learned man to find the origin of the image of the Virgin of the Seven Swords, so popular in Catholic countries, in an image of the Assyrian goddess Ishtar.[134] The genesis of this representation of our Lady of Seven Sorrows, as of the devotion itself, is known in every detail, the date and place of it have been exactly determined : it is scarcely older than the sixteenth century, and it comes from the Low Countries.[135]

Another scholar claims to have discovered numerous analogies, indicative of a common origin, between the cultus of the Blessed Virgin and the cultus of Astarte. He goes so far as to declare that the long embroidered triangular robe worn by our Lady in some images is the continuation of the sacred cone which represented the eastern goddess.[136]

An attempt has been made to prove the descent of the thirteenth-century madonnas from the Gaulish type of mother-goddesses, "through the medium of Gallo-Roman types of more skilful workmanship, which already have a virginal expression".[137] The intermediaries referred to are those carvings which show the goddesses as a seated woman suckling a baby. Surely it is obvious that such a group could very easily suggest the mother of God, and that it would not be surprising if our ancestors were sometimes deceived by the resemblance. But so far were they from needing a model from which to represent the Blessed Virgin in this way that it is precisely the type of the oldest known madonna image, painted on a wall in the catacomb of Priscilla.[138*]

Horus is shown on horseback, driving his spear into a crocodile; St George is shown on horseback, driving his spear into a dragon : but we must not rush to the conclusion that St George is identical with the Egyptian god.[139] Quite apart from the fact that most warrior-saints were represented on horseback[140] and that the sight of any equestrian statue could suggest this iconographic type, the legend of St George the dragon-slayer, which has no connexion whatever with the legend of the god Horus, was bound to lead to Christian artists giving the saint's image that form which has become classical. But it only came later, for as has already been said, there is no mention of the dragon in the older Passions of St George. St Menas with his inevitable companions, the two camels, reminds us of Horus and his crocodiles. It could be that Coptic sculptors took their idea from so widespread a representation to create their popular type of the great martyr; but that is no reason for transforming him into a heathen divinity and making him a sort of substitute for Horus.[141] The classical origin of the statue of St Peter sitting in a chair, carrying the keys in one hand and blessing with the other, is undeniable.[142] But does it follow that St Peter has to be put in the same category as other people represented in a similar way?

NOTES ON CHAPTER VI

[1]One of the most curious relevant cases is that of Demetrius's prayer in Seneca, *De providentia*, v, 5-6. The philosopher expresses the conformity of his will to the will of the gods as follows: "Hoc unum de vobis, di immortales, queri possum, quod non ante mihi voluntatem vestram notam fecistis. Prior enim ad ista venissem, ad quae nunc vocatus adsum. Vultis liberos sumere? vobis illos sustuli. Vultis aliquam partem corporis? sumite. Non magnam rem promitto; cito totum relinquam. Vultis spiritum? Quidni? nullam moram faciam, quo minus recipiatis quod dedistis. A volente feretis, quicquid petieritis. Quid ergo est? maluissem offerre quam tradere. Quid opus fuit auferre? accipere potuistis. Sed ne nunc quidem auferetis, quia nihil eripitur nisi retinenti. Nihil cogor, nihil patior invitus, nec servio Deo sed adsentior, eo quidem magis quod scio omnia certa et in aeternum dicta lege decurrere." If this prayer be compared with the *Suscipe* of St Ignatius of Loyola, with which he concludes his book of *Spiritual Exercises*, the resemblance between the two passages is found to be astonishing. Yet I think I am justified in saying that at the time he was writing St Ignatius was not nurturing himself on Seneca.

[2]Dio Cassius, lx, 23.

[3]C. A. Böttiger, "Isisvesper", in *Kleine Schriften*, vol. ii (Dresden, 1838), pp. 210-230.

[4]*In Verrem*, iv, 43.

[5]Ovid, *Fasti*, iv, 337-346.

[6]L. Deubner, *De incubatione capita quattuor* (Leipzig, 1900).

[7]Collitz-Bechtel, *Sammlung der griechischen Dialekt-Inschriften*, nn. 3339-3341; P. Cavvadias, Τὸ ἱερὸν τοῦ Ἀσκληπιοῦ ἐν Ἐπιδαύρῳ (Athens, 1900), pp. 256-267; A. Defrasse & H. Lechat, *Épidaure* (Paris 1895).

[8]On all this see our *Les recueils antiques de miracles des saints* (Brussels, 1925).

[9]Ibid., p. 72.

[10]*Dial.*, iii, 38. ["One day, as he was making the round of his diocese according to custom, he came to the church of the blessed martyr Eutychius. As night was coming on, he had a bed made close to the martyr's tomb, and there lay down to rest after the day's work. In the middle of the night, he declared, he was neither sleeping nor able to keep wide awake, but was oppressed as usual by drowsiness, while his active mind was troubled by some heavy weight. Then the same blessed martyr Eutychius stood by him, saying, 'Redemptus, are you awake?' He replied, 'I am.' Eutychius said, 'The end of all flesh is come, the end of all flesh is come, the end of all flesh is come.' After this threefold utterance the vision of the martyr, which was seen by the eyes of the bishop's mind, vanished."]

[11]In *Les recueils antiques de miracles ...*, pp. 103-105, we have made detailed examination of Gregory of Tours' texts, in which some

writers have thought they found evidence for the practice of incubation at Tours and Brioude.

[12]We refer to the miracles of SS. Cosmas and Damian, Cyrus and John, Artemius, Therapon, Isaias, Theodore, Menas, Thecla and Demetrius, examined in *Les recueils antiques . . .*, pp. 8-73.

[13]Published by J. Pomjalovskij, *Life of St Paisios the Great* (in Russian; St Petersburg, 1900), pp. 62-89.

[14]*Mémoires pour servir à l'histoire ecclésiastique*, vol. v, p. 760.

[15]Wangnereckius-Dehnius, *Syntagmatis historici de tribus sanctorum Cosmae et Damiani nomine paribus partes duae* (Vienna, 1660), pp. 481-483; L. Deubner, *Kosmas und Damian* (Leipzig, 1907), pp. 162-164.

[16]*In gloria martyrum*, xxx.

[17]Collitz-Bechtel, *Sammlung der gr. Dialekt-Inschriften*, n. 3339. Cf. P. Perdrizet, "Le miracle du vase brisé", in *Archiv für Religionswissenschaft*, vol. viii (1905), pp. 305-309.

[18]See O. Crusius, in *Mélusine*, vol. v, p. 203.

[19]P. Perdrizet, in *Revue des études anciennes*, vol. ii (1900), pp. 78-79. Cf. *Mélusine*, vol. v, pp. 97-100.

[20]*Les recueils antiques de miracles*, p. 70.

[21]H. Gaidoz, *Un vieux rite médical* (Paris, 1892).

[22]*In gloria martyrum*, xxvii. ["For this tomb placed below the altar is accounted a very exceptional thing. But when the railings that surround the place are opened, he who wishes to pray goes above the tomb and, a little *fenestella* thus being seen, he puts his head inside it and prays according to his need." The *fenestella* is a window or opening in a saint's tomb or in the structure (*confessio*) that encloses it.—Tr.]

[23]*In gloria confessorum*, xxxvi.

[24]*De virtutibus S. Martini*, iv, 2. All these examples are given by Gaidoz, op. cit., pp. 36-37.

[25]See for instance Weinhold's studies of the vestiges of ritual nakedness in various superstitious observances, "Zum heidnischen Ritus", in *Abhandlungen der k. Akademie Wissenschaften zu Berlin* (1896) i, pp. 1-50.

[26]Pierre des Vaux de Cernay, *Historia Albigensium*, n. 47, Bouquet, vol. xix, p. 43: "Viderat enim quandam avem, quam indigenae vocant avem sancti Martini, ad sinistram volantem, et perterritus fuit valde. Ipse enim, more Sarracenorum, in volatu et cantu avium et ceteris auguriis spem habebat."

[27]In a collection of omens published by D. Bassi & E. Martini, *Catalogus codicum astrologorum graecorum. Codd. Ital.* (Brussels, 1903), pp. 158-169, invocation of the following saints is recommended: Stephen, Thecla, Michael, Parasceve, George, Irene, Cosmas and Damian, Katherine, Demetrius, Anastasia, the Holy Cross, Ann, the Blessed Virgin, Nicholas, Barbara, Pantaleon, Gregory. These seem to be the saints whose names were given to the stars from which portents were read.

[28]In Egypt the names of the Seven Sleepers of Ephesus and of the Forty

Martyrs of Sebaste have been found more than once mixed up with magical formulas; R. Pietschmann, "Les inscriptions coptes de Faras", in *Recueil de travaux relatifs à la philologie et à l'archéologie égyptiennes et assyriennes,* vol. xxi (1899), pp. 175-176. See also W. Pleyte & P. A. Boeser, *Manuscrits coptes du musée d'antiquités des Pays-Bas* (Leyden, 1897) pp. 441-486.

[29]"Christianorum quoque religio habebat atque habet suos semideos, suos heroas; sanctos scilicet martyresque"; L. Deubner, *De incubatione,* p. 57. "Die Heiligen der christlichen Kirchen, vor allem die der griechischen Kirche, stellen die gerade Fortentwicklung des griechischen Heroenkults dar. Die Heilige sind die Heroen der Antike"; G. Wobbermin, *Religionsgeschichtliche Studien* (Berlin, 1896), p. 18. Cf. E. Maass, *Orpheus* (Munich, 1895), p. 244.

[30]On hero-worship, see F. A. Ukert, "Ueber Dämonen, Heroen und Genien", in *Abhandlungen der k. sächsischen Gesellschaft der Wissenschaften,* vol. i, pp. 138-219; Preller, *Griechische Mythologie,* vol. ii; W. Schmidt, *Der Atticismus,* vol. iv (Stuttgart, 1896), p. 572; and especially F. Deneken, "Heros", in Roscher, *Lexikon der griechischen und römischen Mythologie,* vol. i, cc. 2441-2589; P. Foucart, "Le culte des héros chez les Grecs", in *Mémoires de l'Institut,* vol. xlii (1922), pp. 1-166.

[31]On this special question, see K. T. Pyl, *Die griechischen Rundbauten* (Greifswald, 1861), pp. 67 ff.

[32]Lobeck, *Aglaophamus,* p. 280; Rohde, *Psyche,* vol. i, pp. 161-163.

[33]Plutarch, *Theseus,* 36, *Cimon,* 8.

[34]Pausanias is here the principal source. The most important texts have been set out by Rohde, *Psyche,* vol. i, p. 161, and by Deneken, art. cit.

[35]Herodotus, i, 67, 68.

[36]Pausanias, viii, 29, 4.

[37]The texts have been brought together by Lobeck, *Aglaophamus,* p. 52; Ukert, op. cit., pp. 202-204; Friedländer, *Sittengeschichte,* vol. ii, ch. I: Die Reisen.

[38]J. A. Hild, "La légende d'Énée", in *Revue de l'histoire des religions,* vol. vi, (1882), p. 67.

[39]See *Les origines du culte des martyrs,* pp. 1-119.

[40]For that reason M. Gelzer claims that St Demetrius came to replace the tutelary god of Thessalonika. He says: "Der Typus einer solchen Paganisierung des Christentums ist nun vor allem der heilige Demetrius. Er ist gleichsam die Personifikation oder die Fleischwerdung des antiken griechischen Polisgedankens. Wie Apollon und Herakles führt er den Beinamen Sosipolis"; "Die Genesis der Byzantinischen Themenverfassung," in *Abhandlungen der k. sächsischen Gesellschaft der Wissenschaften,* vol. xviii (1899), n. 5, p. 54.

[41]*Graec. affect. curatio,* viii, Raeder, pp. 194-219.

[42]T. Trede's book, *Das Heidentum in der Römischen Kirche,* 4 vols. (Gotha, 1899-1891), is wearisome to read and is the result of very super-

ficial observation. The author knows the Neapolitans intimately; but his consistent ill-humour is enough to show that he was not the man to understand them and their exuberant devotion; and he never makes any allowances for them.

[43]The texts are brought together in Tillemont, *Mémoires,* vol. iii, p. 405.

[44]*Acta SS.,* Jan., vol. ii, p. 1083; Deubner, *De incubatione,* pp. 80-98. See *Anal. Boll.,* vol. xxx, pp. 448-450.

[45]*In gloria confessorum,* ii.

[46]We are less well informed about the substitution that took place on Mount Gargano; but it has long been recognized that the legend of that sanctuary contains echoes of the oracle of Calchas that made the place famous. See, e.g., F. Lenormant, *A travers l'Apulie et la Lucanie,* vol. i (Paris, 1883), p. 61; G. Gothein, *Die Kulturentwicklung Süd-Italiens* (Breslau, 1886), pp. 67-75.

[47]Marangoni, *Delle cose gentilesche e profane trasportate ad uso e adornamento delle chiese* (Rome, 1744), pp. 256-287; L. Petit de Julleville, "Recherches sur l'emplacement et le vocable des églises chrétiennes en Grèce", in *Archives des missions scientifiques,* 2nd series, vol. v (Paris, 1868), pp. 469-533; P. Allard, *L'art païen sous les empereurs chrétiens* (Paris, 1874), pp. 259-298.

[48]Petit de Julleville, op. cit., pp. 492-493.

[49]Ibid., pp. 504-505.

[50]Homily preached in the church of the Evangelists, *P.G.,* vol. lxxvii-p. 1104.

[51]Pagans made the comparison, as may be gathered from several texts of the Miracles of SS. Cosmas and Damian. These are brought together in Deubner, *De incubatione,* p. 77.

[52]C. Wachsmuth, *Das alte Griechenland im neuen* (Bonn, 1864), p. 23; Petit de Julleville, op. cit., 505-506.

[53]F. Lenormant, *Monographie de la voie sacrée Éleusinienne* (Paris, 1864), p. 452.

[54]Petit de Julleville, op. cit., pp. 488, 514; A. Mommsen, *Athenae christianae,* p. 89. Pausanias, i, 2, 4.

[55]E. de Gubernatis, "Aidoneo e san Donato, studio di mitologia epirotica", in *Rivista Europea,* an. v (1874), vol. ii, pp. 425-438.

[56]There are several reservations to be made about the ideas on this matter expressed by E. Lucius in a posthumous work, *Die Anfänge des Heilegenkults in der christlichen Kirche* (Tübingen, 1904); see *Anal. Boll.,* vol. xxiv, p. 487.

[57]Anything like a full bibliography would be very long; for a few indications, see A. Bertrand, *La religion des Gaulois* (Paris, 1897), pp. 191-212; *Bulletin archéologique du comité des travaux historiques,* 1897, pp. 150-160; 1898, pp. lxv-lxvi. See also the important article by R. C. Hope, "Holy Wells: their Legends and Superstitions", in *The Antiquary,* vol. xxi (1890), pp. 23-31 and following volumes; and by the same author, *Legendary Lore of the Holy Wells of England* (London, 1893).

[58]*Vita S. Gregorii thaumat., P.G.,* vol. xlvi, p. 954.

[59]In Malta at the end of the sixteenth century a festival in honour of St John the Baptist was celebrated whose pagan flavour was very marked. R. Wünsch, *Das Frühlingsfest der Insel Malta* (Leipzig, 1902), saw in it a feast of the returning spring, christianized one knows not when. He may have been right; but I cannot follow him when he claims that the procession of March 12 (op. cit., pp. 68-70) is a continuation of this long-abolished custom. In passing, still less do I like his ideas about Good Friday observance in Athens, which reminds him of the festivals of Adonis; and I like not at all the meticulous parallel between St John the Baptist and Adonis, which moreover is useless for the support of his theory.

[60]Anrich, *Mysterienwesen* (Leipzig, 1894), p. 231; Duchesne, *Origines du culte chrétien,* p. 276.

[61]Duchesne, op. cit., pp. 247-254. See also an article by H. Grisar, "Relazione tra alcune feste cristiane antiche e alcune usanze pagane", in *Civiltà cattolica,* series xvii, vol. xii, pp. 450-458.

[62]Marquardt, *Le culte chez les Romains,* vol. ii, pp. 179-183. Cf. De Bruyne in *Revue Bénédictine,* vol. xxxiv, pp. 18-26. A. Dufourcq, *Études sur les Gesta martyrum* (Paris, 1900), p. 207, queries whether the date of the feast of St Hippolytus might not be determined by that of the pagan festival *Dianae in Aventino* (Marquardt, op. cit., p. 373); his link between the two feasts is of the slightest, and August 13 is certainly the date of the *depositio* of St Hippolytus.

[63]C. Petersen, *Ueber die Geburtstagfeier bei den Griechen* (Leipzig, 1857), pp. 313-314. Cf. A. Mommsen, *Feste der Stadt Athen* (Leipzig, 1898), pp. 1-5.

[64]H. Usener does not share this opinion. He writes: "Die christlichen Heiligen, die an die Stellen von Göttern gesetzt worden sind, gestatten uns in ihrem Gedenktag die Zeit des ursprünglichen Götterfestes mit Sicherheit zu erkennen und dadurch das Wesen des Festes und der Gottheit zu ermitteln." *Archiv für Religionswissenschaft,* vol. vii (1904), p. 14.

[65]J. Rendel Harris, *The Dioscuri in the Christian Legends* (London, 1903), p. 62. The same author afterwards published other works on this subject, which push the theory beyond reason; it was a veritable obsession with the Dioscuri. Cf. *Anal. Boll.,* vol. xxvi, pp. 332-333; xxxviii, 182-183.

[66]*Anal. Boll.,* vol. xxiii, pp. 427-432.

[67]Harris, op cit., pp. 1-19; cf. *Anal. Boll.,* vol. cit., pp. 428-429.

[68]H. Usener, *Legenden der heiligen Pelagia* (Bonn, 1879), p. xxi.

[69]CIG., 4443. ["To the divine Augustus Caesar, to Poseidon the securer and to Aphrodite, guardian of voyagers".]

[70]CIL., iii, 3066: *Signia Vrsa Signi Symphori templum Veneri Pelagiae a solo fecit et signum ipsius deae posuit Falcone et Claro cos. k. mais.*

[71]To give some idea of the discoveries of this kind that can still be made, let me quote from the collection, so well-known in the middle ages, in which St Gregory the Great brought together many curious tales, stories about saints, pious anecdotes, visions and relevations, which he retailed to

his deacon Peter with engaging candour. Chapter xxxvi of the fourth book of the *Dialogues* bears the odd title: *De his qui quasi per errorem educi videntur e corpore;* and one of the things that Gregory relates in it makes its meaning clear. He had it from the mouth of one Stephen, who told it as his own experience. Stephen had died, and seen his soul conveyed to Hell. He came before "the judge who presides there", and was turned away, because, said the judge, "This is not the man I sent for; it was Stephen the blacksmith". The dead man's soul at once returned to his body, and his neighbour and namesake, the blacksmith, died (*P.L.*, vol. lxxvii, p. 384). There is no possibility of mistake: St Gregory's friend Stephen was an unscrupulous man who boasted of being the hero of a story he had read in a book. Not to speak of St Augustine, he might have read it in Plutarch or, more likely, Lucian in his *Philopseudes,* where Cleomenes in similar fashion tells how he was taken before Pluto in Hades and sent back to earth again, whereupon his neighbour, the blacksmith Demylus, was taken away instead. See E. Rhode, *Psyche,* 2nd edn, vol. ii, p. 363; L. Radermacher, "Aus Lucians Lügenfreund", in *Festschrift Theodor Gomperz dargebracht* (Vienna, 1902), p. 204; A. Jülicher, "Augustinus und die Topik der Aretalogie", in *Hermes,* vol. liv (1919), pp. 94-103.

[72]*Acta SS.,* July, vol. vi, p. 376.

[73]F. Becker, *Die heidnische Weiheformel D.M.* (Gera, 1881), pp. 65-67.

[74]*Catalogus codicum astologorum graecorum, II: Codices venetos descripserunt,* G. Kroll et A. Olivieri (Brussels, 1900), p. 214.

[75]Cumont, *Catalogus codd, astrolog.,* vol. iv (1903), p. 159.

[76]Procopius, *Bell. Vandal.,* i, 21 :

Τὸν χειμῶνα οἱ ναῦται . . . ὁμωνύμως τῇ πανηγύρει προσαγορεύειν εἰώθασιν, ἐπεὶ ἐς τὸν καιρὸν ἐπισκήπτειν φιλεῖ, ἐφ, οὗ ταύτην οἱ Λίβυες ἄγειν ἐς ἀεὶ τὴν ἑορτὴν νενομίκασι. Cf. i, 20, Dindorf, pp. 393, 397.

[77]E. S. Hartland, *The Legend of Perseus,* vol. iii (London, 1896), p. 38.

[78]On this, see our *Légendes grecques des saints militaires* (Paris, 1909), pp. 45-50.

[79]Ibid., p. 75.

[80]See *Les recueils antiques de miracles des saints,* pp. 8-18.

[81]The sailors of Aegina wish one another a good voyage in the phrase "May St Nicholas hold your tiller". E. Curtius, "Die Volksgrüsse der Neugriechen", in *Sitzungsberichte der k. Preussischen Akademie,* 1887 p. 154. L. Radermacher, "St Phokas", in *Archiv für Religionswissenschaft,* vol. vii (1904), pp. 445-452.

[82]After a thorough examination of the question, the learned author of *Hagios Nikolaos* (Leipzig, 1913-17), M. Anrich, reaches the same conclusion (vol. ii, p. 505).

[83]H. Usener, *Die Sintfluthsagen* (Bonn, 1899), pp. 168-180. Id., *Legenden der heiligen Pelagia* (Bonn, 1897).

[84]*Hist. eccl.,* ix, 6.

[85]*P.G.,* vol. l, pp. 519-526.

[86]*P.G.,* vol. cxiv, pp. 397-416.

[87]The best work on the acts of St Lucian is that of P. Franchi de' Cavalieri, *Di un frammento di una Vita di Costantino,* taken from *Studi e documenti di storia e diritto,* vol. xviii (1897), pp. 24-45.

[88]*Passio S. Luciani,* n. 12, *P.G.,* vol. cxiv, p. 409.

[89]Ibid., n. 15.

[90]Ibid, n. 16.

[91]O. Keller, *Thiere des klassischen Alterthums* (Innsbruck, 1887), pp. 211-235; A. Marx, *Griechische Märchen von dankbaren Tieren* (Stuttgart, 1889), p. I ff.

[92]*Acta SS.,* Feb., vol. ii, p. 670.

[93]*Acta SS.,* Sept., vol. vii, p. 192.

[94]*Acta SS.,* Mar., vol. i, p. 757; *Synax. eccl. Constant.,* p. 308.

[95]P. Batiffol, "Étude d'hagiographie arienne; La passion de S. Lucien d' Antioche", in *Compte rendu du Congrès scientifique international des catholiques* (Brussels, 1894), vol. ii, pp. 181-186.

[96]P. Franchi, op. cit., pp. 39-43.

[97]In the Syriac martyrology. See De Rossi-Duchesne, *Martyrologium Hieronymianum,* in *Acta SS.,* Nov., vol. ii, p. [lii].

[98]"Durch die Legende des Lukianos wissen wir das die Bithynier die Epiphanie des Dionysos am xv des auf wintersonnenwende folgenden monats Dionysos feierten. Wir wissen daraus auch, unter welchen mythischen bilde die erscheinung des gottes geschaut wurde. Als entseelter auf dem rücken eines gewaltigen delphin zum lande gebracht, das war das bild Bithynischer Epiphanie" (Usener, op. cit.,) p. 178.

[99]*P.G.,* vol. xvii, p. 471 ["This blessed man, after lying outstretched on pounded shards for twelve days, finished his course on the thirteenth day."]

[100]The three legends are summarized in *Synax. eccl. Constant.,* pp. 117-120. The sources in *Bibl. hag. graec.,* pp. 105-106.

[101]Published by H. Usener in *Anal. Boll.,* vol. xii, pp. 10-41.

[102]Ibid., *Acta sanctae Marinae et Christophori* (Bonn, 1886), pp.15-46.

[103]The different redactions of the Passion of St Margaret, *Bibl. hag. lat.,* 5303-5310.

[104]*Acta SS.* Oct., vol. iv, p. 24.

[105]*P.G.,* vol. cxv, pp. 348 ff.

[106]*P.G.,* vol. cxvi, pp. 609 ff.

[107]*Acta SS.,* Jan., vol. i, pp. 257-261.

[108]A. Boucherie, in *Anal. Boll.,* vol. ii, pp. 196-205.

[109]K. Wessely, *Die Vita S. Theodorae* (Vienna, 1889), pp. 25-44. We omit Porphyria of Tarsus, who is not a saint, and Andronicus and Athanasia, who in our opinion complicate Usener's list uselessly. But he could have added St Papula, who lived amongst monks in the diocese of

Tours and was made their abbot. Gregory of Tours, *In gloria confessorum,* xvi.

[110]The date is given in the Syriac martyrology, *Acta SS.,* Nov., vol. ii, p. [lxi].

[111]Chrysostom: *P.G.,* vol. l, pp. 579-585. Ambrose: *De virginibus,* iii, 7, 33, *P.L.,* vol. xvi, p. 229; *Epist.* 27, *ad Simplicianum,* 38, ib., p. 1093.

[112]It cannot be said that no confusion existed and that the proof is the three saints named Pelagia entered in the synaxaries on October 8. The very identity of the date explains the error. The notices concerning the three namesakes are the result of an habitual proceeding by compilers of synaxaries: when they came upon two irreconcilable traditions about the same one saint, they just made him into two different people.

[113]Usener, *Legenden der heiligen Pelagia,* p. xx.

[114]CIL., iii, 3066. Cf. Preller-Robert, *Griechische Mythologie,* vol. i (1894), pp. 364-365. There is nothing in the Greek poets, C. F. H. Bruchmann, *Epitheta deorum quae apud poetas graecos leguntur* (Leipzig, 1893), p. 68.

[115]See I. B. Carter, *Epitheta deorum quae apud poetas latinos leguntur* (Leipzig, 1902), p. 102.

[116]CIG., 3369, 3956, 9497.

[117]Usener, op. cit., pp. xxi-xxii.

[118]Ibid., p. xxiii.

[119]*Acta SS.,* Oct., vol. iii, pp. 147-163.

[120]*Acta SS.,* Feb., vol. iii, p. 174.

[121]*Acta SS.,* July, vol. v, pp. 50-70.

[122]St Gregory, *Dial.,* iv, 13.

[123]Gelzer, *Die Genesis der byzantinischen Themenverfassung, p.* 54.

[124]Sources in H. Mayersahm, *Deorum nomina hominibus imposita* (Kiel, 1891).

[125]H. Usener, *Götternamen* (Bonn, 1896), pp. 358ff.

[126]This is acknowledged by Wirth himself, *Danae in den christlichen Legenden* (Vienna, 1892), pp. 24-26.

[127]*Acta SS.,* June, vol. v, pp. 4-7. Cf. *Synax. eccl. Constant.,* pp. 633-636.

[128]A. Boeckh, *Encyklopaedie der philologischen Wissenschaften* 2nd edn (Leipzig, 1886), p. 560.

[129]"Sardus Hercule procreatus ... Sardiniam occupavit et ex suo vocabulo insulae nomen dedit" (Isidore, *Etymol.* xiv, 6, 39, *P.L.,* vol. lxxxii, p. 519). Isidore's compilation contains many similar examples.

[130]Mustoxidi, *Delle cose Corciresi* (Corfu, 1848), pp. xi-xx.

[131]Boeckh, op. cit., p. 581.

[132]See our *Origines du culte des martyrs,* p. 220.

[133]*Acta SS.,* July, vol. vi, p. 398.

[134]H. Gaidoz, "La Vierge aux sept glaives", in *Mélusine,* vol. vi (1892), pp. 126-138.

[135]*Anal. Boll.,* vol. xii, pp. 333-352; P. Soulier, *La confrérie de N.-D.*

des Sept Douleurs dans les Flandres (Brussels, n.d.); A. Duclos, *De eerste eeww van het broederschap der Zeven Weedommen van Maria* (Bruges, 1922).

[136]Cf. *Mélusine,* vol. iii (1887), p. 503; see also G. Rösch, "Astarte-Maria", in *Theologische Studien und Kritiken,* vol. lxi (1888), pp. 265-299.

[137]J. Baillet, *Les Déesses-Mères d'Orléans* (Orleans, 1904), p. 14.

[138]What is more surprising is that distinguished archaeologists should have let themselves be deceived about the significance of an Egyptian stele representing Isis with Horus at her breast. M. Gayet, in "Les monuments coptes du musée de Boulaq", in the *Mémoires de la mission archéologique du Caire,* vol. iii, pl. xc and p. 24, did not hesitate to recognize it as the Blessed Virgin suckling the divine Child, though with the qualification that "this representation must belong to the earliest period of Coptic development, when the ancient style was still influential." G. Ebers, *Sinnbildliches. Die koptische Kunst,* etc. (Leipzig, 1892), adopted the same interpretation. But C. Schmidt had only to turn the stone round—its back had been used for a Christian epitaph—to eliminate the stele as a Coptic monument and restore it to the worship of Isis and Horus: "Ueber eine angebliche altkoptische Madonna-Darstellung", in *Zeitschrift für aegyptische Sprache,* vol. xxxiii (1895), pp. 58-62.

[139]Clermont-Ganneau, "Horus et saint Georges", in *Revue archéologique,* new series, vol. xxxii (1876), pp. 196-204, 372-399, pl. xvii.

[140]See J. Strzygowski, "Der koptische Reiterheilige und der hl. Georg", in *Zeitschrift für aegyptische Sprache,* vol. xl (1902), pp. 49-60.

[141]A. Wiedemann, "Die Darstellungen auf den Eulogen des hl. Menas", in *Actes du sixiéme Congrès des Orientalistes,* vol. iv (Leyden, 1885), pp. 159-164.

[142]H. Grisar, *Analecta Romana* (Rome, 1899), pp. 627-657.

CHAPTER VII

SOME HAGIOGRAPHICAL ERRORS

Not separating a saint from his legend. Excessive trust in hagio-
graphers. Incautious appeal to local tradition. Confusion bet-
ween a likely and a true narrative. Excessive importance given to
the topographical element. Utter contempt for legend.

To DRAW up a list of the chief errors perpetrated by hagiographers
and critics ever since people have interested themselves in the lives
of the saints would be a heavy undertaking indeed. There is no
form of literature which is more often approached without any
preparation than this; and if it be true that good will suffices to
please the saints, it is less true that nothing more is needed in order
to praise them in a worthy manner, or properly to estimate the
quality of the praise that is accorded them. Hagiographers, unhappily, have been great offenders, and our only consolation is to
believe that much will be forgiven them.

It is too much to hope to coax all of them into the straight paths
of scientific criticism; but let us at least try to forearm them against
certain extremely serious errors which are current among them,
which continually worsen the misunderstandings between history
and poetry and sharpen the conflict between science and religious
devotion. These mistaken beliefs are mostly understood rather
hazily. In the light of the principles that we have attempted to set
out, it should generally be enough to state these errors in precise
terms for their falsity to be at once apparent.

The first and commonest mistake consists in not separating the
saint from his legend. A narrative is accepted because it refers to
a well-authenticated saint; the existence itself of another saint is
questioned because the stories about him are improbable or even
ridiculous. The same principle leads to either of these equally
absurd conclusions, according with the school that applies it.

We need not spend much time in demonstrating its falsity.

Every part of this book goes to show that the saints are continually liable to be compromised by what is written about them, in the degree that the people and the hagiographers wish to do them honour. Moreover, the documents concerning them are at the mercy of all the perils of transmission. So there is no direct proportion between the legitimacy and popularity of a saint's cultus and the historical value of the written documents that testify to it. Martyr A., whose cultus has never spread beyond the walls of his small basilica, lives for us in his authentic and impressively beautiful *acta*. Martyr B., whose tomb draws pilgrims from all over the world, is now known only from stories which are less interesting than the *Arabian Nights* and of just about the same historical value.

Dare I say that the value of the Acts of saints is in inverse ratio to the fame of their cultus? As a general statement this would not be exactly true, but it is unquestionable that, legend being busiest with the most popular saints, it has been more difficult to keep historical tradition inviolate in much-frequented sanctuaries than anywhere else. This is certainly what is found at great pilgrimage-centres; except in certain very special cases, all the particulars that we have about their origins and the patron saint venerated there are fabulous.

We are therefore quite justified in being wary of a legend, while maintaining full trust in the saint.

I do not go so far to say that the existence of a given saint must be accepted whatever his legend may be. I have referred to several hagiographical narratives which are concerned with imaginary people and yet have all the appearance of authentic documents. Consequently other evidence is required to establish that the object of the cultus really lived. When it happens that in the course of centuries all other traces of him have disappeared, we may reasonably be doubtful about it.

A second very common mistake is to put too much trust in the biographers of saints. People seem to carry over to these good men something of the respect due to the saints themselves; the phrase "We read in the lives of the saints . . .", so often repeated and without the speaker troubling to specify the biographer referred to, clearly shows that the very highest qualities as a historian are implicitly attributed to all biographers.

If one inquires why so much faith is put in the writer of a saint's life, one may be told that because of his piety or his public reputation or the high office he held he was one of the most remarkable men of his time. The speaker forgets to add whether there are grounds for thinking him to have been well informed and able to make good use of the sources at his disposal. That is how known writers are judged. Those who are anonymous—and the great majority of legends have no name to back them—benefit from the reputation for knowledge and integrity that has been conferred on hagiographers as a body, a reputation very little deserved, as we have seen.

Need we dwell on the mischief done to the saints themselves by quoting, as their authentic utterances, the words which some obscure scribbler has put into their mouths after laboriously digging them out of his own inferior mind?

It will be said that these remarks are intended for readers with no particular pretensions and no critical sense whatever. Not at all. The same grave error is found at the scientific level, but there it goes by another name: the confusion of authenticity with veracity. First it is proved that certain Acts are authentic, for instance, that St Eucherius was really the author of the Passion of the Martyrs of Agaunum; then this Passion is used as if it were a document of the highest order, and it is thus made to encumber the history of the later persecutions. And so it goes on.

It is not going beyond our subject to call attention to the illusion of those who evince a sort of blind admiration for the collection, no doubt a respectable one, known as the *Acta Sanctorum;* some people have acquired the regrettable habit of quoting it as though it were the Gospel. When a writer wants to speak well of some strange miracle or dubious revelation, how often do we not read the naïve observation: "This fact is admitted by the Bollandists".

An uninformed reader assumes from this that, after a detailed examination of the matter, these "pitiless critics" (that is the stereotyped phrase) have laid down their arms, being unable in face of the evidence to deny the accuracy of the account or to contest the supernatural character of the happening.

It is obvious that it would be doing too much honour to any group of scholars, who are simply using methods known to and within the capacity of everyone, to regard them as a final authority in matters that are of infinite delicacy and little amenable to exact treatment. Neither Bollandus nor Papebroch nor any of their successors have had any such ambitious aims. Generally speaking, they have refrained from trying to solve insoluble problems, regarding it as a sufficient task to classify hagiographical texts, to publish them with scrupulous care, to make known as accurately as possible their origin, sources and characteristics, and when possible to estimate the abilities, integrity and literary probity of their authors.

When then some worthy writer feels the need to gratify his public by informing it that he has not failed to look through the "vast collection" (another stereotyped phrase) of the *Acta Sanctorum*, it is desirable that at least he should not make the editors responsible for all that it contains. Let him be content with some formula that does not compromise anyone, such as : "The account of this incident has been published by the Bollandists". But to infer from this that the Bollandists declare it to be true is to draw an unwarranted conclusion. "If the Bollandists," wrote one of them, "were positively to believe all the miracles and revelations that they publish they would be the most sturdily credulous men in existence."[1]

The third error is to set up the tradition of the church where a saint is specially honoured in opposition to the considered conclusions of scientific research.

Among those who proceed in this way are some who, without noticing it, confuse apostolic tradition, the rule of faith for every

Christian, with popular tradition in their particular church. Such people should be sent back to their theology, there to learn not to use the word "tradition" without qualification except in dogmatic matters.

But there are many who, without going to that extreme, think themselves justified in contesting the conclusions of criticism in the name of respect for local traditions. Unfortunately, what is usually dignified with the name of local tradition is in fact the current version of the patron saint's legend, and the degree of respect claimed for it is that it shall be accepted as an historical tradition without more ado. Such a claim clearly cannot be admitted if it be made without weighing the worth of the evidence, to do which one must go back to its origin. If a saint's history, as officially accepted, belongs to one of the first three categories of hagiographical texts set out in Chapter IV above, then it may be said that the local tradition, at any rate in its main lines, is an historical tradition; if not, it cannot be appealed to at all. Historical tradition is that which goes back to the event itself; popular tradition often does not appear till several centuries after it, and then displaces the most solidly established historical tradition, sometimes with scant ceremony.

History tells us that St Procopius of Caesarea was a cleric. Legend, accepted all over the East, later made him a military officer, and he was soon known by the name of *Procopius dux* and as nothing else.

Prudentius makes Pope St Sixtus II die by crucifixion, and the poet's lines when writing of St Lawrence are well known :

> Fore hoc sacerdos dixerat
> iam Xystus adfixus cruci.[2*]

Yet we know for certain, from a letter of St Cyprian who was a contemporary, and a well-informed contemporary, that Sixtus perished by the sword.[3]

From the fourth century contradictory accounts of St Agnes were in circulation; history would probably disprove all of them, if only history were not, unhappily, silent on the subject.[4]

The traditions of those churches in France which claim apostolic origin date from the time of the acceptance of the legends on which those claims are based. In almost every case this date can be easily ascertained, and to try to substantiate the legend by the tradition to which it gave rise is simply to argue in a vicious circle.

But then it may be objected : "Do you not know what used to be done in the churches during the fifth and sixth centuries? To satisfy the craving of the faithful to hear the acts of the martyrs read at religious gatherings, the old and revered accounts inherited from the preceding age were everywhere rewritten in a more popular and eloquent style. The new editors, writing under the eye of the bishops, would surely have been careful not to add any important particulars not already known to the people".[5]

None of this agrees with the facts.

It takes for granted that the Passions of a later time were derived directly from "the old and revered accounts inherited from the preceding age". This has to be proved in each individual case, and we know how rarely it is possible to do so.

Then again it is assumed that the Acts of the martyrs were generally read at public worship. But it is known that in the great majority of churches this was not the case; consequently we cannot count either on the watchfulness of the bishops or on the sensitive ears of the faithful to have safeguarded historical tradition where the martyrs were concerned. So episcopal control over local hagiography and the people's attachment to a received version of a saint's history are facts to be proved, not an hypothesis to be assented to.

Whenever circumstances enable us to follow the various stages of the birth of a legend, we are able to see perfectly clearly that there was no such twofold conservative influence. Our detailed study of the case of St Procopius is amply conclusive on this point. Should we say that the clergy and people of the diocese of Lyons kept jealous watch over the memory of the Curé of Ars if they gave the slightest credit to a biographer who represented him, not in his presbytery, but at the head of an army?

The old hagiographical legends were undoubtedly a part of

popular literature. They had no official status, and what is known of their origin and development affords no guarantee of their historical value. The faithful found them edifying, and that was all that mattered to them. In our own day how many people are satisfied with those lamentable publications known as the *Petits Bollandistes* or the *Grande Vie des saints,* in which historical truth is given only a small place but whose tales can be used to foster piety!

A fourth error is to declare a hagiographical narrative to be historical simply because it contains no improbabilities.

Let me say at once that the medieval hagiographers, intent above all on impressing their readers with what was miraculous or out of the ordinary, stuffed their passionaries with fabulous matter to such an extent that the mere absence of such extravagances encourages a presumption in the writer's favour. If no one went further than that there would be no occasion for disagreement.

Once again, it is necessary to examine in what form a given document has come down to us. Many Passions of martyrs have been transmitted in texts of varying lengths, some amplified, others considerably shortened or even cut down to the length of a breviary lesson. Now abridged texts often made a better impression than the original, developments which show the handiwork of the editor having largely disappeared. Compare for instance the short Passion of St Theodotus with the longer text that is extant : [6] on the evidence of the abbreviated version by itself one might judge the hagiographer and his work quite differently. The same test can easily be applied to many other abridgements whose original still exists.

Confusion between what is true and what is likely can often be detected in the application of those methods of higher criticism whose users profess to uncover the historical element which lies concealed below the legendary accretions. On the supposition that all improbabilities in a narrative are interpolations, this extraneous element has only to be removed and we shall then have the document in its primitive state.

This may sound a simple-minded proceeding, yet it has been used by men who were far from simple-minded. I will instance only one interesting example : such a scholar as Lami made a judicious selection of passages from the fabulous legend of St Minias and produced a reasonable account of the martyr—but it was no more true than the legend was.[7]

It is not every day that historians so openly go to work in this way, but they often use the method without realizing it. This is what they are doing when, for example, they rely on this or that suspicious document on the specious plea that it includes "good parts". Le Blant did this on a large scale when he was looking for "supplements to Ruinart". If these "good parts" are not vestiges of the historical source which the editor used, then they are useless for rehabilitating the document, as any one can see.

A fifth error is to classify a document as historical simply because its topographical element is accurate.

This mistake has been made hundreds of times, and it must be acknowledged that very often a beguiling argument is educed from topographical exactness. But how often it happens that this is the only aspect of a document that can be verified; and when it is found to be sound in this respect, what is more natural than to conclude that the whole thing is reliable?

If excessive importance be attached to topographical criteria, how far astray one can be led! We could mention many works of fiction the movements of whose heroes about Paris can be easily followed. When, therefore, it has been forgotten that Bourget wrote novels, these stories will have to be taken for real history; and the question whether *David Copperfield* is largely autobiographical will be decided by the fact that the hero's travels can be followed on the map. In good criticism, all that it is allowable to deduce from a topographically accurate narrative is that the author was acquainted with the places in which his story is set;

this means ordinarily that he wrote at Rome, Alexandria or Constantinople, according to the particular knowledge that he shows, and that he had seen the tomb or the basilica which he describes.

After that, it is not difficult to estimate the value of archaeological discoveries which seemed to give support to the *acta* of certain martyrs which had long been suspect. It was satisfactorily proved that these acts were written in the neighbourhood of the sanctuaries whose origins they were supposed to relate (not a very surprising discovery). But this adds nothing to the authority of the narrative; and after, as before, the "confirmation" provided by archaeological research, it can be said that the whole legend sprang from a poet's imagination.

Some time ago there was quite a stir about a discovery which was said to have rehabilitated the Acts of SS. John and Paul. This is what Edmond Le Blant had to say about it : [8]

Little reliance was put on a text deriving in part, it was thought, from the original *acta* but corrupted by the intrusion of a number of untenable particulars. But there was a continuing tradition that the two martyrs had been put to death in their own house; the precise spot where they had been beheaded was pointed out, and in the sixteenth century a marble tablet was let into the floor near the middle of the church, bearing the words *Locus martyrii SS. Ioannis et Pauli in aedibus propriis.* One of the Passionists serving this church, Father Germano, whose intelligent interest cannot be too highly commended, was anxious to find out whether the arrangement of the place bore out this belief. So he excavated and explored beneath the church; and he soon found, under the high altar, two rooms of a house. The materials of which they are built and their internal decoration belong to the beginning of the fourth century, if not to the end of the third. So the church was indeed built on the site of an ancient house, as the *Passio* says.

There is no point in continuing the quotation, for this last sentence tells us the sole result of these excavations. They did nothing to answer the question of whether the John and Paul text derives from original *acta,* though corrupted by "a number of

untenable particulars". Since then it has been proved that the
Passion of SS. John and Paul does not depend on an historical
source, but is simply an adaptation of the story of SS. Juventinus
and Maximinus;[9] and, in spite of the interest of "the martyrs'
house", none of the difficulties of the legend have been cleared
up.[10*]

We have now drawn the reader's attention to several defects of
method, putting him on his guard above all against excessive trust
in hagiographical legends. We have been solely concerned with the
historical point of view, and it has to be recognized that only too
often the history of the saints is obscured by legend. But it would
be one more mistake to think that the legend of the saints—I mean
legend in general—does not deserve any attention at all. A comparison will illustrate what I mean.

Suppose an artist and an archaeologist are looking at a religious
picture, some great work of an Italian or Flemish master.

The artist will wholeheartedly admire the beauty of the general
idea, the skill of the composition, its expressive power, the depth
of religious feeling.

If the archaeologist is a man with no appreciation of painting,
he will give voice to a number of criticisms, perhaps justified in
themselves but of a kind to exasperate the artist. The landscape is
sheer fancy, everybody knows it is not like that; that sort of architecture is unknown amongst those people; those clothes are wrong
for that time and place. The archaeologist is shocked to see St
Lawrence wearing a dalmatic, and in court at that; and perhaps
he ridicules the charming scene of St Peter preaching from a pulpit in a Roman piazza, with St Mark sitting at his feet, taking
down the sermon in shorthand and dipping his pen into an ink-
well held by a kneeling disciple.

That is how our archaeologist might approach Fra Angelico
or Van Eyck or Perugino. No doubt he would examine with
interest the garments worn by the holy women at the tomb, the
weapons of the soldiers taking Christ to Calvary, and the build-

ings lining the route, because in them he would recognize a contemporary record of the painter's time; and perhaps he would be irritated with the admiring artist, not interested in these antiquarian fads but absorbed in the real significance of the work, "what it says and how it says it".

Which man shows the better appreciation of the legend in picture form, he who seeks to read the mind and spirit of the painter or he who reacts in just the same way both to a great work of art and to the antique debris in a museum display-case?

I would not venture to make a strict parallel between these contrasting attitudes and those concerning medieval writings about the saints, on the one hand of simple readers who are sincerely impressed thereby, on the other of those people who condemn all legend out of hand. It must be recognized that the devout writers of saints' lives have not in general produced such happy results as the painters; they have few masterpieces to their credit, or even works which, taken alone and in themselves, attract and hold the attention.

And yet it cannot be denied that, in spite of ignorance of technique and unskilfulness of execution, medieval legend as a whole (not each legend in particular) has something of that mysterious and sublime poetry which pervades our old cathedral buildings, it expresses the Christian feelings for an ideal of holiness with unexampled force.

It must be remembered that there is often considerable discrepancy between what our worthy hagiographers wanted to say and what in fact they said. Their amplifications are often chilly, the bearing of their characters stiff and stilted, the situations unbelievable. But the governing thought is lofty and fine : these writers keep their eyes fixed on that exalted beauty of which pagan antiquity knew nothing, the beauty of a soul decked in God's grace; and their very inability to show it forth in all its glory makes us appreciate it the more.

The *Golden Legend* is a perfect example of the hagiographical work of the middle ages; yet for a long time it was treated with high disdain, and scholars were very hard on the good James of

Voragine. "The man who wrote the Legend", declared Luis Vivès, "had an iron mouth and a heart of lead".

Certainly it is difficult to speak of this book severely enough if it be held that popular works must be judged by the standards of historical criticism. But people are beginning to see that this is an injudicious proceeding, and those who have discerned the spirit of the *Golden Legend* are careful not to speak of it disparagingly.[11] I confess that, when reading it, it is often difficult to refrain from smiling. But it is a sympathetic and friendly smile, which does not at all disturb the religious response aroused by the picture of the goodness and heroic deeds of the saints.

In this picture God's friends are shown us as greatest amongst the things of earth, as beings raised above the material creation and all the wretchedness of the human state. Kings and princes honour and consult them, jostling with the people to kiss their relics and beg their protection. Even in this world they live on familiar terms with God, and he bestows on them, with his blessings, something also of his power; but they use it only for the benefit of their fellow men, and to them men turn to be freed from the ills of soul and body. The saints show forth every virtue in superhuman fashion—gentleness, mercy, forgiveness of wrongs, self-discipline, renunciation of one's own will : they make virtue attractive and ever invite Christians to seek it. Their life is indeed the concrete manifestation of the spirit of the Gospel; and, in that it makes this sublime ideal a reality for us, legend, like all poetry, can claim a higher degree of truth than history.[12*]

NOTES ON CHAPTER VII

[1]C. de Smedt, *Des devoirs des écrivains catholiques* (Brussels, 1886), p. 16.

[2]*Peristeph.*, ii, 21-22. ["The bishop Sixtus, when fastened to the cross, foretold this was to be."]

[3]*Epist.* lxxx, Hartel, vol. iii, p. 840.

[4]P. Franchi de' Cavalieri, *S. Agnese nella tradizione e nella leggenda*, p. 26.

[5][P. Guéranger], *Les Actes des martyrs depuis l'origine de l'Église. ...,* vol. i (Paris, 1856), p. xxxiv.

[6]Both have been published by P. Franchi de' Cavalieri, "I martirii di S. Teodoto e di S. Ariadne", in *Studi e testi*, vol. vi, pp. 61-84, 85-87.

[7]*Sanctae ecclesiae Florentinae monumenta*, vol. i (Florence, 1758). This is what he says on p. 589: "Eius actis insinceris et apocryphis fides adhiberi ab homine cordato non potest; tentare nunc iuvat an ea defaecare, et fabellis, quibus scatent, purgare et ad verosimilem historiam redigere, mihi res ecclesiae Florentinae inlustrare adgresso fortunate liceat."

[8]*Les persécuteurs et les martyrs*, p. iii. See also P. Allard, *La maison des martyrs* (Paris, 1895); taken from *Le Correspondant*.

[9]P. Franchi de' Cavalieri, "Nuove note agiografiche", in *Studi e testi*, vol. ix, pp. 55-65. Cf. *Anal. Boll.*, vol. xxii, p. 488.

[10]We have suggested that in the patron saints of the *titulus Pammachii* we should recognize the apostles John and Paul, transformed by legend into officers at the court of the emperor Julian. This solution has not pleased everyone. We simply prefer it to other hypotheses. See P. Franchi de' Cavalieri, *Note agiografiche*, fasc. 5 (Rome, 1915), pp. 44-62, who proposes two eastern namesakes. Mgr Lanzoni returned to the question in *Rivista di archeologia cristiana*, vol. ii, pp. 209-210: his answer to the riddle hardly differs from ours. But instead of the two apostles John and Paul, he suggests John the Baptist and Paul; we need not discuss his reasons here: cf. *Anal. Boll.*, vol. xliv, p. 250.

[11]*Anal. Boll.*, vol. xxiii, p. 325.

[12]In a letter to Count John Potocki, Joseph de Maistre quoted and commented on an example of what he called "Christian mythology". I cannot do better than quote this fine passage to clarify what I have just been trying to say: "Listen; I will give you one of these examples. It is taken from some ascetical work whose name I have forgotten. A saint, whose name I have also forgotten, had a vision in which he saw Satan standing before God's throne. Listening, he heard the Evil One say, 'Why have you damned me? I have offended against you only once, while you have saved thousands of people who have offended against you many times.' And God answered, 'Have you asked my forgiveness once?' That is Christian mythology! It is an effective expression of truth which keeps its value and power independently of literal truth, which would add nothing to it,

What does it matter whether the saint did or did not hear God speak those sublime words? The great point is to know that *forgiveness is refused only to the man or woman who has not asked for it.*" (*Lettres et opuscules inédits,* vol. i, Paris, 1851, pp. 235-236.)

HIPPOLYTE DELEHAYE

A MEMOIR

FATHER HIPPOLYTE DELEHAYE

A MEMOIR

by

Paul Peeters, s.j.

Father Hippolyte Delehaye, president of the Society of Bollandists, died at Brussels on 1 April 1941. Owing to the circumstances of that time the news of his death spread but slowly, even inside Belgium. The grief that it caused in many circles was necessarily somewhat muted in the face of so many other great bereavements. Abroad, several learned bodies of which Father Delehaye was a member, notably the Académie des Inscriptions et Belles-Lettres[1] and the Pontifical Roman Academy of Archaeology,[2] officially rendered public homage to his memory;[3] here and there individual friends and admirers evoked the character and achievement of the old master in terms of the deepest reverence.[4] But these isolated voices, however warm their praise, were far from expressing in its fullness the unanimous appreciation and respect which were accorded to his high reputation. Our purpose here is not to finish what these eulogies left incomplete; we who were so closely associated with his work are not qualified freely and frankly to do justice to his greatness. We are able here only freely to speak of our own memories.[5]

Hippolyte Delehaye was born at Antwerp on 19 August 1859. His family, originally of Chièvres in Hainaut, had been settled at Antwerp for several generations. Among its forbears it counted Michael Baïus, the too-famous forerunner of Jansenism; the evidence for this is the epitaph of Éloy Delehaye (or de le Haye), who died on 29 November 1650, and his wife Tazele Reghem,

187

whose gravestone is still to be seen in the outside wall of the parish church at Chièvres, against the lateral porch.[6] There was no need to be nervous of uttering the name of Baïus with scant admiration in front of Father Delehaye. He did not boast of this ancestor and had no inclination towards his teaching; but one felt from his way of speaking about Baïus that, the question of orthodoxy apart, he did not find this very learned man's character wholly displeasing.

He found more matter for pride in being by birth a fellow towns-man of Papebroch. His home was not far from the one-time Jesuit house at Antwerp which was the birthplace of the Bollandists' work and the scene of their activity for nearly a century and a half. The fame of the old Belgian hagiographers was still alive in the neighbourhood of the former Musée Bollandien, and more than once did their future successor listen as their story was told. Later on, when he himself talked about their domestic history, one could have believed that by some trick of memory he was speaking from recollections of his own childhood.

Father Delehaye's youth resembled in every respect that of most of his predecessors. Brought up in a modest hardworking family, where the traditional principles of Christian education held undis-puted sway, he did the full course of the humanities at the Collège Notre-Dame in his native city. In every class there he achieved a success that bore witness to his diligence no less than to his pre-cocious talents; and immediately his studies were finished, crowned as he was with scholastic honours, he entered the novice-ship of the Society of Jesus at Arlon, on 28 September 1876. The first stages of his regular training were achieved without any un-usual happening.

During his course of philosophy, at Louvain from 1879 to 1882, he showed, among his other abilities, an uncommon aptitude for the exact sciences, and in consequence he was appointed pro-fessor of mathematics in the Collège Sainte-Barbe at Ghent. He was indeed remarkably well fitted for this post, to which was added the teaching of Flemish and of the natural sciences. Had he been able to consult his tastes they would have led him in a quite different direction; but he made the sacrifice cheerfully and, with the seriousness that he brought to everything, he gave himself unreservedly for four years to duties that he found rather distasteful. According to the recollections of contemporaries it was not in his mathematics class that he learned to control men; but his sense of duty and unbending strength of will enabled him to profit by an experience which might have been discouraging. Feeling that he had a vocation to write, he chose a subject from his teaching material, and in 1885 published a little study of the Plants of the Bible in *Précis historiques* [135]. This youthful effort at least showed an enterprising spirit and an aptitude for work that could be put to better use. Very fortunately he came into contact with a man of good judgement and experience, Father Constantin Van Aken, formerly a professor of theology, who discerned his still unappreciated talent and helped to put him on the right road. Till the end of his life Father Delehaye was fond of recalling what he owed to the kind direction and influence of this wise counsellor. Thus it came about that, in the leisure time left by his duties, he was able by his own efforts to begin an apprenticeship to those historical researches in which he was destined to make his name.

For a beginning he published in the *Messager des sciences historiques de Belgique* in 1886-87 a study of Henry of Ghent that was in part original [137]. The occasion of it was an article of the previous year by Father Franz Ehrle, in the first volume of *Archiv für Literatur und Kirchengeschichte,* which Father Ehrle had just founded with Father Henri Denifle, o.p. In this article the future prefect of the Vatican Library and cardinal librarian of the Holy Roman Church had ground to powder the current fables about the career and historical personality of the *Doctor sollemnis.* It was to Father Delehaye's credit that he appreciated to the full the superiority of the method used by Father Ehrle; and, with the help of material he had found at hand in the archives of Ghent and of Tournai, he was able to add some new particulars to the life-story of the famous doctor of the Sorbonne and archdeacon of Tournai. "Nouvelles recherches sur Henri de Gand" caused something of a flutter among those interested, and several attempts were made to refute the young author, who replied to them in the *Messager des sciences historiques* in 1888 [138]. Altogether, he had the honours in this first skirmish. Father Ehrle followed it with interest, and no doubt from this time he kept Father Delehaye in mind as a future recruit, to be held in reserve for the brilliant *élite* that he was collecting around the Vatican Library.

But already in Belgium another leading scholar was taking a hand. Father Charles De Smedt, whom Father Van Aken had interested in his pupil, agreed to examine the new essays that Father Delehaye's enthusiasm had at once got to work on. Father De Smedt soon perceived a talent unusually well fitted to engage in historical research. Not content with encouraging the beginner, he helped him to clear his writing of certain traces of haste, inexperience and impetuosity. More still, he introduced him into the world of learning. Thanks to Father De Smedt's recommendation, several articles by Father Delehaye on Guibert of Gembloux and the legate Peter of Pavia were readily accepted by the *Revue des questions historiques,* which published them one after another from 1889 to 1892 [140-142].

Even before this success, achieved, one may say, against wind and tide, there could be no mistake about the direction that should be given to the young mathematical professor's abilities. The time was approaching for him to begin his theological studies. Its date was advanced and, to enable him to pursue his preferred historical work at the same time, he was sent to Innsbruck University, to which the teaching of Pastor and of Father Hartmann Grisar then lent particular distinction. He stayed there for the academic year 1886-87; but the arrangement of the courses did not work out as had been hoped, and moreover the Tirolese climate proved bad for Father Delehaye's health. So he was recalled home and, by way of a change, he spent a year teaching mathematics, though this time in the higher scientific course of the Collège Saint-Michel at Brussels.

This year was decisive for the young scholar, on the way to being a master. He was introduced to the Bollandist library, where he was soon quite at home. In addition to several notes or essays on the edge of hagiographical subjects, he wrote a Latin dissertation on Guibert of Gembloux, which was published in vol. vii of *Analecta Bollandiana* [7]; and when in the autumn of 1888 he went to Louvain to finish the courses he had begun at Innsbruck, Father De Smedt and his Bollandist colleagues were authorized to consider him as one of their men. He was ordained priest on 24 August 1890. Preparation for his final examination in theology was hurried on, and on 4 January 1891 he returned to the *Museum Bollandianum*. On the following February 20 Father Delehaye's nomination as hagiographer was confirmed. A wide prospect for his career was now open to him, and henceforth it was interrupted for only a short time when, in 1892-93, he went to Tronchiennes for his third year of noviceship, which was reduced to a few months.

The work of the Bollandist Society which was thus reinforced by Father Delehaye's exceptional gifts was then enjoying a period of growth and prosperity, one of the most tranquil in all its long history. After the trials and hesitations inseparable from a new departure, Father De Smedt's reform had been crowned with complete success,[7] if one may call success the modest satisfaction of being unreservedly approved by those judges whose opinion is worth listening to. The members were faced with a huge programme of work, which clearly bore the guarantee of its own utility and since then has been approved by time. For the carrying out of this work Father De Smedt, who had reached the highest point of his reputation and was still untouched by the handicaps of old age, had under his resolute but gentle authority a group of highly gifted collaborators, who complemented one another excellently by their diversity of character and abilities. Let me here give a last recollection of these fine workers, thanks to whom the Bollandist Society had then recovered the strength and energy of its youth.

Father Joseph De Backer can hardly be counted as a very active

force among them : he was one of the rescue-party which came
with Father De Smedt in 1876 to save the work, which was in
danger of complete collapse. His collaboration in scientific work
was now much reduced; but his experience, his practical judgement, his outspokenness and impartial disinterestedness continued
to make a contribution whose value was yet more apparent when it
was no longer there. Father De Backer's mind and character had
the straightforwardness and simplicity of another age; he was a
living expression of the *mos maiorum* to which the whole of his life
was a tribute. To this good old man the ways and customs of the
house were so many quasi-sacred rites, which he observed auto-
matically through long habit till they became a sort of amiable
mania, at which he was the first to smile and which everyone respected.

Father Joseph Van den Gheyn, on the other hand, concealed
beneath an air of rather imposing solemnity a passion for work
which seemed quite tireless. He was a brilliant man, but inclined
to give too much play to his impetuous, wide-ranging disposition.
He was first attracted by ethnography, comparative linguistics,
mythology and folklore, and his experience in these enterprising
studies had not prepared him to be always sufficiently on his guard
amongst specious hypotheses and delicate balances between the
possible and the probable. Moderated by the stricter critical temper of Father Delehaye, his quickness of mind and dexterous
execution could have done wonders; but in fact the corrective did
not work that way. Feeling that his elbow-room was being constric-
ted, Father Van den Gheyn had no difficulty in finding an out-
let for his activity. In 1896 he was appointed keeper of the manuscripts in the Bibliothèque royale at Brussels and gradually lost
interest in his work as a Bollandist, eventually giving it up altogether.[8]

Unlike Father Van den Gheyn, Father Albert Poncelet was a
model of concentration as a worker. But he too formed a contrast
with Father Delehaye's intellectual temper, a contrast as complete
as could be between two first-class scholars who were in full agreement on the principles of their method. He was more solid than

original, clear-headed, a little dogmatic, with a sort of impassioned ardour; he reached his ends less by flashes of intuitive discernment than by the light of the dark-lantern that he shone with enthusiastic pertinacity into every remote corner of a subject. Scholarship delighted him above all by the solidity of its positive results. He believed in the most complicated techniques, and was not far from thinking that they were weakened if their daunting complexity was simplified.[9]

A rich variety of quite other qualities met and made a unity in the person of Father François Van Ortroy. Of robust temperament, strong-minded, forthright and shrewd, sure of himself, businesslike and immovably self-possessed, he was a man of much resource, producing schemes of all kinds to keep work moving, however heavy the daily burden might be. He had to take his time, in order to go into what he called the *alentours,* surroundings, of a question. But when he had taken his walk round, ears pricked and nose in the air, he would pronounce his judgement with a vigour that no power on earth could shake. His lively mind poured out an endless stream of bewildering discoveries. His was one of those happy natures endowed with the gift of smoothing puckered brows and brightening the most overcast day. His boisterous sallies were sometimes disconcerting, but more usually his solid basis of zeal and kindly obligingness was clearly apparent. The confidence that Father Van Ortroy inspired was well served by a limitless practical good sense and by a sort of beneficent guile, which in the long run rather too often kept him from getting on with his main business.[10]

Such was the very good team to which Father Delehaye found himself assigned. If the mordant of his intellectual excellence had made itself welcome to his fellows, it could have acted as the rare metal which ensures maximum hardness or elasticity to an alloy. But when chosen spirits are engaged in a common undertaking, elective affinities get the upper hand only if there be a mutual condescendence proportionate to the quality of the talents involved. It was found difficult to maintain this proportion, and events did not help the situation. In 1899 Father De Smedt became rector of the Collège Saint-Michel; he had temporarily to give up effective direction of the Bollandist work, and this deprivation did not fail to make itself felt. During his rectorship he had to make up his mind, and—incorrigible optimist that he was—he determined boldly, but fortunately, to move the college to its present site. The migration took place in October 1905, and it was the occasion of Father Van den Gheyn's secession. Father De Backer had not waited for the final event. When it became certain that the uprooting would take place, he had recoiled from the risk of an impossible transplantation and had retired in September 1902, to the unanimous regret of his colleagues. Thus ended the period that had seen the successful renewal of the Bollandists' work.

When Father Delehaye entered on his career in 1891 there was nothing to suggest that this dislocation would come about; and it must be regarded as providential that he should have begun at one of those privileged eras when budding talents are pretty well assured of a future. Those who came to maturity in that generation did not all display outstanding abilities; but the force which urged them on had the inestimable advantage of being supported and guided by a current which swept them away from pretentious fashionable crazes, without drowning them in scepticism or disillusioned resignation. At that time a fine, earnest enthusiasm for the work was widespread. After Pope Leo XIII freely opened the Vatican library and archives to scholars, there was as it were a renewed rising of sap in ecclesiastical historical studies. Young students had found masters who were worthy of their mission, and under their direction these students were gallantly preparing themselves, not to astonish the world, but to take a useful place in their science. Great enterprises were undertaken and prospered, under the gentle breeze of a new spirit which had the bracing effect of light airs in springtime. The little group of Bollandists, inwardly rejuvenated and tightened up, shared abundantly in the general enthusiasm. They were full of activity, rather overworked (as always) but cheerful and confident, and the old-fashioned picturesqueness of their library added the domestic charm of things past to their labours. To all those who experienced the charm of that archaic workshop it left, not an elegaic regret, but a useful lesson that they were not able to forget.[11]

When Father Delehaye arrived, it was decided that he should be responsible principally for the Byzantine Greek part of the work. But before taking this up fully he had first to deal with the Acts of St Wolfgang for the *Acta Sanctorum,* volume ii of November [1] (this saint had been carried over from volume xiii of October). His early work on Guibert of Gembloux and Peter of Pavia had familiarized him with the historical sources for the medieval period and the best studies bearing on it. Accordingly, at this short notice, he wrote a commentary, of somewhat excessive length, which proves he would have had only to turn his mind to it to make his name amongst the recognized explorers of the Germanic middle ages.

From this preliminary undertaking he gained experience which he put to good use in the far less well-known field which he had now to explore. Up till then, Greek hagiography had remained at a great disadvantage when compared with Latin hagiography, which was studied by an older and more numerous body of scholars, who were incomparably better provided with tools for their work and were accustomed to a less accommodating discipline, one which admitted no immunities from criticism. Our predecessors had made praiseworthy efforts to catch up on this lost ground, which in a last analysis went back to the good old days when Latin alone reigned in the *Acta Sanctorum,* as in the Sorbonne and elsewhere. But the inferiority of the Byzantine Greek department was due to a variety of causes, hidden away under the cloak of custom too long established. The situation was seen clearly only when it had been brought to an end and old ways could be compared with a better thought-out practice.

The honour of bringing about this reform belongs to Father Delehaye. The method that he was to inaugurate was not a ready-made one. He was to work it out in the light of his own experience

and with the help of the advice and example of others, for whom
he was always the first to express respect. It was some years since
Karl Krumbacher had begun to employ his genius on putting
Byzantine erudition onto the same footing with classical philology,
applying the same principles to it. From his chair in the University of Munich, and perhaps still more in *Byzantinische Zeitschrift*
which he had founded in 1892, he wielded a vigilant and compel-
ling authority over the whole field of studies concerning the Greek
middle ages. A comparable work, though less striking and well-
known, was being done by Vassily Vassilievsky in Russia. Following Krumbacher, a number of young scholars were turning their
attention to Greek hagiography, among whom Albert Ehrhard,
Pio Franchi de' Cavalieri and several others were to earn a high
reputation. Father Delehaye took his place amongst this *élite* and
soon became a recognized leader of the renascence in Byzantine
studies.

In a very short time the Bollandist editions of Greek Lives and
Passions underwent a complete change in appearance and
arrangement. Hitherto they had been obliged to include a full
Latin translation of the original text. Father Delehaye thought it
desirable to get rid of this cumbrous feature, but he did not gain
his point without encountering opposition. The truth is that the
reasons he advanced gave a slight impression of being arguments
against an obligation that was disagreeable to him personally; in
the long run it certainly would have entailed tiresome complica-
tions. It is not easy to imagine Father Delehaye bending his
mettlesome talent to the task of putting into Latin, for example,
the hundred folio pages of the two Lives of St Lazarus the Galesiot
in volume iii of the *Acta Sanctorum* for November (pp. 508-588,
588-608). But in the event the rightness of his instinct was vindicated. To publish a document and add a translation of it implies
that it is intended for readers of whom many cannot read it in its
original language. The interpreter who makes it available to them
is taken to have accomplished a burdensome task of special difficulty, and this is often true. But the credit that is rightly given him
can make both him and his public forget that the essential business

of criticism does not begin until after this preliminary operation.
The editor who has translated a document whose language calls
for unusual knowledge finds himself, in relation to his own version,
in much the same position as a medievalist confronted by a Latin
text which he fathoms easily. This had sometimes been lost sight of.
The practice of translating, which is useful or even necessary in
particular cases, belongs in fact to the field of "popularization",
and by renouncing it Father Delehaye was put in the position of
having to aim higher and address his publications to their natural
judges. It goes without saying that he took every precaution
that he should have nothing to fear from their verdict.

Whilst still preparing the Acts of St Wolfgang, Father Delehaye
set about an undertaking which was among the things desired by
Father De Smedt. He was charged with the drawing up of a complete list of Greek hagiographical writings that had already been
published. The plan of this catalogue was decided on in December
1891, and in carrying it out Father Delehaye showed the definite-
ness of his standpoint and the judicious poise which characterized
all his work. He knew that "the best is the enemy of the good", and
for the present he confined his aims to what was immediately prac-
ticable. The material he had to bring together and classify was far
from being comparable in bulk to that of Latin hagiography, but
it was scattered to the four winds in rare and abstruse publications
and in great part not easily accessible. Had Father Delehaye been
decoyed by ambition to produce a definitive work straight away he
would have found himself held up for years by preparatory research, and this would have got in the way of more useful enterprises. Rather than make any rash attempt at a forced-march, he
preferred to confine himself at first to what was most urgent. A
first sketch, conscientious but summary, of the *Bibliotheca Hagiographica Graeca* was ready for press in the spring of 1894 and it
was printed off by the beginning of the following year [115].

Armed with this handy tool, Father Delehaye proceeded to a
methodical calendaring of still unpublished Greek hagiographical
writings. In collaboration with Henri Omont, he compiled in 1896
the catalogue of the incomparable Greek hagiographical material

in the Bibliothèque nationale in Paris [116], and in 1899, with Pio Franchi de' Cavalieri, that of the Vatican Library [117]. These two important collections, to which in 1913 was joined the *Catalogus codicum hagiographicorum graecorum Germaniae Belgii Angliae* by Fathers C. Van de Vorst and H. Delehaye [124], are items of the first importance in a long series of similar catalogues, in which are recorded the Greek hagiographical manuscripts of more than thirty libraries in Europe, Asia Minor and Egypt. The whole series, whose continuation was slowed down by the war of 1914, bears the same uniform character of practical utility. It has a small enough place in the interests of bibliophiles; but, apart from the inadvertences and omissions inevitable in an individual investigation, for which the time available was nearly always too limited, hagiographers find in it all the essential information required for their purposes.

Meanwhile the *Bibliotheca Hagiographica Graeca*, which had helped to speed up the business of inventory-making and to lighten its detail, grew from day to day. A second edition, nearly doubled in size, was published in 1909. This was followed by a *Synopsis Metaphrastica*, summarizing the latest state of Father Delehaye's mind about the famous logothete's menology, its probable composition and the historical personality of its author; this was the result of persevering research which at times had led to exchanges of views between Father Delehaye and his competitor Albert Ehrhard, exchanges whose tone speedily grew milder.

This passage of arms about Metaphrastes was only an episode in a very extensive enterprise, one of the most lasting of all those with which Father Delehaye's name will continue to be associated. In order to explore Greek hagiographical literature with all the necessary knowledge, it was essential to have a general framework in which each piece could be given its place or its point of contact with tradition as a whole. It was to answer this fundamental requirement that Father Victor De Buck had thought out the plan of the *Annus ecclesiasticus graeco-slavicus*, whose execution he entrusted to Father Ivan Martinov.[12] But whatever the merits of this first attempt, it had to be recognized that the Greek sources in it had suffered from their fusion with their very much more obscure Slav derivatives, in comparison with which the Byzantine menaia and other hybrid collections appeared like original documents already filtered and strained. Instead of some artificial synthesis, there would be every advantage in providing, in its natural form, a document which by its very purpose was as it were a compendious survey of Greek hagiography at the time of its fullest development. The Synaxary of Constantinople fulfilled all the desired conditions at every point. Nothing then could be more useful than to put this collection within the reach of scholars, in a good edition, established on a sufficiently extensive study of the manuscript tradition. It was a big undertaking, whose numerous difficulties provided food for thought. Father Delehaye gave it very careful consideration, and decided that he was not frightened by it.

At first it was intended that the synaxary should appear at the beginning of volume iii of November. But with its copious prolegomena, its critical apparatus, its numerous complementary extracts, its notes and 70 pages of alphabetical index, the length of the work exceeded all expectations. It was therefore decided to make a separate volume of it, and it appeared in 1902 under the title *Propylaeum ad Acta Sanctorum Novembris* [2].

There is no need to remind our friends and regular readers of the worth of this monumental work, which was welcomed by the Greeks themselves with a warmth that was compounded of admiration and astonishment. Among Western scholars, even those least given to hyperbolical praise, the note of surprise was struck in their expressions of wholehearted gratitude to the courageous editor for a first-class working tool which they had needed but had not dared to hope for. For over half a century the *Synaxarium Ecclesiae Constantinopolitanae* has justified all this high approval by the service it has rendered and continues to render in so many places. At the time of Father Delehaye's death, Hans Lietzmann wrote to the Bollandists, on 13 April 1941, recalling with a full heart that his master Hermann Usener had reserved for him the honour of reviewing this great work,[18] whose author he held in particular esteem.

Nevertheless a less favourable critic has persisted down to our own day in blaming this edition of the synaxary on the ground that it gives insufficient attention to the primitive form of the document and its subsequent evolution.[14] It is only fair to say that this criticism is misconceived. Father Delehaye deliberately left the genesis of the synaxary in the background because the interest of this question of literary history is not proportionate to the interminable and costly research it would have entailed, which would have been to the detriment of more important and more urgent aspects of the work. The synaxary is not one of those individual works whose importance is due to the authority of a person or of some testimony or line of thought. Its chief value is as the official expression of the cultus of saints as practised by the Byzantines when it was at its height. None of the document's known recensions provides a version of it that is free from gaps and omissions, to say nothing of the material errors with which they are riddled. Each of them requires to be completed and corrected one by the other; and the additions with which they enrich the tradition have their own value, which in every case depends solely on the source used by the reviser at that place, and not at all on its degree of conformity with the primitive version of the collection. Father Delehaye took as the basis of his edition the recension called the Synaxary of Sirmond, and this was not simply for the sentimental reason that it had long ago been examined with devoted care by previous Bollandists: it was chosen first and principally because this version reflects better than any other the liturgical usage of the imperial capital, clearly recognizable in the many local rubrics, whose importance had not escaped the notice of Du Cange.[15] For specialists engaged on critical reconstruction, the essential elements of what they find missing is supplied by the variants occurring in a good fifty parallel redactions, which Father Delehaye records by means of a perfectly clear notation. Surely no more need be said for those who wish to have a just estimate of the matter. After a first hesitation, Mgr Ehrhard, with a candour worthy of his character and authority, recognized the full value of Father Delehaye's work,[16] and his final judgement therefore agreed with that which had been Krumbacher's from the moment of publication.[17]

Harnack called it a Herculean achievement,[18] but it did not absorb all Father Delehaye's tireless activity. His collaborators were exhausted; but he still found time and energy for lesser productions. During those same years he wrote continually in *Analecta Bollandiana,* articles which one would have thought were written at leisure, not to mention those which other publications were eager to accept and were soon vying with one another to get hold of.

Father Delehaye's name first appeared on *Analecta Bollandiana* in 1892 (volume xi), and it remained there for half a century. Ten years' experience had shown that, without aiming at giving itself a popular topical interest, a periodical that wants to contribute to contemporary learning must avoid appearing more formidable than its subject matter absolutely requires. The rule of using only Latin, even in the critical dissertations, had been notably modified from 1891, and this innovation facilitated the introduction into each number of the *Analecta* of a bulletin of hagiographical publications, which prompted Abbé Duchesne to remark slyly that there were hard times ahead for incompetent hagiographers.[19] Less satirically, the fact is that during these years the review became, not more bellicose or trenchant, but perhaps more lively and unconstrained, as indeed was required if it was to venture into the day-to-day scrimmage of scholarship. It would be neither exact nor just to attribute all the honour of this to a certain new spirit brought to the review by Father Delehaye, for none of the editors who shared the work during those flourishing years needed to learn from the newcomer among their collaborators; but his hand could be picked out from all the others by the terse and incisive touches with which his pen sparkled.

In the course of fifty years Father Delehaye's contributions to *Analecta Bollandiana* numbered some 115 dissertations, editions of texts, critical researches, catalogues of manuscripts, notes and comments of varying importance. To these must be added numberless reviews of books, of which some appeared in nearly every issue. It is chiefly to him that our *Bulletin des publications hagio-graphiques* owes its distinctive character. Originally it was strictly confined to works and writings coming under a fairly wide interpretation of its title; Father Delehaye judged that the time was ripe for the inclusion of a number of publications of more general interest. The result was a heavy increase of editorial work, of which he usually did more than his fair share. Turning the some 200 pages that the bulletin eventually reached, one year with another, we keep on seeing those characteristic well-turned analyses at the end of which we know we shall read the initials H.D.

It goes without saying that these reviews, always markedly personal and original, did not all go equally deeply into the matters treated in the books; and that only Father Delehaye's vast reading and penetrating mind, as quick as it was sure, enabled him at a swift reading to judge such a variety of publications of such diverse value, and to find in them matter for exact and pertinent comment. But when he was dealing with an author who was adventuring into regions that he, Father Delehaye, knew from A to Z, or whom he had already "caught out", his pen broke well and truly with academic conventions. In his younger days he did not always succeed in curbing a caustic wit, which was not to be rashly provoked. He soon brought this polemical tartness under control; there was left only the quick-witted directness of a ready and resolute intelligence that shot straight at the weak spot, and at one blow disarmed a specious argument or reduced a fallacious system to its proper value. When a thesis or a paradox had irritated him he would jot down a few lines on paper while the impression was still fresh; and his convictions expressed thus had a clarity and exactitude of expression which demonstrated the working and the spontaneous reaction of his mind better than more considered writings. A shrewd judge was right when he said that Father Delehaye's intellectual temper can be seen most clearly and definitely in his critical reviews.[20]

In going through the long list of subjects treated by Father Delehaye in *Analecta Bollandiana* one is overcome by the diversity of this impressive collection of original studies; all the disciplines pertinent to hagiographical criticism are represented : church history, general history, philology, archaeology, epigraphy, paleography, semantics, liturgy, folklore. Even canon law has a place, in the long dissertation on letters of collective indulgence [88]. What is even more wonderful is the unity of inspiration and method which governs this variety of subjects; it gives the aggregate of these separate studies the appearance of a building in course of construction, whose unfinished parts reveal the thought that is in the architect's mind. But this huge many-sided work never overflows, so to say, the area proper to hagiography. Father Delehaye did not have to the same degree as a Victor De Buck the aptitude for improvisation and the daring necessary for keeping one's balance on ground where one is not wholly at home. The discomfort and awkwardness which an apprentice is bound to feel were in the highest degree distasteful to him; and early on he renounced the taking up of any new study which would have involved his going through an elementary stage. These instinctive repugnances of his were in accordance with his idea of scientific work. He was apt to be severe about polygraphs, those erudite jacks-of-all-trades who, stretching their elastic talents to the limit, spread their energy over so many and such disparate objects that they cannot keep a grip on them. He was the first himself to observe the rule he imposed on others. He would certainly have been able to attain more than one kind of excellence; but in order to be a hagiographer as he understood it he confined himself to being a hagiographer only, and whenever necessary restricted his scope, even at the risk of narrowing his outlook.

Several of the detailed studies with which Father Delehaye enriched the *Analecta* owe their interest partly to the exceptional value of unpublished material which he himself had found in manuscripts. One of his most valuable discoveries deserves more emphasis than those who have profited by it have seen fit to give it. Father Delehaye was the first to identify certain historical Passions in the old Greek menologies as belonging to the developed version of Eusebius of Caesarea's book on the martyrs of Palestine. The *editio princeps* that he published in 1897 [19] was soon included in an important series. This documentary contribution and his thorough discussion of the whole question led him to form very definite ideas about *De martyribus Palestinae* and the authority of Eusebius, to which he reconciled those who did not share his downright admiration for the Father of Church History. His fertile ingenuity was again at its best on the numerous occasions when he reopened some much-discussed question which seemed to be exhausted. Thus, when he first came into direct contact with the Christian antiquities of Rome, he was quite ready to write an account full of new and original opinions about *Les Saints du cimitière de Commodille* [15], on the basis of documents which had already been through the hands of many archaeologists : a bold and skilful stroke which obviously left a pleasant memory with him.

However, it was a well-marked characteristic of Father Delehaye that he rarely let himself be tempted by the historical puzzles that scholars pass on from generation to generation to be discussed over and over again. When he met one of them in the course of other work, he did not try to dodge it but brought up all his forces for a frontal attack. Nevertheless this kind of exercise had small attraction for him. He was ill at ease with these subjects that are hemmed in by known and anticipated difficulties; research on them can only proceed by a process of sapping, like a miner, probably to encounter at the end a last decisive question which it is impossible to answer by Yes or No. It was not the slowness nor the hardness of the effort required that repelled him : once he got going he pursued his investigations with a stubborn perseverance that increased with the difficulties. But if by chance he got it into his head that a question was insoluble, it ceased to have any interest for him and he left it, not without a touch of irony, to the unemployed or the wranglers who were willing to waste time over it.

His abilities found their opportunity in subjects that opened out a wide and not too crowded horizon, wherein critical intuition could be exercised side by side with solid and free-ranging learning. Then he showed a mastery of exposition which went straight to what was essential, jettisoning all useless lumber, rejecting abstruse and pedantic apparatus, and never hesitating to thrust aside secondary questions which threatened to get in his way. Confronted by some complex and involved matter, he excelled in finding an observation-point whence the lines were seen to untangle and converge simply through the foreshortening of the perspective. Certain of his dissertations, covering a wide area of still obscure questions, follow a pattern he himself evolved, which it might be rash for anyone else to try to imitate : such, for example, are the volume on *Légendes grecques des saints militaires* [122], and the articles on the saints of Cyprus [53], on the saints of Thrace and Moesia [65], on the martyrs of Egypt [79] and on the stylites or pillar-saints. This last essay appeared first in the *Revue des questions historiques* [145], and was reprinted and augmented in the *Compte rendu du Congrès scientifique des catholiques à Bruxelles* [145] and in Analecta Bollandiana [68, 69], and finally became a book [131]; some of the pages of this volume are perhaps made a little hazy by the Hellenic mirage, but it took and keeps an honoured place in the history of Christian asceticism.

All these publications, full of new things and things made yet newer by the writer's genius for synthesis and co-ordination, are distinguished by a sobriety that Father Delehaye deliberately imposed on himself. When confronted by imposing monographs that affect to be (and generally are not) the last word on every aspect of something, he evinced no admiring astonishment, still less any desire to emulate them. When he had cleared up a saint's dossier and put it in order, verified the evidence for his cultus and elucidated debateable points in his biography or his legend, Father Delehaye felt that his task was finished. He was not indifferent to additional information or lost memories that still remained to be found, but he firmly believed that this further patient work was no business of his. "We have to do the work of pioneers", he used to say, meaning thereby that the work most worthy of a critic is to clear up, if he can, those obscurities, and get rid of those false lights, which make hagiography a thing apart, one that requires a special method and that is full of surprises. The doing of such research so often proves only a snare and a delusion for those who are content to look at a few isolated documents through a magnifying glass. It needs the constant support of a solid, well-organized knowledge of all the abounding literature to which hagiographers go for their models, that is, when they do not find what they want all ready made, matter and form together. And so Father Delehaye came to the conclusion that an explorer in the advance-party, who is obliged to have a mastery of and continually to use this vast collection of material, ought to leave for others the satisfaction of completing at their leisure the researches for which he has prepared the way.

Father Delehaye's persistent meditations on the specific principles of hagiographical method led him to see that they could be expounded to other readers besides professional scholars. Experience enabled him to put his finger on the radical misunderstanding which is bound to make many discussions quite fruitless. Between the defenders of an allegedly ancient tradition and the historians who call it in question, the lively exchanges of controversy are almost the only arguments that reach their mark; everything else is lost in the void or swamped in a confusion of cross-purposes. To justify his doubt, or even to formulate it clearly, the critic needs first of all thoroughly to set out the value of the sources that he admits and uses, and the rules to be followed in their interpretation : these clarifications involve him step by step in what is in effect an introduction to hagiographical studies. So fundamental a statement cannot be improvised in relation to each particular case and by means only of the data relating to that case.

Father Delehaye believed it was possible to draw up a systematic account of the matter in a form assimilable by the average well-educated person : an account that would show in a living way, with topical illustrations taken from everyday experience, the complex of factors by which historical truth eventually becomes corrupted in the people's mind and imagination, especially when ethnical, national, religious or simply poetical feeling is deeply involved. This explains the halo that gradually forms round the memory of saints. The less worthy part of hagiographical literature, which derives from this warping of tradition, is similarly subject to regular influences and processes, which can be reduced to formulas. Once the factors have been properly sorted out and arranged in convergent series, each throwing light on the others, it is found that the critic's job of straightening these crooked shoots is vindicated, or at least clearly defined. Such was the aim of an essay called *Les légendes hagiographiques*, of which the first sketch was published in the *Revue des questions historiques* [161] in 1903. This pungent psychological analysis of the romantic imagination of hagiographers and their public attracted the attention and appreciation that it deserved; it was lengthened into a full study, which appeared two years later under the same title [118].

This little volume aroused more lively interest and curiosity than any other of Father Delehaye's works; but it attracted some rather unfavourable attention as well. Those Catholics who kept their heads realized that the author's judgements were no more severe than the censures and reproofs pronounced by ecclesiastical authority on examples of credulousness or trickery exactly like those he denounced; and it was obvious that in themselves these abuses in no way compromised veneration of the saints. But those were the days when the modernist crisis was in its first ferment, and the audacities, real or supposed, of criticism raised a gale of distrust. Moderate minds, which were ready to listen to reason about each of the impugned legends separately, were frightened to see so many brought together in systematic order, as though they were exhibits at a trial. Some people, who were little familiar with the author's manner of writing, mistook his shrewd liveliness for mockery—why, sometimes he even allowed himself to smile when dealing with this distressing subject. Controversialists, who seemed to be on the look-out for this opportunity, set themselves unscrupulously to aggravate the situation, and at one moment it looked as if they might have succeeded only too well. It did not happen, thank

God! After the first sharp shock and an occasional backwash, the fuss subsided completely; the upshot of it all was to contribute to the book's success. *Les légendes hagiographiques,* three times republished, was translated into Italian, English and German [119—121]; and the longer work written by H. Günter in this last language, under an equivalent title, did not succeed in dethroning it.[21]

On re-reading today the book that provoked so sharp a conflict it seems surprising that the determined fault-finders should have been able to judge it as stamped with an aggressive radicalism. Father Delehaye was inflexible where the rights of historical truth were concerned, and he detected the weak side of a tradition with sharp, cold insight; but he took no pleasure in finding it wanting, and he sometimes even experienced a sort of regret. But he did not feel called on to show much consideration towards hagiographers who knowingly took advantage of popular credulity; and still less towards officious apologists who tried stubbornly to whitewash proven forgers. On the other hand, for the artless faith and often charming fancy which give life to the fictions engendered in the collective mind he had a sympathetic and respectful interest; and the pedant who was so infatuated with his method that he did not understand these things appeared to Father Delehaye as blind as the Boeotian who, in the name of historical realism, would disdain Raphael's St Cecily or Michelangelo's Moses.

Whatever anyone may say, neither scepticism nor ironical unconcern was the natural bent of his mind. Those who, paying too much attention to certain rebukes he addressed to advocates of bad causes, have given him the reputation of a hunter down of saints (*dénicheur des saints*) ought also to remember the battles he fought and won in defence of tradition when he saw it being unjustly attacked. His article on *S. Martin et Sulpice Sévère* [72] is a vigorous speech for the defence in which he disputes every foot of the ground with E. C. Babut, who had impugned the truthfulness of Martin's biographer. Plenty of other cases could be adduced in which his critical spirit displayed its stout conservatism. Despite his friendship with distinguished leaders of the mythologcal school, he hastened to oppose them every time they made an untimely excursion into the field of hagiography. It was he who halted the triumphant progress of the much cried-up theory that the saints were the successors of the pagan gods.[22]

Nearly twenty years after the publication of *Les légendes hagiographiques,* Father Delehaye returned to part of the same subject in a new work, called *Les Passions des martyrs et les genres littéraires* [127]. This time his object was to establish that, in this very special class of document, the historical value of a given piece has a practically fixed relation to its literary form, and to show how, from the best to the worst, the quality of the content degenerates in proportion to the amount of rhetoric that is found in it. It is perhaps not altogether sure that this descending scale corresponds to a fixed scale of degrees set out in the sophistic. But what we wish to remark here is the considerable number of hagiographical documents which emerge nearly or quite unscathed from Father Delehaye's test. As for the rest, a thoughtful reader will derive from the thesis at least this reassuring conclusion, that what he is tempted to dismiss as bogus is very often simply a clumsy, bombastic attempt to express an ideal in hackneyed terms, or, if it be preferred, in a setting that is unsuitable but of the same order as the conventional fictions imposed on Christian art by inadequate means of expression.

The truly methodical spirit that animated all Father Delehaye's critical work appears yet more clearly when he is laying bare the historical foundations of the cultus of saints, most particularly in his book on the *Origines du culte des martyrs,* one of the best things that he gave us [123]. Except for the introduction and a few pages of general conclusions, aimed specially at certain fallacious systems, this volume is almost wholly made up of facts and quotations drawn from the most unexceptionable sources. In it Father Delehaye prefers to let epigraphical texts speak, for they often have the weight of autographic testimony, having been inscribed on the martyrs' tombs by those who buried them. For the uninitiated or for superficial readers who want only to skim, the charm of this work certainly has less appeal than that of the

Golden Legend. But nothing essential has been overlooked within
the scope of the author's inquiry, and the reader who takes the
trouble to follow it step by step realizes how much its value is increased by the rigorous elimination of all doubtful matter. Anyone
who is open-minded, but nervous of the temerities imputed to
scientific criticism, has only to read *Origines* to be convinced that,
in the hands of a real master, hagiographical method does an
eminently constructive work, from which tradition has nothing to
fear. Quite the contrary. Since Father Delehaye triumphantly
elucidated the fundamental conception and practice of the cultus
of martyrs in the primitive Church, such rash theories as those of
Ernst Lucius[23] have become harmless. May their ashes remain
undisturbed! The sallies that slipped from the pen of the man who
did such a service may well seem very venial.

Les Origines du culte des martyrs appeared at the end of 1912,
and its success was like the last ray of sunshine from a happy era
that now belonged to the past. Father De Smedt, worn out by
years and ill-health, had died on 5 March 1911, a few weeks after
the publication of the third volume for November of the *Acta
Sanctorum;* this had the honour of being dedicated to King Albert
I, recently come to the throne of Belgium. Thirteen months later,
the death of Father Poncelet took place at Montpellier, with stun-
ning suddenness, while he was on a journey making studies in
connexion with the *Acta Sanctorum Belgii,* whose publication he
had undertaken. Father Delehaye had become president of the
Bollandist Society on 15 April 1912, and to begin with he had as
soon as possible to fill the gap left by this unforeseen loss. It was a
difficult problem, and the events of 1914 made it impossible.

The war brought all publishing to a complete standstill, and the
inevitable succession of restrictions, difficulties and dangers were
not all trifling or soon over. Father Delehaye himself suffered considerably. He was arrested on 31 January 1918 and was kept in
close confinement until the armistice. During this time he contrived to write a sketch which, rewritten and worked over at leisure

later on, became his biography of *Saint John Berchmans* [128]. This detention for his faithfulness to patriotic duty earned him the sympathy of the whole world of letters, thus adding a new note of admiration and respect to his high prestige as a scholar.

Directly he was free again he turned to the task of reconstruction that had fallen to his lot. It was a long time since the Bollandists had been so near to utter ruin. The senior in age, Father Van Ortroy, had succumbed to wartime hardships on 20 September 1917. All work being stopped for an indefinite time, other urgent needs had prevailed, and Father Charles Van de Vorst, a Bollandist since 1911, had been put at the head of the house of studies at Louvain. Father Delehaye alone, with a single titular collaborator, was left to deal with a situation which seemed little short of desperate.

First he set about finishing volume xxxiii of *Analecta Bollandiana,* of which fascicle 3 had appeared on 22 July 1914. This restarting was difficult, but it showed that the regular publication of the review could be safely gone on with. Anyone but Father Delehaye would have thought that this undertaking was almost enough to occupy the forces at his disposal; he judged differently. He said, rightly enough, that the *Analecta* was only an accessory. Nothing would have been done so long as the *Acta Sanctorum* remained in suspense, and therefore in danger of being regarded as moribund. If one once postponed the decison that sooner or later would have to be made, there would not be wanting pretexts, and even good reasons, for prolonging the delay, till eventually the required effort would be impossible. But what was the good of the most courageous will without outside help to ensure the necessary material resources? This agonizing question was settled with the generous help of the administrative council of the Fondation Universitaire de Belgique, among whose members Father Delehaye's personal influence and authority inspired the fullest confidence. Thereupon volume iv of November was put in hand and printed, with the aid of a handful of helpers recruited at the last moment. It comprised two days of the calendar, November 9 and 10, and included several persons whose exotic dossiers together formed a disconcerting medley. This volume, of which the typographical work was regarded as a *tour de force* at the time, was finished in 1925, after four years of unceasing labour that were not without their hours of stress [4]. It at least proved that Bollandist effort had kept its old vitality, or was on the way to recovering it.

The last sheets of volume iv of November were not yet printed when Father Delehaye, true to his way of doing things, began to talk about beginning the editing of volume v immediately; once he had made up his mind to do something, he was not the man to delay its execution. So volume v had a good quick start. But meanwhile another and more attractive project was taking shape in his restless mind. The first idea of it had come to him long before when, newly arrived among the Bollandists, he had seen from day to day the progress of the diplomatic edition of the Hieronymian Martyrology which De Rossi and Duchesne published in the *Acta Sanctorum*, volume ii of November (1894). Such a lesson in criticism by two such masters, on a subject so full of puzzles, did not come under his notice for nothing. Reviewing this monumental work in the *Bulletin critique* for 15 July 1895 [146], he added to warm expressions of his admiration several acute observations on some problems that the two learned editors had resigned themselves to leaving open. He did not promise to find the key to these riddles, which had mystified the most able commentators for three hundred years, but it could be gathered from what he said that the quest attracted him and that he was not wholly without hope of success. He was as good as his word. The De Rossi-Duchesne edition gave rise to heated controversies, in which there was an element of professional rivalry. Scholars of considerable repute who ranked as leading authorities, and others who claimed to be equally important, had their say in these disputes. Father Delehaye was one of those who were qualified to help bring the debate to a useful conclusion; and when Hans Achelis's learned memorandum on the martyrologies appeared in 1900 it was to him that Krumbacher entrusted it for review in *Byzantinische Zeitschrift* [158].

From then on the Hieronymian Martyrology was one of the chief preoccupations of his mind. He kept on coming back to it, as the dividing-line in the various currents that have deluged all ancient hagiography in the West. A copy of the De Rossi-Duschesne edition always lay on his desk, and he constantly studied its pages; they were covered with conventional abbreviations and signs, scored all over with multicoloured lines, full of marks of transposition and concordance, till the book ended up by being a sort of diagrammatic record of the accidents which had thrown the famous martyrology into confusion. Father Delehaye knew his way about this maze. By trying first one and then another of all possible combinations and permutations amongst these strings of distorted proper names, he generally succeeded in finding a sufficiently plausible explanation, which was afterwards confirmed by other examples. Thus a principle of order gradually emerged from what had been an incomprehensible chaos.

This purely philological work had been backed up all the time by historical study of every aspect of the question. His researches into the Greek synaxaries and menologies had been an occasion for scrutinizing most of the eastern sources of the Hieronymian collection. He had familiarized himself with all the parallel documents. But the heart of the problem involved the essential matter to which the evidence of the texts owes its real significance. One cannot consider the value of a martyrology until one has formed a clear idea of the fact to which it is supposed to testify. By testing his deductions ever more closely, Father Delehaye reached the conclusion that, technically speaking and in the strict meaning of the terms, according to the usage of the earlier generations of Christians, a saint was a person whose burying-place was venerated and whose anniversary was observed by a solemn commemoration. These were what he liked to call the two "hagiographical coordinates".[24] Of course the motive of these honours had to be the heroism displayed by the person's death or in his life. But the admiration aroused thereby, and the praise added by edifying writings, were by themselves insufficient to constitute sainthood : there had to be the liturgical recognition as well.

Therefore the first and principal thing in every problem of historical hagiography is to find solid evidence of cultus, properly so called. This is decided by a number of positive indications taken together. The insertion of a name in a martyrology is a conclusive proof only if it due to authentic testimony of local tradition, and not merely to the personal opinion of a compiler. Tradition may be recognized by those sure signs which confer a sacred character on the memory of the holy persons, whether martyrs or confessors: the manner of their burial, the veneration shown at their tomb or before their relics, miracles which give them the reputation of wonderworkers, the churches and chapels dedicated in their honour, pilgrimages to their shrines, the symbolism of their images, votive inscriptions which name them, place-names which record their patronage: all these traditional elements must be considered, and this can be done profitably only in the light of certain basic principles. Father Delehaye was never tired of coming back to them, tackling them from a different angle each time and so bringing something fresh to them: or rather the new turn he gave to his thought enabled him to go deeper along the same line. We have already referred to his book on the *Origines du culte des martyrs*. The same thought and guiding idea are found in the detailed studies which preceded and followed it: *Sanctus* [57, 132], *Martyr et Confesseur* [75], *Loca Sanctorum* [95] and others.

After thirty-five years of converging researches, unwearyingly returned to and checked, Father Delehaye was entitled to feel assured that he had neglected nothing that would enable him to draw every secret from the Hieronymian Martyrology which one might reasonably hope to wrest from it. There was nothing useful to be gained by yet again going through the residue that had defeated all attempts at clearing up. It happened that just at that time Dom Henri Quentin had finished making, with his usual mastery, a critical reconstruction of the *Hieronymianum*. Father Delehaye suggested to him that they should join together in producing an annotated edition, which would make a pendant to the diplomatic edition of De Rossi and Duchesne. This proposal could not have been accepted in a more friendly spirit, and this great work was finally published in 1931 [5], a lasting honour to the *Acta Sanctorum.*

Father Delehaye's historical commentary followed the text restored by Dom Quentin line by line, one might say word for word, and threw light on everything that was capable of being elucidated. Nobody can be surprised that occasionally a little impulsiveness has crept into the conjectural deductions which had to be attempted at every step, and that the peremptory words *nudum nomen,* a bare name, should here and there have slipped from the commentator's tired pen a little too quickly. But as a whole the work proved once more that, in the words attributed to Buffon, "Genius is simply a great aptitude for patience". Father Delehaye's patience had at least achieved prodigies of ingenuity. It was rewarded with as much fame as could be hoped for a work whose merit could be appreciated to the full only by very learned scholars. Pope Pius XI was among them, and as a token of the regard with which he honoured the two authors, he allowed the book to be dedicated to himself.

Other scholars, old friends of Father Delehaye, seized the opportunity to ask him for the fulfilment of a half-promise they had previously dragged out of him. Now that the *Hieronymianum* was no longer a closed book, they wanted an historical commentary on the Roman Martyrology. Father Delehaye succumbed to the temptation; and he believed at first that this work, of which the most ticklish part seemed to be already done, could be condensed into one or two volumes of the *Subsidia Hagiographica,* and that it would not interfere with the preparation of volume v of the *Acta Sanctorum Novembris,* which he was not resigned to leaving dormant.

This illusion was shortlived. As soon as he got to work on the projected commentary it became clear that it would much exceed the anticipated length, and also that it would require a great deal of new research. To be carried out properly it would require a concentration of all the forces that could be brought to bear on it. It was, too, decided to publish it as *propylaea* in the principal series of the *Acta Sanctorum;* consequently the notices for January and February, which had already been written in French, had to be recast and translated into Latin. Father Delehaye got ahead with his preparations with anxious haste, so that printing could begin on the date fixed, and by so doing cut off his own line of retreat. *Fata viam invenient* was the motto which (without saying so) he adopted in such cases. The massive enterprise was started on its way and continued in it, but it was longer and harder than anyone had foreseen.

It was during the constant toil and harassment of this work that Father Delehaye began seriously to feel the effects of old age. Already in 1934 his health had been gravely threatened, so much so that there was thought of relieving him of the burden. Happily, the danger passed and he returned to his element with renewed ardour, quite determined to leave the helm only with life. But his repeated spurts of energy could not disguise the failing of his powers. Increasingly often he forgot matters that he had decided to deal with himself. Questions he had not himself studied, or had dropped for a long time, he could no longer take up with the quickness which had formerly enabled him to find his bearings at a glance and make up his mind with safety. He was still able to cope with unforeseen contingencies in his work, thanks to the steadiness of his judgement and his limitless resources of acquired knowledge; but the soaring flight which once had carried him gaily over obstacles had given place to wearisome effort, which gave him the new sensation of stooping under a load. But no advice could induce him to moderate his application to work, which was much too intense. He even found time and energy to return to old drafts that were waiting in his files; and to give a solid basis to the commentaries for November and December which had not yet been undertaken in the *Acta Sanctorum,* he pressed on energetically with his *Étude sur le Légendier romain* [134], to which he attached special importance. And well it was that he did so, for in the event this much-needed work was finished at a time when it would have been practically impossible for him to enter on it.

By dint of unremitting toil and keeping everyone up to the mark he came within sight of the end of the laborious work on the Roman Martyrology. The last of the manuscript was sent to the printer on 7 May 1940. Two days later the final corrected proofs of the commentaries for November 14-16 followed. The next day, at dawn, a bomb fell and exploded less than a hundred yards from the library : the spectre of war had suddenly arrived on the door-step.

Father Delehaye could not be unmoved by the shock of this staggering surprise; but after quieting his conscience by an inspection of safety measures that no one could now regard seriously, he wanted to go back to work, not failing to rally those who, unable to achieve such self-composure, were seemingly forgetful of the job in hand. However, his superiors, remembering the previous war, judged it wise to send him away for the time being. After a journey in atrocious conditions he arrived in France in mid-August, and within a few days was taking steps to prevent his nearly-finished volume from being sunk in harbour. The danger, thank God, was averted. Thanks to the printer's energy and devotedness, the *Propylaeum ad Acta Sanctorum Decembris* was ready to appear by the last days of 1940 [6]. On the following February 5, Father Delehaye had the satisfaction of delivering it in person at the office of the Académie Royale [239].

This presentation proved to be his swan-song. It was fifty years almost to a day since he had joined the continuators of Bollandus; and this half-century, for thirty years of which he had been their president, had unquestionably been one of the highwater marks of Bollandist achievement. Had he closed his eyes, he would have seen what everyone saw, that this prosperity was in the nature of a personal success for himself. He had made the *Acta Sanctorum* respected and, if we may be allowed to say so, admired in many circles which up till then had known the work almost only through the memory of its old repute; and the better part of this respect and admiration certainly belonged to Father Delehaye. In every sense he had extended its influence and its authority, and he had himself attained a place in the highest rank of the founders of

Byzantine hagiography. The exceptional brilliance of his work had given him a more and more preponderant place among his Bollandist brethren, to such a degree that the activity of the whole group had come to be absorbed in his activity. Wherever the great and old-established Belgian school of hagiography was more than a name, Father Delehaye was looked on as its outstanding representative and its living personification. He was awarded the ten-yearly prize in history in 1910 and the five-yearly prize in philology in 1921. Almost immediately after Father De Smedt's death he was elected a corresponding member of the Académie Royale de Belgique, in May 1913, and he became a full member six years later. Similar honour was conferred on him by the Académie des Inscriptions et Belles-Lettres, of which he became a correspondent in 1914 and, a more uncommon distinction, a foreign associate in 1925. He was also a member of the Pontifical Roman Academy of Archaeology (1919), a correspondent of the British Academy (1920), of the Academy of Bucharest (1924) and of the Mediaeval Academy of America (1926), an associate of the National Academy *dei Lincei* of Italy (1928), a member of the Society of Byzantine Studies of Athens (1925) and of several other learned societies, and a doctor *honoris causa* of the Universities of Oxford (1920) and of Louvain (1926). In fact, he accumulated more honorific titles on his own head than had fallen to the whole of the Bollandist work since it first started.

The credit of these distinctions was reflected onto the institution which was proud to have Father Delehaye at its head, and he accepted them without false modesty. He appreciated their high significance, and it was doubled for him by the more substantial satisfaction of not having gone out of his way in quest of them; he had never withheld or toned down frank expression of truth for fear of displeasing certain powerful dispensers of fame.

What meant far more to him than these marks of honour were the friendships he had formed with scholars in many lands, some of whom have since become very eminent indeed. Did discretion allow them to be named, they would be found to belong to all degrees in the intellectual world, from the highest ranks in the

Church to those unknown and modest workers whom Father Delehaye knew so well how to appreciate. What is left of his voluminous correspondence could one day be a valuable source for the history of scholarship over more than fifty years.

Outside the exalted spheres where his reputation was solidly established, public opinion as a whole showed something of the indifference to Father Delehaye that he showed to it. The fact is that he made little effort to humour the general public, not through any pretentious superiority, but because he had an invincible repugnance for those little contrivances and compromises at the price of which true learning itself has sometimes gained a sort of popularity. All his convictions led him in an opposite direction to that which has seduced some popular favourites of the moment. His unusual talent for exposition was distinguished above all by naturalness and simplicity. He could not abide the least affectation, preciosity, stale unction or the fripperies of sham elegance, still less excessive emphasis, the trenchant manner, the provocative hyperbole, the passion for something new and sensational. In literature as in art, his taste was wide and inclusive; he had his preferences, and on them he did not budge. His convictions were inflexibly classical; he looked on a sincere and discerning admiration for the ancients and the masters of the great eras as an obligation. This was like a touchstone, by which he tested a man's seriousness and right-mindedness.

Thus entrenched in his high ideal of intellectual activity, he cut himself off rigorously from the intriguing of cliques and the allurements of fashion. He found it very difficult to put up with show and ceremony, which even the world of scholarship cannot wholly dispense with. He was seldom seen, and more seldom heard, at congresses and other formal gatherings at which reputations, whether deserved or not, are made much of, not always quietly. Scornful of all publicity, dreading to have to speak in public, not a good conversationalist except on the subjects that preoccupied him, he shunned any intercourse which he saw to be a waste of time.

But the quiet reserve into which he withdrew—less from natural disposition than on principle—had nothing to do with misanthropy. He lived for over fifty years in the Collège Saint-Michael, and he took a most sympathetic interest in the life and activities of the young men around him. Like the great Newman before him, he was not above taking charge of the music in the chapel. Generation after generation of pupils remembered him as a very great scholar, simple-mannered and affable, whom the shyest could approach without nervousness. Father Delehaye had a word of good advice and encouragement for each of them, and never missed an opportunity of spurring them on in their studies. Many of these youths owed the beginning of a promising career to his counsel and influence.

On 14 January 1927 he celebrated the fiftieth anniversary of his entry "into religion," and this family occasion became quite an event, of which the Belgian press of all shades of opinion took notice. King Albert associated himself with it in an autograph letter expressed in very eulogistic terms; the apostolic nuncio, Mgr Clement Micara, presided at the jubilee ceremony; and the prime minister, M. Henri Jaspar, attended in person to invest Father Delehaye with the scarf of a commander of the Order of Leopold. Similar manifestations of regard were expressed more privately, at his diamond jubilee in 1937; during the years between he had acquired new titles to the respect and admiration which everyone had for him.

So Father Delehaye's long and gallant career had, notwithstanding hindrances and hard trials, been exceptionally favoured. He did not wholly escape the sorrows of declining years. At times, those who saw him at close quarters perceived in him a certain regret, mingled with apprehension, about which there could be no mistake. He was worried because he had only partly succeeded in forming a school. One would have liked to be able to suggest to him that the relative isolation that depressed him, and gave him the distressing feeling that he was not understood, was like the clear space found around the roots of a great forest tree. He tried to find some other explanation, feeling sure there must be one. It would have been out of place to tell him that he had been asking a lot when he counted on Providence sending him only disciples who were specially made to his own measure and likeness. It was not so much that he lacked forbearance and understanding in guiding a beginner's first steps. With the chance visitor he was remarkably easy of access. He treated the old servants in the house as friends. But where professional matters were concerned he went straight to his target by the shortest route, without looking for a way round that would enable him to get into a person's mind.

His faith was unfailing, without any attenuation of the supreme importance of his mission as a hagiographer, which for him was a transcendent interest before which every personal consideration had to give way. Held in thrall by this ideal of absolute devotedness to his life's work, he did not notice that, interpreted according to his views, the table of duties involved included more things, and less interesting ones, than he took into account. He was unsparing of his own labour and pains, and it came natural to him not to trouble much about sparing other people's. He knew the value of his approval, and did not waste it on those who would have over-rated themselves. He was sometimes a little abrupt in giving orders, but he was not a grumbler. His most forceful rebukes were usually provoked by the impact of a first impression, which he did not dream of keeping to himself. He was not at his most welcoming when in the heat of composition; simply at the scratching of his pen one knew what to expect : at such times he was possessed by a passion of inspiration that it was wiser not to interrupt. One had to be very sure of oneself before venturing to put forward an opinion that differed from his, or even to suggest to him an idea for which he was unprepared. His rather imperious turn of mind went with a liveliness of perception befitting an artist or a poet. He was both, in the acute sensibility which made him feel the ugliness of an error or a defect of method to the very fibres of his being. An objection, or sometimes a new suggestion advanced at the wrong moment, at once put him on the defensive, and if the person concerned was insistent he was liable to be given a refusal, which could mean the definitive end of it. To get over this instinctive repulsion, it was necessary for him to be induced to reconsider his own point of view and to study the question at issue when his mind was at rest. But how could he have found such real leisure?—the day was always too short for him, and he lived in a state of endless tension through overwork. What he may have lacked as a guide and director of others was no more than the almost inevitable price of the prodigious activity to which we owe most of his achievements. Simple justice requires us to recognize that in giving precedence to his own works he did but accord them an importance that is theirs by rights.

To indicate Father Delehaye's place in the line of successors of Bollandus, we have to look amongst the greatest. Papebroch was his ideal, and in unguarded moments he would let it be seen that he had taken him as his model. But it is doubtful whether he would have been pleased to hear that, resembling this Titan, he also resembled Father De Buck, who too was authentically like him.[25] The penetrating power and sureness of Father Delehaye's comprehensive general view of any matter certainly was reminiscent of Papebroch, as was the fearlessness of his criticism. To these outstanding qualities, which relieved his labours of the more elementary burdens of erudition, he added the best of those which distinguished some of his more illustrious predecessors : the methodical regularity which gave such orderliness to Du Sollier's vast reading, the flowing ease of expression of Stiltingh, the highly personal originality of Victor De Buck, whom it would be unjust not to compare with him. All this was crowned by a well-balanced clearness of exposition that was all his own and gave a sort of austere elegance even to the most deeply laboured of his works.

In ranking Father Delehaye with the highest figures in Bollandist history posterity will be doing the justice to him that he did to others. He had a grateful reverence for Bolland and his immediate successors, which in private conversation he expressed still more warmly than when he was writing about them in his account of the Bollandist work [125]. He too had opened up new paths in hagiographical criticism, and had himself experienced the surprises and

dreadful perplexities that dog the pioneer's every step in a virgin
forest that has not known the axe. At the very end of his life, when
preparing to deal with those weeks of the Roman Martyrology
which follow the point where at present the *Acta Sanctorum*
leaves off, he declared how much he was missing the help he had
had up till then from the folio volumes of our predecessors, especially from their modest lists of *praetermissi*. He made it an occasion for expressing his homage to those dauntless explorers who
had first made their way into the unknown lands of hagiography,
and who did so without any of the resources which today aid and
support the most ill-found scholar on his way. *Gigantes erant super
terram in diebus illis* he repeated time and again when talking of
those incomparable masters. In this way did he testify to his duti-
ful admiration for those who began the work, men whose vast
knowledge was their own, because they had had to get it at first
hand from unpublished or almost inaccessible sources, who knew
them thoroughly because they had themselves read and re-read
them from one end to the other. This impressive thought might
well be brought to the notice of presumptuous or unthinking
people who, from the height of their little learning easily acquired
at secondhand, give themselves the cheap satisfaction of reading a
lesson to the pioneers who cleared the way for them.

Father Delehaye's respect for the masters of the past was part
of a deeper thing. Where matters of soul and conscience were
concerned, he was before all else a man of the old Christian tradition. He read the acts of the martyrs more than treatises on the
lesser virtues, he felt more at home with Theodoret's solitaries
than amongst the refinements of the latest devotional practices.
There was nothing demonstrative, still less formalist, about his
piety; it was as solid as his other convictions. In him, the dedicated
religious and the intellectual worker walked in step along the same
road. He was as wide-spirited as any one can be; but when an
essential principle was at stake he was unbending and strict to the
verge of scrupulousness, if not of rigorism. He had the highest and
most austere conception of the duty of one's state, and his immovably tenacious strength was concentrated on that above all. To

shrink or hesitate when given an order was to forfeit his esteem, for
that was a failing that for him touched the rule of conduct that he
had made the law of his whole life.

Father Delehaye was spared that most trying ordeal of old age,
having to spend one's last years in inactivity. Like our great forbears, Bolland, Henschenius and especially his chosen model Papebroch, he was able to work to the end, by dint of an indomitable
struggle against his infirmities. On 26 March 1941 he was struck
down by an illness that was serious enough to make it prudent for
him to receive the last sacraments. He rallied for a short time, and
then got so much worse that all hope was gone. He bore considerable pain with the rather casual stoicism which was the
characteristic form his patience took; he showed no sign of anxiety,
except that he should not be a burden to those who were looking
after him. After a brief struggle, he died peacefully, towards even-
ing on April 1.

The passing of Hippolyte Delehaye marked the close of one of
the most memorable periods of Bollandist history. He had fulfilled his task, he had run his long race, straight and to the end;
in his hands, the trust for which he had been made responsible had
been more than conserved : well did he deserve the rest to which
God called him. Reflecting on the past which vanished with him,
those who witnessed his death could only repeat the words he had
written at the beginning of *Les origines du culte des martyrs,*
dedicating it to the memory of Father De Smedt and Father
Poncelet, *In pace cum sanctis.*

NOTES ON MEMOIR

[1]Institut de France. Académie des Inscriptions et Belles-Lettres. *Discours de M. Marcel Aubert, président de l'Académie, à l'occasion de la mort du P. Hippolyte Delehaye, associé étranger de l'Académie* (read at the session of 25 April 1941).

[2]Through the mouth of Dom Cunibert Mohlberg. See the *Osservatore Romano,* 10 January 1942.

[3]The eulogy of Father Delehaye read at a joint session of the three classes of the Académie Royale de Belgique on 22 July 1942 appeared in its 1943 Annual.

[4]É. De Strycker, s.j., "Het werk van een Bollandist. In memoriam Pater H. Delehaye, s.j.", in *Streven* (1941), pp. 459-473; id., "L'œuvre d'un Bollandiste. Le Père Hippolyte Delehaye, s.j. (1859-1941)", extracted from *l'Année Théologique* (Paris, 1942); id., in the *Revue d'histoire ecclésiastique,* vol. xxxvii (1941), pp. 333-335; J. Coppens, "Hippolyte Delehaye, s.j.", in *Ephemerides theologicae Lovanienses,* vol. xviii (1941), pp. 186-188; E. Lamalle, in *Archivum historicum Societatis Iesu,* vol. xi (1942), pp. 207-208; Anonymous, in *Scuola cattolica,* vol. xlix (1941), p. 446.

[5]In the following pages the numbers between square brackets refer to the bibliography at the end.

[6]L. Devillers, "Notice historique sur la ville de Chièvres", in *Annales du cercle archéoligique de Mons,* vol. vii (1867), p. 186.

[7]"Le P. Charles De Smedt", in *Analecta Bollandiana,* vol. xxx (1911), pp. i-x; "Après un siècle. L'œuvre des Bollandistes de 1837 à 1937", ibid., vol. lv (1937), pp. xxxiv-xl; P. Peeters, s.j., "L'œuvre des Bollandistes", in *Mémoires de l'Académie Royale de Belgique,* Classe des Lettres et des Sciences morales et politiques, vol. xxxix, 4 (1942), pp. 112-120.

[8]P. Peeters, "Le R.P. Joseph Van den Gheyn", in *Revue des questions scientifiques,* vol. lxxiii (1913), pp. 389-396.

[9]"Le R.P. Albert Poncelet", in *Anal. Boll.,* vol. xxxi (1912), pp. 129-141.

[10]"Le R.P. François Van Ortroy", ibid., vol. xxxix (1921), pp. 4-19.

[11]We are glad here to recall the moving tribute by Father A. Lapôtre, for many years a guest and frequenter of the *musée bollandien:* "La Critique", in *Un siècle. Mouvement du monde de 1800 à 1900* (Paris, 1900), pp. 367-368.

[12]Published in 1863 on the occasion of the millenary celebrations of SS. Cyril and Methodius, and in the following year at the beginning of volume xi of the *Acta Sanctorum Octobris.*

[13]*Theologische Studien und Kritiken,* vol. lxxx (1907), pp. 144-148.

[14]A. Baumstark, *Liturgie comparée* (Chevetogne, 1939), pp. 188-189.

[15]H. Delehaye, "Le synaxaire de Sirmond", in *Anal. Boll.,* vol. xiv (1895), pp. 421-434.

[16]*Ueberlieferung und Bestand der hagiographischen und homiletischen Literatur der griechischen Kirche,* vol. i (*Texte und Untersuchungen,* vol. 1), pp. 52-53.

[17]*Byzantinische Zeitschrift,* vol. xii (1903), p. 675.

[18]*Theologische Literaturzeitung,* 1903, cc. 300-301.

[19]*Bulletin critique,* vol. xii (1891), p. 417.

[20]É. De Strycker, in *Streven,* vol. cit. note 4, p. 472; *Année Théologique,* cit. note 4, p. 18.

[21]*Legenden-Studien* (Cologne, 1906). Cf. *Anal. Boll.,* vol. xxv, p. 397.

[22]In 1935, in an article commemorating the centenary of H. Usener, Carl Clemen frankly made his own the objections brought by Father Dele-haye against the celebrated Bonn professor's system ("Hermann Usener als Religionshistoriker", in *Studi e materiali di storia delle religioni,* vol. xi, pp. 110-124).

[23]*Die Anfänge des Heiligenkults in der christlichen Kirche,* published posthumously by G. Anrich (Tübingen, 1902); cf. *Anal. Boll.,* vol. xxiv (1905), pp. 487-488.

[24]"La méthode historique et l'hagiographie", in *Bulletins de l'Académie royale de Belgique,* vol. xvi (1930), pp. 218-231.

[25]P. Peeters, "L'œuvre des Bollandistes" (1942), in the *Mémoires de l'Académie royale de Belgique,* vol. cit., note 7, pp. 101-111.

BIBLIOGRAPHY
OF SCIENTIFIC WORKS BY
HIPPOLYTE DELEHAYE

BIBLIOGRAPHY

OF SCIENTIFIC WORKS BY HIPPOLYTE DELEHAYE

I. IN THE *ACTA SANCTORUM*

1. Acta Sanctorum Novembris, collecta, digesta, illustrata a
Carolo DE SMEDT, Iosepho DE BACKER, FRANCISCO VAN
ORTROY, Iosepho VAN DEN GHEYN, Hippolyto DELEHAYE
et Alberto PONCELET, Societatis Iesu presbyteris. Tomi II
pars prior, qua dies tertius partim et quartus continentur[1].
Praemissum est Martyrologium Hieronymianum, editi-
bus Iohanne Baptista DE ROSSI et Ludovico DUCHESNE. —
Bruxellis, 1894, in-fol., [12]-LXXXII-195-[4]-624 pp.
2. Propylaeum ad Acta Sanctorum Novembris, ediderunt
Carolus DE SMEDT, Iosephus DE BACKER, Franciscus VAN
ORTROY, Iosephus VAN DEN GHEYN, Hippolytus DELE-
HAYE et Albertus PONCELET, presbyteri Societatis Iesu.
Synaxarium Ecclesiae Constantinopolitanae e codice Sir-
mondiano, nunc Berolinensi, adiectis Synaxariis selectis,
opera et studio Hippolyti DELEHAYE. — Bruxellis, 1902,
in-fol., LXXV pp., 1184 col.
3. Acta Sanctorum Novembris, collecta, digesta, illustrata a Carolo
DE SMEDT, Francisco VAN ORTROY, Hippolyto DELEHAYE,
Alberto PONCELET et Paulo PEETERS, Societatis Iesu presbyteris. Tomus III, quo dies quintus, sextus, septimus et
octavus continentur[2]. — Bruxellis, 1910, in-fol., XII-1001
pp.

[1]Only one commentary by Fr Delehaye in this volume: De S. Wolf-
kango, episcopo Rastisponensi (p. 527-97).
[2]Principal commentaries by Fr Delehaye: De SS. martyribus Galactione
et Episteme (p. 33-45); De S. Demetriano ep. Chytraeo in Cypro (p. 298-
308); De S. Prosdocimo ep. Patavino (p. 350-59); De S. Lazaro monacho
in Monte Galesio (p. 502-608); De SS. Quattuor Coronatis Romae in
Monte Coelio (p. 748-84); De S. Matrona monialium magistra Constantinopoli (p. 786-823); De S. Euphrosyna Iuniore virgine Constantinopoli
(p. 858-89).

4. Acta Sanctorum Novembris, collecta, digesta, illustrata ab Hippolyto DELEHAYE et Paulo PEETERS, Societatis Iesu presbyteris. Tomus IV, quo dies nonus et decimus continentur[1]. — Bruxellis, 1925, in-fol., XII-767 pp.

5. Acta Sanctorum Novembris, collecta, digesta, illustrata ab Hippolyto DELEHAYE, Paulo PEETERS et Mauritio COENS, Societatis Iesu presbyteris. Tomi II pars posterior, qua continetur Hippolyti DELEHAYE Commentarius perpetuus in Martyrologium Hieronymianum ad recensionem Henrici QUENTIN, O.S.B. — Bruxellis, 1931, in-fol., XXIII-721 pp.

6. Propylaeum ad Acta Sanctorum Decembris, ediderunt Hippolytus DELEHAYE, Paulus PEETERS, Mauritius COENS, Balduinus DE GAIFFIER, Paulus GROSJEAN, Franciscus HALKIN, presbyteri Societatis Iesu. Martyrologium Romanum ad formam editionis typicae scholiis historicis instructum[2]. — Bruxellis, 1940, in-fol., XXIII-660 pp.

II. IN *ANALECTA BOLLANDIANA*

More than a thousand reviews and bibliographical notices which appeared in the Bulletin of hagiographical publications in Analecta Bollandiana *are omitted here. At first they were anonymous; they are signed with the initials H.D. from volume XXII* (1903) *to volume XXXIII* (1914), *and from volume XXXVIII* (1920) *to volume LVII* (1939).

7. Guiberti Gemblacensis epistula de S. Martino et alterius Guiberti item Gemblacensis carmina de eodem. — VII (1888), 265-320.

[1]Principal commentaries by Fr Delehaye: De S. Theodoro martyre Euchaïtis Helenoponti (p. 11-89); De SS. martyribus Eusebio, Marcello, Hippolyto, Hadria, Paulina, Neone, Maria, Maximo, Martana et Valeria, Romae via Appia (p. 90-99); De S. Ursino primo Biturigensi episcopo (p. 101-115); De S. Agrippino ep. Neapolitano (p. 118-28); De S. Theoctiste Lesbia in insula Paro (p. 221-33); De S. Thomaide Lesbia matrona Constantinopoli (p. 233-46); De SS. Tryphone, Respicio et Nympha mm. Romae cultis (p. 318-83); De S. Oreste m. Tyanis in Cappadocia (p. 391-99); De S. Constantino quondam Iudaeo monacho in Bithynia (p. 627-56); De S. Blasio Amoriensi mon. Constantinopoli (p. 656-69); De S. Michaele m. Alexandriae (p. 669-78); De S. Iohanne Iuniore mon. in Thracia (p. 678-87).

[2]Fr Delehaye treated most of the notices going back to the Hieronymian Martyrology, and some others.

8. Vita S. Pauli Iunioris, in monte Latro, cum interpretatione latina Iacobi Sirmondi s.i. — XI (1892), 5-74, 136-82. — See below, n° 178.

9. La Vierge aux sept glaives. — XII (1893), 333-52.

10. S. Romanos le Mélode. — XIII (1894), 440-42.

11. Vita S. Nicephori episcopi Milesii saeculo x. — XIV (1895), 129-66. — See below, n° 178.

12. L'inscription de sainte Ermenia. — Ibid., 322-24.

13. Le Synaxaire de Sirmond. — Ibid., 396-434.

14. Vita Sanctae Olympiadis et narratio Sergiae de eiusdem translatione. — XV (1896), 400-423; XVI (1897), 44-51.

15. Les Saints du cimetière de Commodille. — XVI (1897), 17-43.

16. De versione latina Actorum S. Demetrii saeculo xii confecta. — Ibid., 66-68.

17. La *Notitia fundorum* du titre des SS. Jean et Paul à Rome. — Ibid., 69-73.

18. L'inscription d'Abercius. — Ibid., 74-77.

19. Eusebii Caesariensis *De martyribus Palaestinae* longioris libelli fragmenta. — Ibid., 113-39. — See also n° 148 below.

20. L'Amphithéâtre Flavien et ses environs dans les textes hagiographiques. — Ibid., 209-252.

21. Catalogus codicum hagiographicorum graecorum bibliothecae Chisianae de Urbe. — Ibid., 297-310.

22. Les Ménologes grecs. — Ibid., 311-29.

23. S. Anastase, martyr de Salone. — Ibid., 488-500. — See translation, n° 151, below.

24. Le Ménologe de Métaphraste. — XVII (1898), 448-52.

25. Note sur le Typicon de Bova. — Ibid., 453-55.

26. La patrie de S. Jérôme. — XVIII (1899), 260-61.

27. Saints d'Istrie et de Dalmatie. — Ibid., 369-411. — See translation, n°s 154 and 155, below.

28. Les deux saints Babylas. — XIX (1900), 5-8.

29. Catalogus codicum hagiographicorum graecorum bibliothecae Barberinianae de Urbe. — Ibid., 81-118.

30. De codicibus hagiographicis graecis bibliothecae civitatis Lipsiensis. — XX (1901), 205-207.

31. Acta graeca SS. Dasii, Gai et Zotici, martyrum Nicomediensium. — Ibid., 246-48.

32. Ad Catalogum codicum hagiographicorum graecorum bibliothecae Vaticanae supplementum. — XXI (1902), 5-22. — See n° 117, below.

33. Un synaxaire italo-grec. — Ibid., 23-28.

34. S. Sadoth episcopi Seleuciae et Ctesiphontis Acta graeca. — Ibid., 141-47. — See also n° 165, below.

35. Catalogus codicum hagiographicorum graecorum Bibliothecae nationalis Neapolitanae. — Ibid., 381-402.

36. S. Melaniae Iunioris Acta graeca. — XXII (1903), 5-50.

37. S. Barlaam martyr à Antioche. — Ibid., 129-45.

38. La Passion de S. Théodote d'Ancyre. — Ibid., 320-28.

39. SS. Ionae et Barachisii martyrum in Perside Acta graeca. — Ibid., 395-407. — See also n° 165, below.

40. Un fragment de ménologe trouvé à Jérusalem. — Ibid., 408-410.

41. L'hagiographie de Salone d'après les dernières découvertes archéologiques. — XXIII (1904), 5-18. — See also n°ˢ 164 and 174, below.

42. Catalogus codicum hagiographicorum graecorum monasterii Sancti Salvatoris, nunc bibliothecae Universitatis Messanensis. — Ibid., 19-75.

43. Passio sanctorum Sexaginta martyrum. — Ibid., 289-307.

44. Castor et Pollux dans les légendes hagiographiques. — Ibid., 427-32.

45. S. Grégoire le Grand dans l'hagiographie grecque. — Ibid., 449-54.

46. Catalogus codicum hagiographicorum graecorum bibliothecae D. Marci Venetiarum. — XXIV (1905), 169-256.

47. Hesychii Hierosolymorum presbyteri laudatio S. Procopii Persae. — Ibid., 473-82.

48. S. Expédit et le Martyrologe hiéronymien. — XXV (1906), 90-98.

49. Sanctus Silvanus. — Ibid., 158-62.

50. Catalogus codicum hagiographicorum graecorum bibliothecae comitis de Leicester, Holkhamiae in Anglia. — Ibid., 451-77.

51. Notes sur un manuscrit grec du Musée britannique. — Ibid., 495-502.

52. Le témoignage des martyrologes. — XXVI (1907), 78-99. — See also n° 133, ch. III. — For the Italian translation, see n° 119.

53. Saints de Chypre. — Ibid., 161-301.

54. Le pèlerinage de Laurent de Pászthó au Purgatoire de S. Patrice. — XXVII (1908), 35-60. — See also n° 169, below.

55. Une version nouvelle de la Passion de S. Georges. — Ibid., 373-83.

56. Les femmes stylites. — Ibid., 391-92.
57. Sanctus. — XXVIII (1909), 145-200. — See also n° 132, below.
58. Catalogus codicum hagiographicorum graecorum regii monasterii Sancti Laurentii Scorialensis. — Ibid., 353-98.
59. L'invention des reliques de S. Ménas à Constantinople. —
   XXIX (1910), 117-50.
60. Les Actes de S. Barbarus. — Ibid., 276-301.
61. Les premiers *Libelli Miraculorum*. — Ibid., 427-34. — Again in
   n° 123, below, chap. IV. — See also n° 84.
62. Gaianopolis. — Ibid., 435-40.
63. L'aqueduc de S. Socrate à Zénonopolis. — XXX (1911),
   316-20.
64. Les saints d'Aboukir. — Ibid., 448-50.
65. Saints de Thrace et de Mésie. — XXXI (1912), 161-291.
66. Le calendrier lapidaire de Carmona. — Ibid., 319-21.
67. Le culte des Quatre Couronnés à Rome. — XXXII (1913), 63-
   71.
68. Vita S. Danielis Stylis Stylitae. — Ibid., 121-216. — Reprinted
   in n° 131, below.
69. De fontibus Vitae S. Danielis Stylitae. — Ibid., 217-29.
70. Martyrologium hieronymianum Cambrense. — Ibid., 369-407.
71. S. Almachius ou Télémaque. — XXXIII (1914), 421-28.
72. Saint Martin et Sulpice Sévère. — XXXVIII (1920), 5-136.
73. Les martyrs de Tavium. — Ibid., 374-87.
74. Le Typicon du monastère de Lips à Constantinople. — Ibid.,
   388-92. — See also n° 126, below.
75. Martyr et confesseur. — XXXIX (1921), 20-49. — See also
   n° 132, below.
76. La Passion de S. Félix de Thibiuca. — Ibid., 241-76.
77. Cyprien d'Antioche et Cyprien de Carthage. — Ibid., 314-32.
78. Catalogus codicum hagiographicorum graecorum bibliothecae
   Patriarchatus Alexandrini in Cahira Aegypti. — Ibid.,
   345-57.
79. Les martyrs d'Égypte. — XL (1922), 5-154, 299-364. — The
   offprint, with its own pagination, is dedicated to Pio
   Franchi de' Cavalieri (Brussels, 1923, 221 pp.).
80. Les Actes de S. Marcel le Centurion. — XLI (1923), 257-87.
81. Le calendrier d'Oxyrhynque pour l'année 535-536. — XLII
   (1924), 83-99.
82. Synaxarium et Miracula S. Isaiae prophetae. — Ibid., 257-65.
83. S. Hédiste et S. Oreste. — Ibid., 315-19.
84. Les recueils antiques des Miracles des saints. — XLIII (1925),
   5-85, 305-325. — See also n° 61, above.

234   BIBLIOGRAPHY

85. Catalogus codicum hagiographicorum graecorum bibliothecae Scholae theologicae in Chalce insula. — XLIV (1926), 5-63. — Seel also n° 91, below.
86. La personnalité historique de S. Paul de Thèbes. — Ibid., 64-69.
87. Hagiographie et archéologie romaines. — Ibid., 241-69; XLV (1927), 297-322.
88. Les lettres d'indulgence collectives. — XLIV (1926), 342-79; XLV (1927), 97-123, 323-44; XLVI (1928), 149-57, 287-343. — These five articles were brought together in an offprint, with its own pagination, dedicated to Mgr J. H. Ryan, rector of the Catholic University at Washington (Brussels, 1928, iv-156 pp.).
89. Une Vie inédite de S. Jean l'Aumônier. — XLV (1927), 5-74.
90. Trois dates du calendrier romain. — XLVI (1928), 50-67.
91. Ad Catalogum codicum hagiographicorum graecorum bibliothecae Scholae theologicae in Chalce insula supplementum. — Ibid., 158-60. — See n° 85, above.
92. L'hagiographie ancienne de Ravenne. — XLVII (1929), 5-30.
93. Nouvelles fouilles à Salone. — Ibid., 77-88.
94. La *Vigilia Sancti Martini* dans le Martyrologe hiéronymien. — Ibid., 368-75.
95. Loca Sanctorum. — XLVIII (1930), 5-64.
96. Quelques dates du Martyrologe hiéronymien. — XLIX (1931), 22-50. — See also n° 224, below.
97. Une lettre d'indulgence pour l'hôpital della Vita de Bologne. — Ibid., 398-406.
98. Le nouveau volume des *Acta Sanctorum* [above, n° 5]. — L (1932), 59-66.
99. La châsse de S. Commodus. — Ibid., 147-51.
100. S. Romain, martyr d'Antioche. — Ibid., 241-83.
101. S. Bassus, évêque et martyr, honoré à Nice. — Ibid., 295-310.
102. Recherches sur le Légendier romain. La Passion de S. Polychronius. — LI (1933), 34-98.
103. Constantini Acropolitae, hagiographi byzantini, epistularum manipulus. — Ibid., 263-84.
104. Stoudion-Stoudios. — LII (1934), 64-65.
105. Domnus Marculus. — LIII (1935), 81-89.
106. Saints et reliquaires d'Apamée. — Ibid., 225-44.
107. Contributions récentes à l'hagiographie de Rome et d'Afrique. — LIV (1936), 265-315.
108. Quatre Miracles de S. Martin de Tours. — LV (1937), 29-48.

109. De codice rescripto Barrocciano 96. — Ibid., 70-74.
110. Sainte Théodote de Nicée. — Ibid., 201-25.
111. Hagiographie napolitaine. — LVII (1939), 5-64; LIX (1941), 1-33.
112. Passio sancti Mammetis. — LVIII (1940), 126-41.
113. Les Actes des martyrs de Pergame. — Ibid., 142-76.
114. Le nouveau volume des *Acta Sanctorum* [above, n° 6]. — Ibid., 205-206.

III. SEPARATE WORKS

Offprints of articles mentioned elsewhere in this bibliography are not repeated here.

Later editions of a work are included under the same number as the first edition thereof.

All these books are in medium 8vo, and, unless otherwise stated, published at Brussels.

115. Bibliotheca hagiographica graeca, seu elenchus Vitarum Sanctorum graece typis impressarum. Ediderunt Socii Bollandiani. — 1895, x-143 pp. — Second edition, under the title: Bibliotheca hagiographica graeca. Editio altera emendatior. Accedit Synopsis Metaphrastica. — 1909, xv-299 pp.
116. Catalogus codicum hagiographicorum graecorum Bibliothecae nationalis Parisiensis. Ediderunt Hagiographi Bollandiani et Henricus Omont. — 1896, VIII-372 pp.
117. Catalogus codicum hagiographicorum graecorum bibliothecae Vaticanae. Ediderunt Hagiographi Bollandiani et Pius Franchi de' Cavalieri. — 1899, VIII-324 pp.; appeared as a supplement to *Analecta Bollandiana*, volumes XVII (1898) and XVIII (1899). See also n°. 32, above.
118. Les Légendes hagiographiques. — 1905, XI-264 pp. — Second edition, 1906, XI-264 pp. — Third edition, revised, 1927, xv-227 pp. (in the collection *Subsidia hagiographica*, n°. 18). See also n°. 161, and the translations, n°s. 119-121, below.
119. Le Leggende agiografiche. Con appendice di Wilhelm Meyer. Traduzione italiana. — Firenze, 1906, 360 pp. — Seconda edizione italiana con notevoli aggiunte, appendice sui martirologi e indice onomastico. — Firenze, 1910, XVIII-391 pp. Translation by Giuseppe Faraoni of n°. 118, above. — The appendix to the 2nd edition (p. 337-83) is the Italian translation of n°. 52, above.

120. The Legends of the Saints. An Introduction to Hagiography. Translated by Mrs V. M. Crawford. — London, 1907, xv-241 pp. (in the Westminster Library . . . for Catholic Priests and Students). — Translation of n°. 118, above.

121. Die hagiographischen Legenden. Übersetzt von E. A. Stückelberg. — Kempten and München, 1907, ix-234 pp. — Translation of n°. 118, above.

122. Les Légendes grecques des Saints militaires. — Paris, 1909, ix-271 pp.

123. Les Origines du culte des martyrs. — 1912, viii-503 pp. — Second edition, 1933, viii-443 pp. (in Subsidia hagiographica, n° 20). — See also n° 61, above.

124. Catalogus codicum hagiographicorum Germaniae Belgii Angliae. Ediderunt C. VAN DE VORST et H. DELEHAYE. — 1913, viii-415 pp. (in the same collection, n° 13).

125. A travers trois siècles. L'œuvre des Bollandistes, 1615-1915. — 1920, 284 pp. — See also nos 130, 181 et 184, below.

126. Deux Typica byzantins de l'époque des Paléologues. — 1921, 213 pp. — Mémoires de l'Académie royale de Belgique, Classe des Lettres, collection in-8°, 2nd series, vol. XIII (1921), n° 4. — See also n° 74, above.

127. Les Passions des martyrs et les genres littéraires. — 1921, viii-448 pp.

128. Saint Jean Berchmans (1599-1621). — Paris, 1921, vi-171 pp. (in the series Les Saints). — Many editions (the eighth in 1932). See translation, n° 129, below.

129. St John Berchmans. Translated from the French by Henry Churchill Semple, s.j. — New York, 1921, 189 pp. — Translation of n° 128, above.

130. The work of the Bollandists through three centuries. 1615-1915. From the original French. — Princeton, 1922, 269 pp. — Translation of n° 125, above.

131. Les saints stylites. — 1923, [vii]-cxcv-276 pp. (in Subsidia hagiographica, n° 14). — See also nos 68, 145, 185.

132. Sanctus. Essai sur le culte des saints dans l'antiquité. — 1927, viii-266 pp. (in the same collection, n° 17). In part a reworking of nos 57 and 75, above.

133. Cinq leçons sur la méthode hagiographique. — 1934, 147 pp. (in the same collection, n° 21). — See also nos 52, above, 210 and 216, below.

134. Étude sur le Légendier romain. Les saints de novembre et de décembre. — 1936, 273 pp. (in the same collection, n° 23). — See also nos 231 and 232, below.

IV. PRINCIPAL ARTICLES
ELSEWHERE THAN IN *ANALECTA BOLLANDIANA*

135. Les Plantes de la Bible. — *Précis historiques*, vol. XXXIV (1885), p. 353-72.
136. Philippe II d'après sa correspondance intime. — Ibid., vol. XXXV (1886), p. 175-94.
137. Nouvelles recherches sur Henri de Gand. — *Messager des Sciences historiques ou Archives des arts et de la bibliographie de Belgique*, vol. LX (1886), pp. 328-55. 438-55; vol. LXI (1887), p. 59-85.
138. Notes sur Henri de Gand. — Ibid., vol. LXII (1888), p. 421-56.
139. Les Registres des Papes. À propos de quelques travaux récents. — *Précis historiques*, vol. XXXVII (1888), p. 193-212.
140. Guibert, abbé de Florennes et de Gembloux. — *Revue des questions historiques*, vol. XLVI = N. S. vol. II (1889), p. 5-90.
141. Pierre de Pavie, légat du pape Alexandre III en France. — Ibid., vol. XLIX = N. S. vol. V (1891), p. 5-61.
142. Le légat Pierre de Pavie, chanoine de Chartres. — Ibid., vol. LI = N. S. vol. VII (1892), p. 244-52.
143. Le Bullaire et l'histoire du pape Calixte II. — *Messager* [see n° 137], vol. LXVI (1892), p. 225-29.
144. La Vie de Saint Paul le Jeune (d. 956) et la chronologie de Métaphraste. — *Revue des questions historiques*, vol. LIV = N. S. vol. X (1893), p. 49-85.
145. Les Stylites. Saint Syméon et ses imitateurs. — Ibid., vol. LVII = N. S. vol. XIII (1895), p. 52-103. — Also appeared under the title "Les Stylites" in *Compte rendu du troisième Congrès scientifique international des Catholiques, tenu à Bruxelles du 3 au 8 septembre* 1894 (Bruxelles, 1895), vol. V, p. 191-232. — See also n° 131, above.
146. Review of: Martyrologium Hieronymianum. Ad fidem codicum adiectis prolegomenis ediderunt Iohannes Baptista De Rossi et Ludovicus Duchesne. [Extracted from n° 1, above]. — *Bulletin critique*, 2nd series, vol. I (1895), p. 385-89.
147. Une épigramme de l'Anthologie grecque (I, 99). — *Revue des Études grecques*, vol. IX (1896), p. 216-24.
148. Il libro di Eusebio *De Martyribus Palaestinae*. — *Civiltà cattolica*, 16th series, vol. XII (1897), pp. 56-65, 177-88. — See also n° 19, above.

149. La Vie d'Athanase, patriarche de Constantinople (1289-1293, 1304-1310). — *Mélanges d'archéologie et d'histoire publiés par l'École française de Rome*, vol. XVII (1897), p. 39-75.

150. Mercurian (Evrard), général des Jésuites. — *Biographie nationale*, vol. XIV (1897), col. 444-50.

151. S. Anastasio martire di Salona. — *Bullettino di archeologia e storia dalmata*, vol. XXI (1898), p. 57-72. — Translation of n° 23, above.

152. Note sur la légende de la lettre du Christ tombée du ciel. — *Académie royale des Sciences, des Lettres et des Beaux-Arts de Belgique. Bulletins de la Classe des Lettres et de la Classe des Beaux-Arts*, 3rd series, vol. XXXVII, 2nd part (1899), p. 171-213.

153. The Forty Martyrs of Sebaste. — *American Catholic Quarterly Review*, vol. XXIV (1899), p. 161-71.

154. Santi dell' Istria e della Dalmazia. — *Bullettino di archeologia e storia dalmata*, vol. XXIII (1900)), p. 85-111. — Translation of n° 27 above, except for the two chapters about Istria. — There is an offprint having as title on the outside: Santi della Dalmazia.

155. Santi dell' Istria e Dalmazia. — *Atti e memorie della Società Istriana di archeologia e storia patria*, vol. XVI (1900), p. 372-403. — Translation of the two chapters about Istria in n° 27 above. — An offprint of this translation, with the French title of n° 27 (Parenzo, 1901, 32 pp.), forms a supplement to vol. XXIV (1901) of the *Bullettino di archeologia e storia dalmata*.

156. Simon Metaphrastes. — *American Ecclesiastical Review*, vol. XXIII (1900), p. 113-20.

157. Papebrochius (Daniel), hagiographe. — *Biographie nationale*, vol. XVI (1901), col. 581-89.

158. Review of: H. Achelis, Die Martyrologien, ihre Geschichte und ihr Wert. — *Byzantinische Zeitschrift*, vol. X (1901), p. 614-17.

159. Une question à propos d'une épitaphe du cimetière de Domitille. — *Atti del II° Congresso internazionale di archeologia cristiana tenuto in Roma nell' aprile* 1900 (Rome, 1902), p. 101-103.

160. Saint Cassiodore. — *Mélanges Paul Fabre* (Paris, 1902), p. 40-50.

161. Les Légendes hagiographiques. — *Revue des questions historiques*, vol. LXXIV = N. S. vol. XXX (1903), p. 56-122. — Articles returned to in the book of the same title, n° 118 above.

162. Périer (Jean), hagiographe. — *Biographie nationale,* vol. XVII (1903), col. 20-21.

163. Pien (Jean), hagiographe. — Ibid., col. 396-97.

164. L'hagiographie de Salone d'après les dernières découvertes archéologiques. — *Jahreshefte des österreichischen archäologischen Instituts,* vol. X (1907), col. 77-100. — Reproduction of n° 41 above, with 16 illustrations added. There is an offprint with its own pagination.

165. Les versions grecques des Actes des martyrs persans sous Sapor II. Greek texts and translations. — *Patrologia Orientalis* (R. Graffin and F. Nau, vol. II, Paris, 1907), p. 403-560 (this fasc. 4 appeared in 1905). — N°s 34 and 39 above, with other texts added.

166. (Collaboration in) *The Catholic Encyclopedia* (New York, 1907-1914)[1].

167. La *Translatio S. Mercurii Beneventum.* — *Mélanges Godefroid Kurth* (Liège, 1908), vol. I, p. 17-24.

168. A Fifteen-Century Pilgrimage to St Patrick's Purgatory. — *The New Ireland Review,* N. S. vol. XXXI (1909), p. 1-9.

169. Correspondence. — *Revue celtique,* vol. XXX (1909), p. 188. — À propos n° 54, above.

170. Review of: H. Lietzmann and H. Hilgenfeld, Das Leben des heiligen Symeon Stylites. — *Byzantinische Zeitschrift,* vol. XIX (1910), p. 149-53.

171. (Collaboration in the 11th edition of the) *Encyclopaedia Britannica* (Cambridge, 1910-1911)[2].

[1] Articles: Hagiography (vol. vii, p. 107-108; Henschen, Godfrey (ibid., p. 240); Martyrology (vol. IX, p. 741-42).

[2] Articles: Bollandists (vol. IV, p. 177-78); Canonization (vol. V, p. 192-93); Denis, St (vol. VIII, p. 21-22); Fiacre, St (vol. X, p. 309); Florian, St (ibid., p. 539); Giles, St (vol. XII, p. 17-18); Hagiology (ibid., p. 816-17); Helena, St (vol. XIII, p. 219); Hubert, St (ibid., p. 846); Januarius, St (vol. XV, p. 155); Kilian, St (ibid., p. 792); Lawrence, St (vol XVI, p. 304); Linus (ibid., p. 736); Lucia, St (vol. XVII, p. 100); Marcellinus, St (ibid., p. 684); Margaret, St (ibid., p. 700); Martyrology (ibid., p. 805); Pelagia, St (vol. XXI, p. 62); Roch, St (vol. XXIII, p. 425); Rupert, St (ibid., p. 855); Saint (ibid., p. 1010-1011); Sebastian, St (vol. XXIV, p. 566),; Sergius, St (ibid., p. 667); Symeon Metaphrastes (vol. XXVI, p. 285); Synaxarium (ibid., p. 292); Thecla, St (ibid., p. 742-43); Valentine (vol. XXVII, p. 850-51); Veronica, St (ibid., p. 1037-38); Vincent, St (vol. XXVIII, p. 89-90); Vitus, St (ibid., p. 152). —The American editions of the *Encyclopaedia Britannica,* notably the 14th (1929-32), have summarized or used these articles without referring them to the author; some of those summarized no longer carry a signature.

172. Les Martyrs d'Interamna. — *Bulletin d'ancienne littérature et d'archéologie chrétiennes*, vol. I (1911), p. 161-68.

173. Les Légendes de S. Eustache et de S. Christophe. — *Le Muséon*. vol. XXXI = N. S. vol. XIII (1912), p. 91-100.

174. L'agiografia di Salona secondo le ultime scoperte archeologiche. — Spalato, 1912, 29 pp. — Supplement to vol. XXXV of *Bullettino di archeologia e storia dalmata*. — Translation of n° 41, above, with the same illustrations as in n° 164.

175. Review of: Karl Krumbacher and A. Ehrhard, Der heilige Georg in der grichischen Ueberlieferung. — *Byzantinische Zeitschrift*, vol. XXI (1912), p. 226-31.

176. Review of: Michael Huber, Die Wunderlegende von den Siebenschläfern. — *Deutsche Literaturzeitung*, vol. XXXIII (1912), col. 27-29.

177. Review of: Karl Schmeïng, Flucht und Werbungssagen in der Legende; and of: Franz Ostendorf, Überlieferung und Quelle der Reinoldlegende. — *Ibid.*, vol. XXXIV (1913), col. 156-58.

178. Monumenta Latrensia hagiographica. — *Milet. Ergebnisse der Ausgrabungen und Untersuchungen seit dem Jahre* 1899, herausgegeben von Theodor Wiegand, vol. III, 1st part: *Der Latmos*, von Theodor Wiegand (Berlin, 1913), p. 97-176. — Includes a new edition of n°s 8 and 11, above.

179. Review of: Godefroid Kurth, Étude critique sur la Vie de Sainte Geneviève. — *Archives belges*, vol. XV (1913), p. 177-79.

180. Une inscription de Fortunat sur S. Martin (I, 5). — *Mélanges Camille de Borman* (Liège, 1919), p. 19-26.

181. Les *Acta Sanctorum* des Bollandistes. — *Études*, vol. 158 (1919), p. 660-88; vol. 159 (1919), pp. 191-207, 441-57, 692-714; vol. 160 (1919), pp. 163-89, 444-58. — See also n° 125, above.

182. *ΜΙΕΡΕΥΣ*. Note sur un terme hagiographique. — *Académie des Inscriptions et Belles-Lettres. Comptes rendus des séances de l'année* 1919, p. 128-35.

183. La Légende de saint Eustache. — *Académie Royale de Belgique. Bulletin de la Classe des Lettres et des Sciences morales et politiques*, 5th series, vol. V (1919), p. 175-210.

184. Note bibliographique sur: Hippolyte Delehaye, À travers trois siècles. L'œuvre des Bollandistes, 1615-1915 [above, n° 125]. — *Ibid.*, 5th series, vol. VI (1920), p. 28-29.

185. L'origine des stylites. — Ibid., p. 67-76. — Reproduced in n°
131, above, ch. IX.

186. Bibliographical note on: Bruno Lefebvre, Notes d'histoire des
mathématiques. — Ibid., 5th series, vol. VII (1921), p. 69-
71.

187. La persécution dans l'armée sous Dioclétien. — Ibid., p. 150-
56.

188. Bibliographical note on: Hippolyte Delehaye, Les Passions des
martyrs et les genres littéraires [above, n° 127]. — Ibid.,
p. 241-42.

189. Greek Neomartyrs. — The Constructive Quarterly, vol. IX (1921),
p. 701-712.

190. Stals (M.-J.), prémontré de Tongerloo, hagiographe. — Biographie nationale, vol. XXIII (1921-1924), col. 585-86.

191. Report on: [Georges Hinnisdaels], L'Octavius de Minucius
Felix. — Bulletin [see n° 183], 5th series, vol. VIII (1922),
p. 50-51.

192. Les Horrea Agrippiana à Rome. — Integral text unpublished;
summarized ibid., p. 450.

193. Bibiliographical note on: Paul Peeters, Histoires monastiques
géorgiennes. — Ibid., 5th series, vol. IX (1923), p. 27-29.

194. Une Vie grecque de S. Dominique. — Miscellanea Dominicana,
1221-1921 (Rome, 1923), p. 4-9.

195. Euchaïta et la Légende de S. Théodore. — Anatolian Studies
presented to Sir William Ramsay (Manchester, 1923), p. 129-34.

196. Notice sur la vie et les travaux du Père Charles De Smedt. —
Annuaire de l'Académie royale des Sciences, des Lettres et des
Beaux-Arts de Belgique, vol. XC (1924), 2nd part, p. 93-121.

197. Bibliographical note on: Gabriel Millet, L'École grecque dans
l'architecture byzantine; Id., L'Ancien art serbe. —
Bulletin [above, n° 183], 5th series, vol. X (1924), p. 9-11.

198. Report on: [Paul Bonenfant], La Suppression de la Compagnie
de Jésus dans les Pays-Bas autrichiens en 1773. — Ibid.,
p. 51-56.

199. La Vie de sainte Théoctiste de Lesbos. — Byzantion, vol. I
(1924), p. 191-200.

200. Servus Servorum Dei. — Bulićev Zbornik. Strena Buliciana,
(Zagreb-Split, 1924), p. 377-78.

201. Le Martyre de saint Nicétas le Jeune. — Mélanges offerts à
M. Gustave Schlumberger (Paris, 1924), p. 205-211.

202. Bibliographical note on: Paul Graindor, Henri Grégoire, etc.,
Byzantion, vol. I. — Bulletin [see n° 183], 5th series, vol.
XI (1925), p. 94-96.

203. Report on: [Alfred Poncelet], Étude sur l'établissement de la Compagnie de Jésus en Belgique et sur ses développements jusqu'à la fin du règne d'Albert et Isabelle. — Ibid., p. 150-51.

204. À propos de Saint-Césaire du Palatin. — *Rendiconti della Pontificia Accademia Romana di Archeologia*, anno III (1925), p. 45-48.

205. Bibliographical note on: Hippolyte Delehaye et Paul Peeters, Acta Sanctorum Novembris, vol. IV [above, n° 4]. — *Bulletin* [see n° 183], 5th series, vol. XII (1926), p. 18-19.

206. Refrigerare, Refrigerium. — *Journal des Savants*, N. S. vol. XXIV (1926), p. 385-90.

207. La Légende de saint Napoléon. — *Mélanges d'histoire offerts à Henri Pirenne* (Bruxelles, 1926), p. 81-88.

208. Pronomen. — *Bulletin Du Cange. Archivum latinitatis medii aevi*, vol. III (1927), p. 28-29.

209. Les martyrs Épictète et Astion. — *Académie roumaine. Bulletin de la section historique*, vol. XIV (1928), p. 1-5.

210. Les caractéristiques des Saints dans l'art. — *Le Correspondant*, vol. CCLXXVII (1928), p. 481-500. — Reproduced in n° 133, above, chap. V.

211. Une page du "Martyrologe Hiéronymien". — *Bulletin* [see n° 183], 5th series, vol. XV (1929), p. 20-33.

212. Note sur une inscription chrétienne de Milan. — Ibid., p. 313-20.

213. Les ampoules et les médaillons de Bobbio. — *Journal des Savants*, N. S. vol. XXVII (1929), p. 453-57.

214. La Légende de la bienheureuse Ida de Toggenburg. — *Nova et Vetera, Revue catholique pour la Suisse romande*, vol. IV (1929), p. 359-65.

215. Report on: L. Rochus, Étude lexicographique et grammaticale sur la latinité de Salvien. — *Bulletin* [see n° 183], 5th series, vol. XVI (1930), p. 129-30.

216. La méthode historique et l'hagiographie. — Ibid., p. 218-31. — Reproduced in n° 133, above, chaps. I and II.

217. Tusco et Basso Cons. — *Mélanges Paul Thomas* (Bruges, 1930), p. 201-207.

218. La dédicace de la basilique de Fossombrone. — *Rendiconti della Pontificia Accademia Romana di Archeologia*, vol. VI (1930), p. 109-111.

219. Bibliographical note on: Paul Faider et Mme Faider-Feytmans, Catalogue des Manuscrits de la Bibliothèque publi-

que de la Ville de Mons. — *Bulletin* [see n° 183], 5th series, vol. XVII (1931), p. 380-82.

220. Bibliographical note on: Alfred Poncelet, Nécrologe des Jésuites de la Province flandro-belge. — Ibid., p. 458-59.

221. "In Britannia" dans le Martyrologe hiéronymien. — *Proceedings of the British Academy*, vol. XVII (1931), p. 289-307.

222. Réfractaire et martyr. — *Bulletin de l'Amicale Saint-Michel*, avril 1932, p. 5-8.

223. Rapport sur les travaux de la Commission pour la publication d'un Catalogue général des Manuscrits. — *Bulletin* [see n° 183], 5th series, vol. XIX (1933), p. 8-10.

224. Notizie milanesi in alcune date del Martirologio Geronimiano. — *Ambrosius*, vol. IX (1933), p. 29-34. — Translation by Luigi Mainardi of extracts from n° 96, above.

225. Le refus de servir et l'Église primitive. — *Hauteclaire*, octobre 1933, p. 192-97.

226. Un groupe de récits "utiles à l'âme". — *Annuaire de l'Institut de philologie et d'histoire orientales*, vol. II (= *Mélanges Bidez*) (Bruxelles, 1933-34), p. 255-66.

227. Rapport sur l'activité de la Commission du "Catalogue général des Manuscrits des Bibliothèques de Belgique". — *Bulletin* [see n° 183], 5th series, vol. XX (1934), p. 153-55.

228. Bibliographical note on: Hippolyte Delehaye, Cinq leçons sur la méthode hagiographique [above, n° 133].—Ibid., p. 195-96.

229. Rapport sur les progrès du Catalogue des Manuscrits des Bibliothèques de Belgique. — Ibid., 5th series, vol. XXI (1935), p. 20-21.

230. Bibliographical note on: Paulus Grosjean, Henrici VI Angliae regis Miracula postuma. — Ibid., p. 225.

231. Bibliographical note on: Hippolyte Delehaye, Étude sur le Légendier romain. Les saints de novembre et de décembre [above, n° 134]. — Ibid., 5th series, vol. XXII (1936), p. 48-49.

232. Presentazione del volume: Étude sur le Légendier romain [above, n° 134]. — *Rendiconti della Reale Accademia Nazionale dei Lincei*, 6th series, vol. XII (1936), p. 372-74.

233. Bibliographical note on: Catalogue général des Manuscrits des Bibliothèques de Belgique, vol. III, par Paul Faider, avec la collaboration de Pierre-P. Debbaudt et de Mme Faider-Feytmans. — *Bulletin* [see n° 183], 5th series, vol. XXIII (1937), p. 362-63.

234. Bibliographical note on: Stéphane Binon, Documents grecs inédits relatifs à S. Mercure de Césarée; Id., Essai sur le

Cycle de S. Mercure. — Ibid., p. 460-61.

235. La Passion de sainte Anastasie la Romaine. — *Studi dedicati alla memoria di Paolo Ubaldi* (Milan, 1937), p. 17-26.

236. À propos de la Vie de S. Charles. Lettre à Monseigneur Giovanni Galbiati (11 juillet 1938). — *Echi di San Carlo Borromeo*, fascicule 18 (1938), p. 630-33.

237. La Vie gracque de saint Martin de Tours. — *Atti del V Congresso internazionale degli Studi Bizantini (Roma, 20-26 sett.* 1936), vol. I (1939), p. 428-31. — This vol. I of the *Atti* forms vol. V of *Studi Bizantini e Neoellenici.*

238. Les Actes de S. Timothée. — *Anatolian Studies presented to William Hepburn Buckler* ([Aberdeen], 1939), p. 77-84.

239. Bibliographical note on: H. Delehaye, P. Peeters, etc., Propylaeum ad Acta Sanctorum Decembris [above, n° 6]. — *Bulletin* [see n° 183], 5th series, vol. XXVII (1941), p. 27-30.

INDEX OF SAINTS' NAMES

INDEX OF SAINTS' NAMES

Florian of Bologna, m., 22, 41n., 76
Florian of Lorsch, m., 76
Florus and Laurus, mm., 141. 142
Fortunata, m., 53, 79n.
Francis Xavier, 22, 42n.
Frodoberta, 30
Fronto of Perigueux, 41n., 73
Fructuosus, m., 61-2, 81n., 94
Fursey, 20, 35, 41n.

G

Galla, v., 155-6
Gallus, ab., 75
Gaugericus, 34
Genesius the Actor, m., 95
Genesius of Arles, m., 96
George, m., 30, 43n., 56, 88, 114,
134, 145-6, 159, 162n.
George of Suelli, 25
Gervase and Protase, mm., 141
Géry. See Gaugericus
Gordian, m., 83n.
Gordius, m., 83n., 94
Gregory the Great, p., 51, 80n., 87,
122-3, 162n., 165-6n.
Gregory the Wonderworker, 139

H

Harvey, 25
Helen, emp., 142
Hermogenes, m., 56
Hilary of Poitiers, 133, 134, 139
Hippolytus, m., 58, 93, 165n.
Honorius of Buzençais, 22
Hubert, 21, 75
Hyacinth, m., 82n.

I

Ignatius of Antioch, m., 37, 94,
100n.
Ignatius of Loyola, 74, 161

Irenaeus, bp., 93
Irenaeus, m., 95
Irene, m., 76, 162m.
Isaac, m., 35
Isaias the prophet, 122, 162n.
Isodore of Seville, 24

J

James the Greater, 23
James the Less, 93
James of the March, 25
James (with Marian), m., 94
Januarius, bp.m., 29
Januarius (with Faustus), m., 96
Jason, m., 157
Jerome, 25
Joasaph (with Barlaam), 51, 70,
79n., 91, 144
John of Alexandria, 113-114, 116
John the Baptist, 35, 56, 165n.
John Berchmans, 211
John Chrysostom, 92, 94, 150, 152
John Colombini, 74
John and Cyrus, mm., 33, 121, 133,
134, 162n.
John and Paul, mm., 178-9, 182n.
John of Réomé, 80n.
Joseph of Arimathea, 78
Judas Thomas, 141
Julian of Anazarbus, m., 34, 35, 94
Julian (with Florentius), m., 76
Julian the Hospitaller, 31, 46n.
Julitta, m., 94
Julitta (with Cyricus), 95
Julius, m., 95
Junian, ab., 34
Justin, m., 94
Juvenal of Cagliari, 113
Juventinus, m., 94

K

Katherine, 38, 56, 89, 162n.
Kentigern, 24
Kümmernis. See Liberata